NORTHERN ROCKY MOUNTAIN

Wildflowers

A FIELD GUIDE TO
SPECIES OF THE NORTHERN ROCKIES,
INCLUDING WATERTON-GLACIER
INTERNATIONAL PEACE PARK AND
BANFF, JASPER, GLACIER, KOOTENAY,
MOUNT REVELSTOKE, AND
YOHO NATIONAL PARKS

by H. Wayne Phillips

FALCON®

Copyright 2001 by The Globe Pequot Press
Printed in Korea

Falcon and FalconGuide are registered trademarks of Falcon Publishing, Inc.

1 2 3 4 5 6 7 8 9 0 SI 06 05 04 03 02 01

Inside photos by H. Wayne Phillips
Illustrations by DD Dowden
Front cover photo of Fairy Slipper by H. Wayne Phillips

Cataloging-in-Publication Data is on file at the Library of Congress.

Project Editor: Gayle Shirley
Copyeditor: Julianna Schroeder
Map by Tony Moore
Page compositor: Darlene Jatkowski
Book design by Falcon Publishing, Inc.

CAUTION

Ingesting plants or plant parts poses a potentially extreme health hazard and could result in sickness or even death. No one should attempt to use any wild plant for food or medicine without adequate training by a fully qualified professional. The author, publisher, and all others associated with the production and distribution of this book assume no liability for the actions of the reader.

All participants in the recreational activities suggested by this book must assume responsibility for their own actions and safety. The information contained in this guidebook cannot replace sound judgment and good decision-making skills, which help reduce risk exposure; nor does the scope of this book allow for disclosure of all the potential hazards and risks involved in such activities.

Learn as much as possible about the recreational activities in which you participate, prepare for the unexpected, and be cautious. The reward will be a safer and more enjoyable experience.

CONTENTS

To my sons and their wives,
Kelly Phillips and
Laura Martin and
Rob Phillips and
Monika Mahal,
and my grandchildren,
present and future—
with love to you all.

ACKNOWLEDGMENTS

The most enjoyable part of writing this book has been the association with my wildflower-loving friends. Thanks so much to all of you for sharing your enthusiasm and knowledge of native plants, for your encouragement, and for your help with the critical local information on locations and flowering times for the plants that I wanted to find and photograph for the book. In some cases you have even assisted me in the field. Thanks especially to Lillian Pethtel and Michelle Craig of Kamiah, Idaho; Drake Barton and Kathy Lloyd of Clancy, Montana; Pattie Brown and Sam Culotta of Bigfork, Montana; Jerry DeSanto of Babb, Montana; Peter Stickney and Steve Shelly of Missoula, Montana; Earle and Pattie Layser of Alta, Wyoming; Maria Mantas and Steve Wirt of Whitefish, Montana; Dennis Nicholls and Jill Davies of Noxon, Montana; and Tom Kotynski and Katie Myers of Great Falls, Montana. For their generous assistance in identifying and verifying plant specimens, I owe a debt of gratitude to Peter Stickney and Matt Lavin. Thank you very much.

Thanks to Susan Spady of Pro Photo in Great Falls for her fast and superior slide developing.

I am especially grateful to Marilyn Schneider for her help in the field and her support, patience, and understanding over the long days while I was chained to the word processor.

Most important, thanks to Bill Schneider of Falcon Publishing, Inc. for inviting me to write this book and for the support of editors Gayle Shirley, Julianna Schroeder, Laura Ottoson, and the rest of the Falcon staff.

THE NORTHERN ROCKY MOUNTAIN REGION

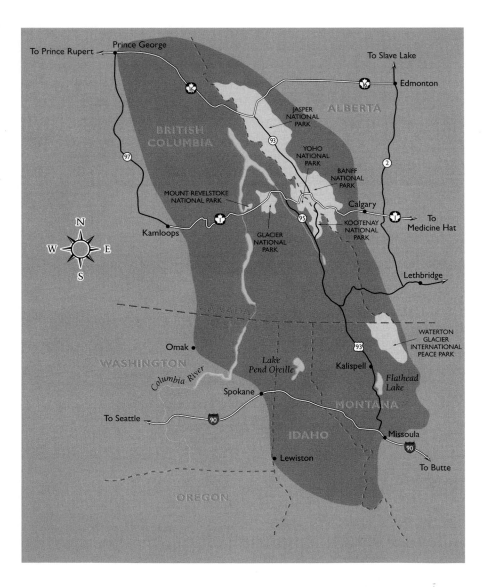

$\mathcal{J}$NTRODUCTION

The Northern Rocky Mountain Region

Geography

The Northern Rocky Mountain region is a land of forested mountain ranges interspersed with deep canyons and valleys. It includes northwestern Montana, northern Idaho, northeastern Washington, southeastern British Columbia, and southwestern Alberta.

The region stretches from Lost Trail Pass on the Idaho-Montana border northward to Prince George, British Columbia, and from the Okanogan River in Washington and the Fraser River in British Columbia eastward to the eastern slope of the Rocky Mountains in Alberta and Montana. The southern boundary lies along the watershed divide between the Salmon and Clearwater Rivers in Idaho. The western boundary is a line drawn between Lewiston, Idaho; Spokane, Washington; Omak, Washington; Kamloops, British Columbia; and Prince George, British Columbia. The eastern boundary follows the eastern slopes of the Rocky Mountain Front from the Alberta–British Columbia border (east of Mount Buchanan) southeastward to Waterton-Glacier International Peace Park. It then follows the Continental Divide south to Scapegoat Mountain; turns westward and follows the Blackfoot River to Missoula, Montana; and then goes southward up the Bitterroot Valley to Lost Trail Pass.

In designating the Northern Rocky Mountain region, I have generally followed Robert G. Bailey's *Description of the Ecoregions of the United States* (1995). However, I have moved the southern boundary farther south to follow the Salmon-Clearwater watershed divide in Idaho. A significant change in climate and vegetation occurs along this line, as described by Ray J. Davis (1952) and Rexford Daubenmire (1968).

When compared with the valleys and peaks of the Central Rocky Mountains, those of the Northern Rockies are generally lower in elevation. Elevation extremes in the Northern Rockies range from less than 750 feet above sea level at the confluence of the Clearwater and Snake Rivers at Lewiston, Idaho to 12,972 feet at the summit of Mount Robson in British Columbia. However, within the Northern Rockies in Washington, Idaho, and Montana (outside of Glacier National Park), few peaks rise above 7,000 or 8,000 feet in elevation. These mountains typically comprise a repetitive series of ridges and narrow V-shaped canyons, fully covered with dense forest on all but the highest ridges and summits. Slopes are often steep, with 3,000 to 5,000 feet or more of vertical relief between the valleys and summits.

The major mountain ranges within the area are:

Idaho: Bitterroot, Clearwater, Coeur d'Alene, Purcell, Selkirk, Selway, and St. Joe.

Montana: Apgar, Bitterroot, Cabinet, Coeur d'Alene, Continental Divide, Flathead, Lewis, Livingston, Mission, Ninemile, Purcell, Rattlesnake, Reservation, Salish, Swan, and Whitefish.

Washington: Kettle River, Okanogan, and Selkirk.

Alberta: Rocky.

British Columbia: Cariboo, Columbia, MacDonald, Monashee, Okanagan, Purcell, Rocky, Selkirk, and Shuswap.

The Northern Rocky Mountain region is the headwaters of five great river systems: the Columbia, Fraser, Peace, Athabasca, and Saskatchewan. However, most of the land drains into the Columbia River and its major tributaries: the Bitterroot, Clark Fork, Clearwater, Coeur d'Alene, Duncan, Flathead, Granby, Kettle, Kootenay, Okanagan/Okanogan, Pend Oreille, Saint Joe, Sanpoil, Spokane, and Swan rivers.

Climate

The climate in most of the Northern Rocky Mountains is cool and temperate with a maritime influence. Precipitation comes in spring, fall, and winter. Winters are relatively mild considering the northern latitude, with snow and rain alternating to produce a dense snowpack. Summers are dry and hot. When compared with the area east of the Continental Divide, most of the Northern Rocky Mountain region sees more days of rain and higher overall precipitation, less wind, and more days of fog and overcast skies, especially in the fall and winter.

The annual precipitation in the Northern Rocky Mountains ranges from 16 to 40 inches in the valleys and on the lower slopes, while up to 100 inches or more falls on the higher mountains. In Missoula (elevation 3,200 feet), on the southeastern fringe of the region in Montana, annual precipitation averages less than 14 inches, while in Wallace, Idaho (elevation 2,770 feet), 118 miles to the northwest on the western slope of the Bitterroot Range, it averages 46 inches.

Winter temperatures are often milder in the Northern Rockies than at the same latitudes east of the Continental Divide. For example, the average minimum temperature in January at West Glacier, Montana, is 14 degrees F, or 38 degrees warmer than at East Glacier, 55 miles to the east over the Continental Divide. Temperature extremes from summer to winter are also more moderate here. The difference between the mean high temperature in July and the mean low temperature in January is 115 degrees F at East Glacier but only 65 degrees at West Glacier.

The generally moderate temperatures in the Northern Rocky Mountains are the result of the inland maritime influence—that is, the westerly flow of air from the Pacific Ocean. However, arctic air masses sometimes do push down from the north and overpower the maritime air flow, resulting in much colder temperatures. Sometimes extreme temperatures of 20 to 35 degrees below zero or more are experienced.

Normally, this Pacific flow of air brings cloudy, wet winter weather to the Northern Rockies, with temperatures near freezing and precipitation alternating between snow and rain in the valleys. Fog and high humidity are normal conditions. Northern Idaho is one of the cloudiest places in the United States in the winter. It is overcast 70 percent of the time on average, and some winters it is cloudy close to 90 percent of the time. The moist climate of the Northern Rocky Mountains is also strongly influenced by its narrow canyons, which milk the moisture from the clouds.

In sharp contrast, summer is usually hot and dry, with clear blue skies. A northward shift in the West Coast subtropical, high atmospheric pressure system causes the prevailing westerly winds to carry dry, subsiding air across the region. Orofino, Idaho, holds the record high summer temperature for the state: 118 degrees F. Thunderstorms during this period are usually of the "dry lightning" variety, and it is not uncommon for the lightning to start forest fires. Significant precipitation during this period is often nonexistent. It averages less than 1 inch per month.

The climate in the region shows the greatest maritime influence north of the Clearwater River in northern Idaho. This influence gradually declines as one goes eastward into northwestern Montana, westward into Washington to the Okanogan River, southward in Idaho to the Salmon River divide, and northward into British Columbia. East of the Continental Divide, in the Alberta Rockies, the climate is drier.

Soil

The same westerly flow of air from the Pacific that brings moisture to this region has also showered the area with volcanic ash from the many eruptions in the Cascades. The eruption of Mount St. Helens in 1980 is a prime example; ash continued to filter down from the trees for months after the explosion. Similar volcanic ash falls have rained down on the Northern Rockies over eons of volcanic activity, especially after the great eruption of ancient Mount Mazama, which formed Crater Lake in Oregon about 7,000 years ago. Ash is an important component of the surface soils in the Northern Rockies. It helps retain moisture and encourages plant growth. This ash layer in the soil is most pronounced on the downwind northerly and easterly slopes, where it is up to 36 inches deep in some parts of northern Idaho. It tapers off to a depth of 6 to 18 inches in northwestern Montana. Where this ash does occur, it is a key factor in vegetation development.

Glaciers and glacially dammed lakes have also influenced the surface geology and, in turn, the plant distribution in the Northern Rockies. During the ice age that began about 2.5 million years ago and ended 10,000 years ago, the great Cordilleran ice sheets, which advanced through the Northern Rockies of Canada and into far northern Idaho and northwestern Montana, filled the valleys and dammed the Clark Fork of the Columbia far up the Bitterroot Valley. Distinctive soils developed from the deep layers of fine-textured lake sediments and glacial tills that this glacial activity created. This led to the formation of distinctive vegetation patterns.

Bedrock geology is also influential in soil and vegetation development in the region. The Precambrian Belt series of sedimentary argillites (mudstones) and quartzites (sandstones) often formed deep, fine-textured soils that predominate in large areas of the Northern Rockies, while other areas developed on coarse sands of granitic origin. Understanding geology and soil development can be helpful in predicting vegetation patterns and finding particular wildflowers.

Vegetation

The Northern Rockies region is richer in coniferous tree species than the central and southern parts of the Rocky Mountain chain. Ponderosa pine, lodgepole pine, limber pine, Douglas-fir, subalpine fir, Engelmann spruce, and Rocky Mountain juniper are common to all three zones. Whitebark pine is found in both the Northern and Central Rockies. Four additional conifers are found in abundance in the Northern Rockies (and in the Cascades to the west) but are absent from the Central and Southern Rockies. These are western hemlock, mountain hemlock, western red cedar, and Pacific yew. In addition, the natural ranges of grand fir, white spruce, western white pine, alpine larch, and western larch fall largely within the Northern Rockies but overlap the boundaries to the south and east (Fig. 1).

The vegetation of the Northern Rocky Mountains is distributed in zones (Fig. 2) based on elevation, slope exposure (the cardinal direction a slope faces), precipitation, and soil.

The drier, broad mountain **valleys** (Fig. 3) are dominated by ponderosa pine and Douglas-fir forests, as well as grasslands and shrublands that support vegetation adapted to the dry soil and temperature extremes of this region. Snowberry, ninebark, oceanspray, wheatgrasses, fescues, sagebrush, rabbitbrush, balsamroot, lupine, and many other xerophytic grasses, low shrubs, and wildflowers are found in this driest zone. Growing along the rivers and streams are black cottonwood trees, willows, western birch, thin-leaved alder, woods rose, and red osier dogwood.

Many other valleys (like Montana's Swan Valley and the Kootenay-Columbia-Fraser River Valleys in British Columbia) are moist enough to support a continuous cover of moist montane forest vegetation on all but the driest slopes.

Figure 1. Among the many conifers blanketing the Northern Rockies are (from left to right) the western larch, western red cedar, and Pacific yew.

Figure 2. Vegetation zones of the Northen Rocky Mountains

Alpine	Treeless vegetation consisting of low shrubs, cushion plants, heaths, and turfs.
Upper Subalpine	Grassy parklands, heath/cushion vegetation, krummholz, and forests of subalpine fir, spruce, whitebark pine, alpine larch, mountain hemlock, and lodgepole pine.
Lower Subalpine	Forests of subalpine fir, mountain hemlock, spruce, lodgepole pine, western larch, western white pine, Douglas-fir, and grand fir; with meadows, fens, and bogs.
Moist Montane	Forests of western red cedar, western hemlock, grand fir, western white pine, western larch, lodgepole pine, spruce, ponderosa pine, and Douglas-fir; with meadows, fens, and bogs.
Dry Montane	Grassy parks and forests of ponderosa pine and Douglas-fir, with or without grand fir, lodgepole pine, and western larch.
Valleys	Dry valleys with grasslands and forests much like those of the dry montane; moist valleys with vegetation more like that of the moist montane forests.

Dry montane forests (Fig. 4) are found on steep south- and west-facing slopes and thinner soils at low elevations in the mountains. Douglas-fir and ponderosa pine trees often grow widely spaced here in open woodlands or savannahs. At the lowest elevations, especially on steep, south-facing slopes, the vegetation under the trees is often similar to that in the broad valleys. Grasses, balsamroot, lupine, and showy phlox are common. With increasing elevation and deeper soils, lodgepole pine, western larch, and grand fir may also be found growing with the ponderosa pine and Douglas-fir trees. Growing under the trees here are a variety of low, flowering shrubs and wildflowers, including ninebark, ocean-spray, snowberry, spiraea, beargrass, pinegrass, arnica, fairybells, Oregon grape,

Figure 3. Wildflowers flourish beneath the ponderosa pines and Douglas-firs that dominate the dry mountain valleys of the Northern Rockies.

and kinnikinnick. Spruce trees are found along the streams, along with red osier dogwood, willows, birch, and aspen.

Moist montane forests (Fig. 5) are found along streams, on northern and eastern exposures, and on all slopes where there is a strong inland, maritime climatic influence and deeper soils (usually with significant ash layers). The lush forests here have great diversity in both tree species and understory vegetation. Western red cedar, western hemlock, and/or grand fir are the dominant trees in older (climax) forests. Giant cedars thousands of years old are found in old-growth groves in this zone. Western white pine, western larch, ponderosa pine, lodgepole pine, Douglas-fir, and Engelmann spruce form early successional forests here following wildfires, blow-downs,

Figure 4. Dry montane forests are found on steep south- and west-facing slopes at low elevations in the region.

and other disturbances. Without further disturbance, these trees are gradually replaced by the climax forest trees, a process called forest succession, which usually requires hundreds of years. A great variety of wildflowers, shrubs, and vines covers the forest floor in these forests. Some understory plants prefer the deep, cool shade of the older forests (queen's-cup beadlily, wild ginger, gold-thread, Pacific yew, Piper's anemone, fairy slipper), while others do their best in the increased sunlight found in disturbed forests (red-stem ceanothus, paper birch, mountain golden-pea, self-heal, lupine, serviceberry).

Wet meadows (Fig. 6) along streams and ponds are often brilliant with blue camas, elephant's head, false hellebore, and monkeyflowers.

Figure 5. Moist montane forests grow where the climate is influenced more strongly by maritime weather patterns.

Figure 6. Blue camas is among the wildflowers that thrive in wet meadows, like this one in northern Idaho.

The **lower subalpine forests** (Fig. 7) at the lowest elevations look much like the moist montane forests, except western red cedar and western hemlock are replaced by subalpine fir and/or mountain hemlock as the species dominating the climax. The other trees, shrubs, and wildflowers are very similar to those in the adjacent moist montane forests. Openings in the forest canopy often take the form of fens, bogs, and other wetlands where cotton sedge and other unusual plants are found.

With increasing elevation there is a gradual shift to plants more adapted to shorter growing seasons, harsher winter conditions, and deeper snowpack. Trees in the **upper subalpine forests** (Fig. 8) are limited to subalpine fir, mountain hemlock, spruce, lodgepole pine, whitebark pine, and alpine larch. Fool's huckleberry and white rhododendron are common on moist slopes, while beargrass and huckleberry species are more abundant on drier slopes. Steep stream courses and snow chutes are often filled with dense alder glades.

In the years when beargrass flower displays are at their best, the upper subalpine forests and parks are a wildflower enthusiast's dream. Fireweed, mountain hollyhock, and other sun-loving flowers brighten

Figure 7. Wet meadows and ponds are often found within subalpine forests at lower elevations.

Figure 8. Plants growing in the upper-elevation subalpine forests must adapt to shorter growing seasons, harsher winter conditions, and deeper snow.

the slopes after a fire. Under the tree canopy, shade-tolerant plants such as arnica, meadowrue, wintergreen, rattlesnake plantain, and various huckleberry and orchid species are more abundant. The streams in this zone are often lined with brook saxifrage, mountain bluebells, and arrow-leaved groundsel.

South of the U.S.-Canadian border, few mountain ranges in the Northern Rocky Mountains stretch above timberline and form a true alpine zone. However, the higher ridges of many ranges in the region are often open subalpine parklands with only scattered, stunted, and slow-growing coniferous trees and groves. Forest succession following forest fires is exceedingly slow here, and vegetation development is limited by high winds and the short growing season. On the summits and in the cirques on the leeward side of these high ridges, **subalpine heath/cushion vegetation** (Fig. 9) develops with many of the same wildflowers found on a true alpine tundra. Red mountain heather and moss campion often fill these slopes with vibrant color during the short summer. The windward, south- and west-facing slopes of these subalpine summits are dry, grassy, bald mountain parklands, where green fescue, alpine knotweed, and/or beargrass are abundant.

Figure 9. Subalpine heath/cushion vegetation, such as red mountain heather, grows on high ridges and in cirques.

Figure 10. At timberline, the wind twists coniferous trees into bizarre, stunted shapes known as krummholz.

At timberline, the upper limit of tree growth, the wind deforms the coniferous trees into horizontal pygmy forests called **krummholz** (Fig. 10). The elevation of timberline (and the other vegetation zones) varies considerably with latitude.

In the Waterton-Glacier International Peace Park (49 degrees latitude), stunted krummholz tree growth gives way to **alpine tundra** (Fig. 11) at about 7,500 to 8,000 feet in elevation, depending on exposure. Farther north, in Jasper National Park in Alberta (53 degrees latitude), alpine vegetation begins between 6,500 and 7,500 feet in elevation. Here in the high mountains of the southern Canadian Rockies, many peaks rise well above timberline. Well-developed alpine tundra vegetation occurs here, along with extensive rocklands, icefields, and glaciers.

Alpine tundra vegetation is generally low growing, but species composition varies considerably depending on exposure to the wind and available moisture. Cushion plants like alpine forget-me-not and moss campion survive in fellfields, where the thin, rocky soil is exposed to the full blast of the high alpine winds. Where there is more soil development, turf plants like alpine avens and curly sedge thrive. Wetland species, such as arctic gentian, swamp laurel, marsh marigold, and globeflower, grow below snowbanks and along alpine streams and lakes.

Plant Characteristics

In the plant descriptions in this guide, I have kept technical botanical terms to a

Figure 11. Above timberline, low-growing plants hug the rocklands and icefields of the alpine tundra.

minimum. However, knowledge of a few terms is helpful, just as learning the names of tools makes a carpenter's work easier. Terms most often used are outlined below. Further definitions can be found in the glossary at the end of this book.

Life Form

Is the plant woody (tree, shrub, or vine) or is it herbaceous (grass, grasslike, or forb)? Forbs are broad-leaved, nonwoody herbaceous plants that die back to the soil surface at the end of the growing season.

Is the plant annual, biennial, or perennial? Annual plants complete their life cycle in a single year. Biennials grow vegetatively for one year and then produce seed and die the second year. Perennials are capable of living for more than two growing seasons and usually produce seed for two years or more. Trees, shrubs, and vines are always perennial. Herbaceous plants may be annual, biennial, or perennial. Most plants described in this book are perennial herbaceous plants, unless specifically described otherwise.

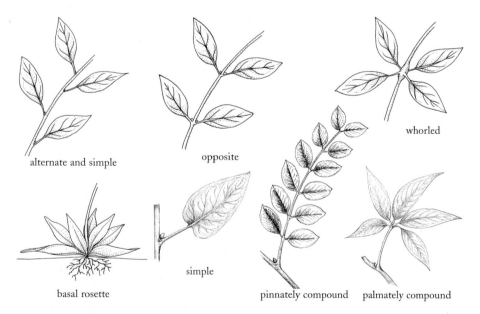

Figure 12. Leaf type and arrangement

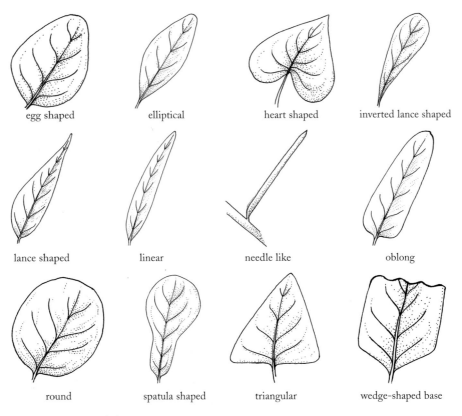

egg shaped   elliptical   heart shaped   inverted lance shaped

lance shaped   linear   needle like   oblong

round   spatula shaped   triangular   wedge-shaped base

Figure 13. Leaf shapes

Leaf Type and Arrangement

Leaves may be simple or compound (Fig. 12). A simple leaf has a single blade. This one blade may be cut or lobed, but not all the way to the midrib. A compound leaf consists of two or more blades called leaflets. Compound leaves may have their leaflets arranged palmately, ternately, or pinnately. Buds and shoots form in the axil of a leaf, but not in the axil of the leaflets of a compound leaf. The base of a leaf stalk (petiole) often has a pair of appendages called stipules. The stalk of a leaflet never has stipules. To determine whether you are looking at a simple leaf or at a leaflet of a compound leaf, look for the location of the bud and the stipules.

The arrangement of leaves on the stem is also important to note. Leaves may be arranged alternately on a stem, in pairs opposite each other, or in whorls. In a whorled arrangement, several leaves are attached to the stem at a common point.

Leaves vary in shape from needlelike or linear to round, egg shaped, or triangular, etc. (Figs. 13 and 14).

toothed

double-toothed

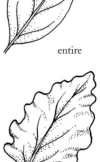

entire

lobed

cleft

wavy

Figure 14. Leaf margins

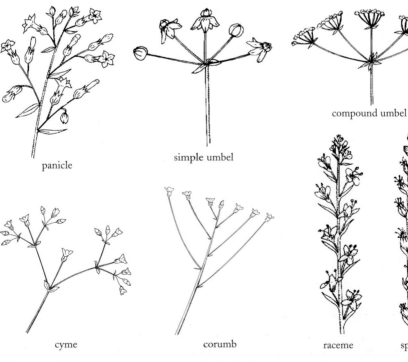

panicle

simple umbel

compound umbel

cyme

corumb

raceme

spike

Figure 15. Flower arrangement, or inflorescence

Flower Arrangement, or Inflorescence

Recognizing how flowers are arranged on the flowering stem is often necessary to correctly identify a wildflower. Flowers may be solitary on the end of the stem; located in the leaf axil (axillary); or arranged in a spike, raceme, panicle, cyme, umbel, or head (Fig. 15).

Flower Parts*

A complete flower has floral parts arranged in four whorls. The outer whorl consists of the sepals, which are often green but may be showy and petal-like. Inside the whorl of sepals are the petals, usually the showiest part of the flower. Next are the stamens, the male parts of the flower, which produce the pollen. A stamen consists of a filament and an anther. Finally, in the most protected position, there is the pistil (or pistils), the female part(s) of the flower. The pistil includes the stigma, style, and ovary. Within the ovary are the ovules, which develop into seeds after fertilization by the pollen (Fig. 16).

Sepals and petals may be separate, or they may be united into various shapes (for example, tubelike, cuplike, or urnlike). Likewise, the stamens may be entirely separate or their filaments or anthers may be joined together. For example, mountain hollyhock (and other plants in the mallow family

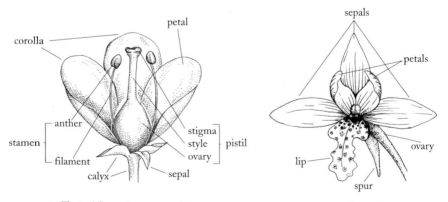

Typical flower in cross section Flower of the Orchid Family (Orchidaceae)

Figure 16. Flower parts

---

*Examination of tiny flower parts is enhanced with the use of a 10x hand lens.

[Malvaceae]) have filaments that are joined to form a tube, at least on the lower portion.

Often, the petals of a flower look much alike. In this case, the flower is referred to as regular. Irregular flowers have petals that are very different from one another. For example, plants in the bean family (Fabaceae) have flowers with five petals: one shaped like a banner, two shaped like wings, and two joined to form a boatlike keel (Fig. 17).

When the sepals, petals, and stamens are attached at the base of the ovary, as in blue camas and other lilies, the flower is said to have a superior ovary. The sepals, petals, and stamens are attached at or near the top of the ovary when the ovary is inferior, as in fireweed and other evening primroses.

Not all flowers are complete (with sepals, petals, stamens, and a pistil). Flowers missing one or more of these parts are referred to as incomplete. Unisexual flowers are incomplete, missing either the stamens or the pistils. Other incomplete flowers may be missing the sepals, the petals, or both. Male and female unisexual flowers are sometimes found growing on the same plant (which is described as monoecious), or they may reside on separate plants (which are referred to as dioecious).

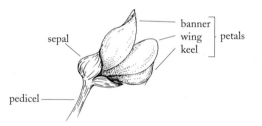

Figure 17. Flower of the bean family (Fabaceae), side view

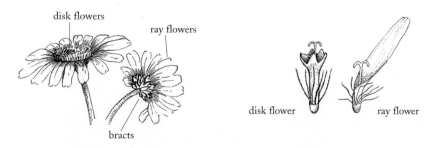

Figure 18. Flowers of the aster family (Asteraceae)

Bracts are modified leaflike structures that lie just below the flower or flower arrangement (Fig. 18). In members of the aster family (Asteraceae), the structure of the bracts is often a key feature in identification. The bracts of asters surround the base of the flower head, which is a composite of many tiny flowers. The sepals of the individual flowers on the heads of asters are reduced to scales or hairlike bristles called pappus. Flowers in the aster family are found in two types, disk flowers and ray flowers. Some aster family species have flower heads with both ray and disk flowers (like sunflowers), while other species have only ray flowers (like dandelions) or only disk flowers (like pussytoes).

How to Use This Guide

Included in this guide are photographs and descriptions of more than 300 plant species from an estimated flora of more than 2,000 species in the Northern Rocky Mountain region. I have attempted to represent most of the terrestrial flowering plant families and a sample of the genera most likely to be encountered in the region. The plants include representatives from all of the vegetation zones, from the valleys to the alpine tundra. Most of the plants are common and widespread, but a few are rare or restricted in distribution. To produce an illustrated book that can be carried in the field with ease severely limits the number of species that can be included. If the species you are searching for cannot be found here, you may wish to consult the Selected References section at the back of the book.

Flower Color

Plants are grouped in this book according to flower color (blue and purple; pink; red and orange; yellow; white; and green and brown). Flower color is a convenient means of quickly grouping plants for identification purposes, but a word of caution is needed. Wildflowers, like all living things, are variable. No two individuals are exactly alike. Color variation is common in all plant species. For example, many white-flowered species have pale pink or lavender color variations. Also, many flowers fade from white to pink or even purple as they age. Some flowers even change color in response to pollination; this color change is a signal to the insect pollinator not to waste energy revisiting a flower that has already been attended to. Some plants have multicolored flowers; in this case, the plants are placed in the color group that seems most prominent.

Within each color grouping, the flowers are arranged in alphabetical order by scientific name, first by family, then genus, and then species. For example, all yellow flowers in the aster family (Asteraceae) are grouped together and arranged alphabetically from *Arnica* to *Tanacetum.*

Plant Names

The first name listed for each plant in this field guide is a common name. There is no universally accepted list of common names for plants. Any common name in general use for a plant in a local area is as valid as another name for the same plant in a different area. For example, serviceberry is known as "sarvisberry" in Montana, "juneberry" or "shadbush" farther east, and "Saskatoon" in Canada. Additional common names applied to a species are often listed in the comments section of the plant description.

Carolus Linnaeus (1707–1778) was the great Swedish naturalist who created the descriptive system that standardized the terminology and naming of plants and animals. He also developed a way to systematically organize the information. His system, which provides a common language for the scientific naming of organisms, has been adopted worldwide. For example, the scientific name of the mockorange is *Philadelphus lewisii*, which is a combination of *Philadelphus*, the generic name, followed by the specific epithet, *lewisii*. Although there are other species in the genus *Philadelphus*, the binomial scientific name *Philadelphus lewisii* defines only the one species that is the state flower of Idaho, the mockorange, or syringa.

The scientific name is followed by the last name (often abbreviated) of the authority who first published an account describing the species. The mockorange first became known to the science of botany after Meriwether Lewis collected a specimen in 1806, near present-day Missoula, Montana. The species was first described in the literature in 1814, in *Flora Americae Septentrionalis,* by Frederick Pursh. Thus, the complete scientific name and authority of the mockorange is *Philadelphus lewisii* Pursh.

Although there is only one valid scientific name for a species, sometimes botanists find it necessary to change the family or the scientific name of a species. For example, if botanists find that a species was named in a previous publication that had been overlooked, the name would be changed to the earlier published name. The second name would then become a synonym or an invalid name for the species. In this field guide I have also listed some of the more familiar synonyms, or currently invalid names, in parentheses, as in the example below:

CLUSTERED ELKWEED
Frasera fastigiata (Pursh) Heller
(also *Swertia fastigiata* Pursh)
Gentian Family (Gentianaceae)

Notice in the example above that the scientific name and synonym of the species are followed by the common name of the family and then, in parentheses, the scientific name of the family. Family names were created using the name of a genus in the family, followed by *-aceae*. Thus, the gentian family, Gentianaceae, is named for the genus *Gentiana*.

In a very few cases in this book, the scientific name for a plant will include the variety. Varieties are plants that differ slightly but consistently from other plants within the species. They are usually found within distinct geographic ranges within that of the species as a whole. In most cases I have not described the many varieties of plant species. When you use a description and photograph to identify a plant, remember that many species have wide variations in plant characteristics.

In assigning a family and scientific name to the plants in this book I have attempted to use the most recently accepted names. In doing so I have consulted the following floral manuals: *Flora of the Pacific Northwest* (Hitchcock and Cronquist, 1973), *Vascular Plants of Montana* (Dorn, 1984), *Flora of Idaho* (Davis, 1952), *Flora of Alberta* (Moss, 1959), and *Flora of North America*, volumes 1, 2, and 3 (Morin, 1993–1997). For more sources of information, see the Selected References section at the end of this book.

Description

In the description section of each wildflower entry, I present the key characteristics of the plant as well as its unique features, including its leaves, bracts, flowers, and sometimes its fruit. I give the dimensions of the leaves and flowers in inches. Please note that these measurements are averages. Since plants are variable in all of their features, take measurements of a number of representatives and then average them before deciding if the plant fits within the range given. A 10x hand lens is sometimes necessary to see some of the tiny plant parts described in this section.

These descriptions are necessarily brief and incomplete and are intended for use with the photograph to identify the plant. Closely related plants are often also described. There may be occasions when a plant does not exactly match an entry, but it is close. In many cases this will be because the plant in question is of a different species in the same genus as the plant that is photographed and described. Botanical manuals listed in the Selected References section may be required to resolve these identification problems. These manuals include more complete botanical keys, descriptions, and often fine line drawings of all of the species in the Northern Rocky Mountains. These manuals are readily available through the public library in most communities.

Bloom Season

The blooming period is given as a range of months, for example: July–September. This means that this particular species can be found blooming someplace within the Northern Rocky Mountains during this period. In any one area, the blooming period may be much shorter, sometimes only a week or two. Blooming and other phenologic events, such as leafing out and fruit ripening, differ according to the latitude and elevation in which the plant is growing. Most of us have noticed the flowers of any given species blooming later in the mountains than they do in the foothills. According to A. D. Hopkins's bioclimatic law, blooming (and other spring-summer events) occurs four days later for each degree of latitude northward or each elevation gain of 400 feet. This assumes that other habitat variables are equal, such as slope exposure. With autumn events, such as leaf color change, the sequence is reversed, with fall colors showing earlier at higher elevations and more northern latitudes. Life activity in the arctic or alpine zones is thus compressed into a very short period of six to eight weeks.

Habitat/Range

This section describes the characteristic environment and geographic range of the plant species. Some plants found in the Northern Rocky Mountains also grow in suitable habitats around the world; others are unique to the Northern Rocky Mountains.

Plants in this book are native to the Northern Rocky Mountains unless I have specifically stated otherwise. Introduced species usually include those imported from Europe and Asia that have escaped cultivation or have accidentally spread into the wild and are now found growing in disturbed or undisturbed habitats in the region. Some introduced species are native to other geographic regions of North America but have only been established in the Northern Rocky Mountains since European settlement of this continent. Information about the conservation of the native wildflowers of the Northern Rocky Mountains is available from the native plant societies of Alberta, British Columbia, Montana, Idaho, and Washington, as well as from the natural heritage data center of each state and province. Contact information for these organizations is listed in the Native Plant Directory at the end of this book.

Comments

This section offers additional information about the plant, including the origin of its name, the history of its discovery, and its traditional or historical uses as food or medicine. This information is included solely to help the reader learn the plant species through association with interesting information about the plant.

This book, or any book, does not contain enough information to enable you to safely experiment with using plants for food or medicine. In 1984, six out of eight men on a float trip on the Owyhee River in eastern Oregon were poisoned after eating what they thought were wild parsnips. One of them died. In 1985, a hiker in Yellowstone National Park who used a plant guidebook to identify edible plants died a painful death from water hemlock poisoning. Please heed this warning.

In addition to posing possible health hazards, picking wildflowers and harvesting plants reduces the reproductive capacity of the native species and also the enjoyment of other wildflower enthusiasts. The large-scale commercial harvesting ("wildcrafting") of wild medicinal plants and products for the herb and floral industry is reducing populations of certain native species of plants in the Northern Rocky Mountains. Please practice "zero impact" wildflower study: Leave plants as you found them for others to enjoy.

BLUE AND PURPLE FLOWERS

Clustered Elkweed

This section includes flowers ranging from pale blue to deep indigo and from lavender to violet. Since lavender flowers grade into pink, you should check the pink section if you do not find the flower you are looking for here.

Wild Ginger

WILD GINGER
Asarum caudatum Lindl.
Birthwort Family (Aristolochiaceae)

Description: The shy flowers of wild ginger are found hiding under the plant's leaves and under dead conifer needles on the forest floor. The flowers consist of 3 brownish purple sepals that are broad at the base but taper to long tail-like appendages at the tip. No true petals are present, but there are 12 stamens and a 6-celled inferior ovary. The plants also reproduce vegetatively by creeping horizontal stems that root at the nodes, forming leafy mats. The heart-shaped leaves are up to 4" long and 6" wide. They occur in pairs on long petioles that are attached opposite each other on the stems. When crushed, the plant emits a strong, distinctly gingerlike aroma.

Bloom Season: April–July.

Habitat/Range: Moist montane forests, often under old-growth cedar or hemlock.

Comments: Because its flower parts are in threes, wild ginger appears to be a mono-cotyledon (like a lily). However, its strongly net-veined leaves reveal its true classification as a dicotyledon (more like a pea). Wild ginger is a medicinal herb used much the same as the true ginger herb *(Zingiber officinalis)*. It is useful in promoting sweating to break a fever, as a poultice applied to cuts and bruises, and as a drink to treat colds and indigestion. On June 27, 1806, when on the Lolo Trail, Meriwether Lewis described the treatment of the inflamed leg of expedition member John Potts by writing in his journal: "we applied the pounded roots and leaves of the wild ginger & from which he found great relief."

LONG-LEAVED ASTER
Aster ascendens Lindl.
(also *Aster chilensis* Nees)
Aster Family (Asteraceae)

Description: The long, narrow leaves of this aster are mostly less than ⅜" wide and 7 times longer than wide. The basal leaves are widest above the middle, tapering toward the base. Surrounding the base of the flower heads are green-tipped bracts in several overlapping series, like shingles. The outer bracts are shorter and more bluntly tipped than the longer, sharply pointed inner bracts. The flower heads consist of violet to pink rays surrounding a yellow disk.

Bloom Season: July–October.

Habitat/Range: Valleys and dry montane forests.

Comments: Long-leaved aster spreads by creeping underground stems, making it well adapted to surviving wildfires. It often increases in abundance and flowers profusely in the years following forest fires.

Long-Leaved Aster

Showy Aster

SHOWY ASTER
Aster conspicuus Lindl.
Aster Family (Asteraceae)

Description: Showy aster has erect stems, 1–3' tall, arising from an extensive system of underground stems or rhizomes. Through the vegetative reproduction of these creeping rhizomes, the plants form large communities on the forest floor. The leaves are egg shaped with sharp teeth on the margin and taper to both the base and the pointed tip. A sandpaper-like texture on the leaf surface is a key identifying characteristic. Flowers are arranged in a cluster of heads on the top of the plant, with purple to lavender rays and a yellow disk. The bracts of the flower head are rather broad, with a paperlike base and a green, pointed tip.

Bloom Season: July–September.

Habitat/Range: In woods from the montane forests to the subalpine zone.

Comments: While this aster is indeed showy when in bloom, it more often forms a leafy ground cover which is rather "inconspicuous." However, following a wildfire the plants respond by sprouting and flowering abundantly.

Leafy Aster

LEAFY ASTER
Aster foliaceus Lindl.
Aster Family (Asteraceae)

Description: Leafy aster has large, entire leaves; the middle and lower ones are mostly over ½" wide and 2–5" long. There are varying amounts of hair on the surface of the seeds, bracts, leaves, and stems. The bracts are pointed, green, and leaflike, especially the outer ones. The bases of the inner bracts have white margins. The rays of the flower heads vary in color from rose-purple to blue or violet, surrounding a yellow disk. There are several varieties of this species. The one illustrated (var. *lyallii*) has leaves that strongly clasp the stem and soft hairs on the bracts, leaves, and stems.

Bloom Season: July–September.

Habitat/Range: Near streams, from moist montane forests to the alpine.

Comments: A common similar species, smooth aster *(A. laevis)*, also has clasping leaves, but it is hairless and has blue-green foliage with a white powdery substance on the surface that rubs off. American Indians used leafy aster to treat wounds and stomachaches.

BULL THISTLE
Cirsium vulgare (Savi) Ten.
Aster Family (Asteraceae)

Description: There are short, bristly hairs on the surface of the leaves of bull thistle that make it rough to the touch. Spiny winged ridges line the stems, originating below the base of the leaves. The bracts around the base of the flower heads occur in several overlapping series, each one with a long, stiff, sharp spine. The large flower heads consist of numerous, small, purple disk flowers and lack any ray flowers. The plants are biennial weeds, growing vegetatively in flat rosettes on the ground the first year; then bolting, flowering, producing seed, and dying the second year.

Bloom Season: July–September.

Habitat/Range: Introduced weed, usually occurring on disturbed soils in valleys and montane forests, often along streams and seepage areas.

Comments: *Cirsium* is named from the Greek *kirsos,* meaning "swollen vein," which thistles were supposedly used to treat.

Bull Thistle

SHOWY FLEABANE DAISY
Erigeron speciosus (Lindl.) DC.
Aster Family (Asteraceae)

Description: Showy fleabane is distinguished by its entire leaves (not lobed or toothed) that are well distributed along the full length of the stem. There is no hair on the leaves, except for a sparse fringe along the leaf margin. There are 1–13 flower heads on each flowering stem. Each flower head has but a single row of narrow green bracts of equal length, and numerous blue to lavender petal-like ray flowers surrounding a golden yellow disk.

Bloom Season: June–early August.

Habitat/Range: Valleys to subalpine forests.

Comments: *Erigeron* comes from the Greek *eri-*, meaning "early," and *geron*, meaning "old man," named presumably because of the early flowering and fruiting habit of fleabane daisy. Some American Indians used species of *Erigeron* as an astringent herb by boiling the root to make a strong tea. The cooled tea was used as an eyewash and to treat diarrhea or childbirth hemorrhage.

Showy Fleabane Daisy

Parry's Townsendia

PARRY'S TOWNSENDIA
Townsendia parryi Eat.
Aster Family (Asteraceae)

Description: Townsendias have a taproot, basal leaves, and flower bracts with a distinct fringe along the margin. Parry's townsendia has an erect stem up to 12" tall. The flower heads are huge, from 1½" to 3½" in diameter from the tips of the colorful ray flowers across the center of the head. The flowers are lavender to purplish or blue, and very showy. Most leaves are basal and broadened toward the tip, tapering toward the base. Leaves on the flowering stem are usually progressively smaller up the stem.

Bloom Season: June–August.

Habitat/Range: Valleys, dry montane, and subalpine forests.

Comments: Parry's townsendia was named for Charles C. Parry (1823–1890), a native of England who came to America in 1832 and contributed much to our knowledge of the native flora. He was a botanist with the Mexican Boundary Survey.

Many-Flowered Stickseed

MANY-FLOWERED STICKSEED
Hackelia floribunda (Lehm.) Johnst.
Borage Family (Boraginaceae)

Description: Many-flowered stickseed has blue flowers and is distinguished by having flower stalks that turn downward as the prickly nutlet fruit forms after flowering. Many-flowered stickseed is a tall, robust plant 1–3' tall. It has a single, or few, flowering stems arising from a taproot. It is a short-lived plant, often completing its life cycle in 2 years.

Bloom Season: June–August.

Habitat/Range: Moist meadows and stream banks, from valleys to subalpine forests.

Comments: The plant is called "stickseed" because of the prickles on the nutlets that stick to animal hair, socks, and almost anything else. In this way the seeds are carried to new places to germinate and propagate the species.

STREAMSIDE BLUEBELLS
Mertensia ciliata (Torr.) G. Don
Borage Family (Boraginaceae)

Description: Bluebells have long, tubelike, blue (or pink) petals that extend well beyond the green sepals. This species is a tall, robust plant from less than 1' to as much as 5' tall. The middle and upper leaves of the flowering stems are up to 2" wide, mostly without a leaf stem (petiole), and are tapered toward the base. Several other closely related bluebell species grow in the Northern Rocky Mountains, including mountain bluebells *(M. oblongifolia),* which is a smaller plant (16" high or less) that grows in the valleys and dry montane forests.

Bloom Season: June–August.

Habitat/Range: Near streams within moist montane and subalpine forests.

Comments: The tender, fresh leaves and flowers of bluebells are edible fresh or cooked, and the taste is said to be like that of oysters. They should not be consumed in large quantities, though, because of possible toxic properties.

Streamside Bluebells

WOODS FORGET-ME-NOT
Myosotis sylvatica Hoffm.
Borage Family (Boraginaceae)

Description: Woods forget-me-not has blue flowers with a yellow "eye" that strongly resemble alpine forget-me-not *(Eritrichium)* and stickseeds *(Hackelia* and *Lappula)*. However, woods forget-me-not does not form dense leafy cushions like alpine forget-me-not, and it has smooth nutlet fruits without the prickles of stickseeds. Woods forget-me-not plants are 2–16" tall. They are covered with hair that often has tiny hooks.

Bloom Season: July–August.

Habitat/Range: Moist meadows, from montane forests to the alpine.

Comments: *Myosotis* means "mouse ear" in Greek, probably because of the hairy appearance and shape of the leaves. *Sylvatica* comes from the Latin component *sylva*, referring to its woodland or forest habitat. This plant is the floral emblem of Alaska.

Woods Forget-Me-Not

Harebell

HAREBELL
Campanula rotundifolia L.
Harebell Family (Campanulaceae)

Description: Harebell has blue to white, bell-shaped flowers. There are usually several (up to 20) flowers per plant. The leaves on the flowering stem are long and less than ¼" wide. The basal leaves are broader, round to heart shaped, but these often dry up by the time the plants are in full flower. The leaves exude a milky juice when broken. The fruit is a capsule that hangs downward and opens by pores near the base.

Bloom Season: June–September.

Habitat/Range: Valleys to subalpine forests.

Comments: Harebell is easy to cultivate and seeds freely. However, it can become weedy in the garden. It is also called "bluebell," but it is not related to bluebells of the genus *Mertensia* in the borage family. A closely related species, creeping bellflower *(C. rapunculoides),* was imported from Europe as a garden flower. This exotic relative of harebell has spread into lawns, where it is difficult to control.

Alpine Milkvetch

WESTERN SWEETVETCH

Hedysarum occidentale Greene
Bean Family (Fabaceae)

Description: Western sweetvetch has rose-pink to magenta-purple "bean flowers" that droop downward from one side of the main flower stalk. Leaves are pinnately compound, consisting of many leaflets arranged "featherlike" on either side of the main leaf axis. Sweetvetch is easily distinguished from milkvetch by having wing petals that are much shorter than the keel petal and by having fruit pods that are constricted between the seeds. The large pods of western sweetvetch have a thin, membranous margin or wing, which helps to separate this species from the similarly colored northern sweetvetch *(H. boreale)* and alpine sweetvetch *(H. alpinum)*.

Bloom Season: June–August.

Habitat/Range: Montane and subalpine forests.

Comments: The name *Hedysarum* is derived from the Greek *hedy-* (sweet) and *saron* (broom). Sweetvetches are good forage plants for both wild and domestic animals.

ALPINE MILKVETCH

Astragalus alpinus L.
Bean Family (Fabaceae)

Description: The distinctive bean-family flowers of alpine milkvetch are bicolored. The banner and keel tip are lavender, contrasting with the white wings and keel base. Unlike most milkvetch species, the wing petals are somewhat shorter than the keel petal, resembling sweetvetch (*Hedysarum* species). However, the pods are usually covered with black hairs and are not constricted between the seeds. The leaves are pinnately compound. The egg-shaped leaflets often have a slight indentation in the tip.

Bloom Season: June–August.

Habitat/Range: Stream banks and meadows, from subalpine forests to the alpine.

Comments: Alpine milkvetch is somewhat of a misnomer, since in the Northern Rockies it is more often seen in moist meadows in the subalpine forest zone rather than in the alpine. However, the full range of the species includes arctic and montane forests in northern latitudes around the globe.

Western Sweetvetch

SILVERY LUPINE
Lupinus argenteus Pursh
Bean Family (Fabaceae)

Description: Lupines have palmately compound leaves and a raceme flower arrangement. The flowers of silvery lupine are usually blue but sometimes pink or white. The banner petal is usually smooth (hairless) on most of the back surface. The banner is only slightly reflexed from the wings and keel to form a narrow V-shaped opening of 45 degrees or less. The plants are usually 24" or less tall. The leaflets are 1–2" long and ⅛–⅝" wide.

Bloom Season: May–July.

Habitat/Range: Valleys, dry montane, and subalpine forest meadows.

Comments: *Argenteus* is Latin for "silvery," probably because of the sheen of the leaves in certain light. Silvery lupine was first described to Western science by Frederick Pursh, from a specimen collected by Meriwether Lewis in the upper Blackfoot River drainage of Montana on July 7, 1806, on the return voyage of the Lewis and Clark Expedition.

Silvery Lupine

Meadow Lupine

MEADOW LUPINE
Lupinus polyphyllus Lindl.
Bean Family (Fabaceae)

Description: Meadow lupine flowers are blue to violet, sometimes lighter colored toward the middle. The banner is broadly reflexed from the wings and keel, forming a wide V-shaped opening of about 60 degrees or more. The palmately compound leaves have numerous large leaflets, 4–6" long and ½–1" wide. The upper surface of the leaf is usually hairless, while the lower surface is variously hairy. Meadow lupine is 20–60" tall and has hollow stems.

Bloom Season: June–August.

Habitat/Range: Streamsides and wet meadows, from montane to subalpine forests.

Comments: *Lupinus* is derived from the Latin *lupus* (wolf). Many lupines have poisonous alkaloids concentrated in their seeds. More sheep losses have been reported from lupine poisoning than from any other genus of plants in the Rockies. Entire bands of 1,000 sheep have died from eating the plants under certain unfavorable conditions.

Red Clover

RED CLOVER
Trifolium pratense L.
Bean Family (Fabaceae)

Description: This is a common clover, with 50–200 deep red to purple flowers arranged in dense, stalkless heads 1" or more in diameter, arising at the ends of leafy branches. Sometimes the heads are attached to a short stalk, less than the length of the 2 leaves that lie immediately underneath. The leaflets appear in threes (as in all clovers), and the foliage and sepals are covered with long, soft, and silky hair. A lighter green, crescent-shaped spot lies within the darker green background color of each leaflet. These short-lived perennial plants are 1–3' tall.

Bloom Season: June–August.

Habitat/Range: Introduced from Europe, it grows in disturbed places from the valleys to the moist subalpine forests.

Comments: This is a nutritious forage plant that has been planted for hay and green manure. Where it escapes cultivation, it competes with the native vegetation. Herbalists value red clover as a remedy for skin problems in both children and adults. It is also an effective expectorant for treating coughs, bronchitis and whooping cough.

American Vetch

AMERICAN VETCH
Vicia americana Muhl. ex Willd.
Bean Family (Fabaceae)

Description: True vetches (*Vicia* species) are herbaceous vines with pinnately compound leaves. The leaf has a slender coiling or twining tendril on the end, which is used for climbing and grasping for support. Sweet peas (*Lathyrus* species) also have leaves with tendrils. However, a careful look at the flowers with a hand lens will show true vetches to be equally hairy all around the end of the style, while sweet peas have hair only on the inner, flattened style surface. The blue flowers of American vetch are rather large (½" long or more) and are arranged in groups of 4–10.

Bloom Season: May–August.

Habitat/Range: Valleys to subalpine forests.

Comments: Like other members of the bean family, the roots of vetches have nodules that house bacterial colonies in a symbiotic relationship. The bacteria take elemental nitrogen from the air and incorporate it into compounds that dissolve in water, making the nitrogen usable for plant growth.

Clustered Elkweed

CLUSTERED ELKWEED
Frasera fastigiata (Pursh) Heller
(also *Swertia fastigiata* Pursh)
Gentian Family (Gentianaceae)

Description: Clustered elkweed is a large plant, with a single flowering stem 20–60" tall and large basal leaves 8–18" long by 2–5" wide. Leafy whorls of 3 leaves each garnish the stems, with pale to dark blue flowers densely clustered at the top. The plants have smooth (hairless) and rather soft, tender foliage. There are 4 sepals, 4 petals, and 4 stamens in each flower. Near the base of each petal is a circular nectary gland surrounded by a tiny fringed membrane. A longer fringe lines the base of the petal. Nonflowering plants, consisting of rosettes of basal leaves at the ground surface, are often seen growing near the plants in flower. In the related species green gentian *(F. speciosa)*, this vegetative stage lasts from 20 to 60 years or more. The plants apparently grow without flowering for many years, while storing food for their one climactic flowering event, and then die.

Bloom Season: May–July.

Habitat/Range: Moist montane forests and meadows.

Comments: The name *Frasera* honors John Fraser (1750–1811), an Englishman who collected plants in North America. During the Lewis and Clark Expedition, clustered elkweed was collected by Meriwether Lewis on June 14, 1806, "in moist wet places, on Squamash flats," near present-day Weippe, Idaho.

NORTHERN GENTIAN
Gentianella amarella (L.) Boerner
(also *Gentiana amarella* L.)
Gentian Family (Gentianaceae)

Description: Northern gentian is a small, annual or biennial plant 4–16" tall. There are numerous, small flowers in crowded cymes on the end of the stems and in the leaf axils, often nearly to the base of the plant. Each tubular flower has 4 (sometimes 5) sepals, petal lobes, and stamens. Flower color varies from purplish blue to pale blue. Just inside the throat of the flower is a crown of fringe.

Bloom Season: June–September.

Habitat/Range: Meadows and moist areas, from valleys to subalpine forests.

Comments: Plants in the genus *Gentianella* have flowers without the pleats between the petal lobes characteristic of the related genus *Gentiana,* and they lack the fringe on the margin of the petal lobes found in *Gentianopsis.* All are commonly called "gentian."

Northern Gentian

Explorer's Gentian

EXPLORER'S GENTIAN
Gentiana calycosa Griseb.
Gentian Family (Gentianaceae)

Description: The flowers of explorer's gentian are funnel shaped, deep blue, and rather large (about 1½" long). Before opening, the upper petal tube has a lovely, pointed, spiral form, like a swirled ice cream cone. Once the flower opens, there are conspicuous pleats between each of the 5 petal lobes. The leaves are opposite and somewhat egg shaped. The leaves, stems, and sepals are smooth, without any hairs. Plant stems are usually unbranched with a single flower on the end, or sometimes with a compact, few-flowered cluster.

Bloom Season: July–early September.

Habitat/Range: Wet meadows and stream banks in subalpine forests and the alpine tundra.

Comments: *Gentiana* was named in honor of King Gentius of ancient Illyria in the Adriatic, who is credited with discovering its medicinal properties. Gentians have been used for centuries as a bitter herb to improve digestion.

Bog Swertia

BOG SWERTIA
Swertia perennis L.
Gentian Family (Gentianaceae)

Description: Bog swertia is a perennial, herbaceous plant with a cluster of basal leaves with petioles (leaf stalks), and a few leaves attached directly to the flowering stem without petioles. The flowers have 5 purple petals and 5 green sepals. The flowers are wheel shaped and flat, with a very short tube. Two fringed nectary glands occur near the base of each petal. The purple petals are streaked with white or green.

Bloom Season: July–early September.

Habitat/Range: Wet meadows, bogs, and along streams in subalpine forests.

Comments: *Swertia* is named in honor of Emmanuel Sweerts, a 16th-century Dutch gardener and engraver. It is often found growing in association with bog orchids.

Sticky Geranium

STICKY GERANIUM
Geranium viscosissimum Fisch. & Mey. ex Mey.
Geranium Family (Geraniaceae)

Description: Sticky geranium is a perennial, herbaceous plant with a thick, woody taproot. Petal color varies from pink to lavender or violet, with dark red veins. The leaves are deeply parted into 5–7 coarsely toothed segments. Glandular hairs cover the sepals and often the leaf stems and other parts of the plant. When touched, the glands exude a sticky, aromatic substance with a strong "geranium bouquet."

Bloom Season: June–August.

Habitat/Range: Moist to moderately dry, open slopes, from the valleys to subalpine meadows.

Comments: *Geranium* comes from a Greek word for "crane," in reference to the long, pointed style or persistent beak of the pods; "crane's-bill" is another common name for plants in the genus. Herbalists use the astringent herb to treat many conditions, including sore throat, tonsillitis, external sores, abrasions, hemorrhoids, gum inflammations, and tooth infections. American Indians used a species of *Geranium*, boiled to yield an astringent tea, to treat dysentery. Other folk uses of geraniums include treating diabetes and as an aphrodisiac.

Ballhead Waterleaf

BALLHEAD WATERLEAF
Hydrophyllum capitatum Dougl. ex Benth.
Waterleaf Family (Hydrophyllaceae)

Description: Ballhead waterleaf has a distinctive, fuzzy, ball-shaped cluster of lavender to bluish flowers underneath the leaves near the ground. The stalk of the flower arrangement is seldom over 2" long. The filaments are conspicuous, extending well beyond the flower petals. The deeply divided and toothed leaves, 4–16" long, often have a lower pair of segments that are somewhat remote from the upper ones.

Bloom Season: April–June.

Habitat/Range: Woodlands and open slopes, from the valleys to the subalpine forests.

Comments: *Hydrophyllum* is derived from the Greek *hydr-* (water) and *phyllon* (leaf), which is fitting for this plant with its tender, succulent leaves. Several species of *Hydrophyllum* were used by American Indians for both food and medicine, especially for combating diarrhea.

THREADLEAF PHACELIA
Phacelia linearis (Pursh) Holz.
Waterleaf Family (Hydrophyllaceae)

Description: This is a slender, annual plant with showy, blue flowers. Some of the leaves are narrow and entire, while the larger ones have 1–4 lateral lobes below the middle. The plant is erect, 4–20" tall, with numerous small clusters of flowers originating in the upper leaf axils.

Bloom Season: April–June.

Habitat/Range: Dry and open, often rocky places, in valleys and dry montane forests.

Comments: Because of its curved or spiraled flower arrangements, *Phacelia* species are often called "scorpionweeds." This species was first collected for science on April 7, 1806, by Meriwether Lewis at his Rock Fort Camp, near what is now The Dalles, Oregon. Some American Indians prepared a tea from this plant to treat colds.

Threadleaf Phacelia

SILKY PHACELIA
Phacelia sericea (Grah.) A. Gray
Waterleaf Family (Hydrophyllaceae)

Description: Silky phacelia is a perennial, herbaceous plant having leaves deeply divided into many segments, covered with silky hairs, and with a taproot. The numerous purple to blue flowers are arranged in clusters of coiled branches, like scorpion tails, that uncoil as blooming progresses. Individual flowers have stamens with long filaments that extend well beyond the petals.

Bloom Season: June–August.

Habitat/Range: Open, rocky slopes at moderate to high elevations in the montane and subalpine forests.

Comments: *Phacelia* comes from the Greek *phakelos,* which refers to the dense flower arrangement. The plants make attractive ornamentals for the rock garden and are easily grown from seed. Some species of *Phacelia* are reported to irritate the skin when handled.

Silky Phacelia

Missouri Iris

MISSOURI IRIS
Iris missouriensis Nutt.
Iris Family (Iridaceae)

Description: Missouri iris has parallel-veined leaves and flower parts in threes; an inferior ovary (floral parts attached to the top); and petal-like style branches. The blue flowers are more than 2" long. It has thick underground rhizomes. This is the only native iris in the Northern Rocky Mountains. However, a yellow-flowered domestic iris *(I. pseudacorus)* has escaped cultivation and is seen along low-elevation streams and lakes.

Bloom Season: May–July.

Habitat/Range: Moist meadows in valleys and dry montane forests.

Comments: *Iris* is Greek for "rainbow," referring to the many colors of iris flowers. Also called "blue flag" and "fleur-de-lis," it is the national flower and emblem of France and the state flower of Tennessee. Missouri iris is both a dangerous poisonous plant and valuable medicinal herb.

Montana Blue-Eyed Grass

MONTANA BLUE-EYED GRASS
Sisyrinchium montanum Greene
Iris Family (Iridaceae)

Description: Like iris, the leaves of blue-eyed grass are folded together lengthwise in 2 ranks and are mostly basal. However, unlike iris, the petals and sepals of blue-eyed grass are short (less than 1¼" long) and similar in shape, and the style branches are not petal-like. The leaves are long and narrow, like grass leaves, but stiffer. The flowers are blue to purple with a yellow center and a bristle tip on each petal. The outer flower bract of Montana blue-eyed grass is nearly twice the length of the inner one.

Bloom Season: April–July.

Habitat/Range: Meadows and stream banks, from valleys to montane forests.

Comments: Other names for blue-eyed grass include "eyebright," "grass-widows," and "blue star." Rocky Mountain plants were previously referred to as *S. angustifolium,* which is now recognized as an eastern species.

FIELD MINT
Mentha arvensis L.
(also *Mentha canadensis* L.)
Mint Family (Lamiaceae)

Description: Field mint is an aromatic herb with square stems and opposite leaves, which are typical of the mint family. However, the flowers of field mint have petals that are similar in size and shape, unlike the 2-lipped flowers of most other plants in the mint family. The small blue, purple, or pink flowers of field mint form in clusters located in the leaf axils.

Bloom Season: July–September.

Habitat/Range: Stream banks and wet areas, from the valleys to the subalpine forests.

Comments: In Greek mythology, the nymph Minthe, daughter of Cocytus and a favorite of Pluto, was changed into one of these plants by the jealous Proserpine. Hikers and canoeists often smell the strong aroma of field mint, crushed underfoot, before they see it. The herb is gathered for its flavor and medicinal value; it is useful for stomachache, colds, and fever.

Field Mint

SELF-HEAL
Prunella vulgaris L.
Mint Family (Lamiaceae)

Description: Square stems, opposite leaves, and irregular, 2-lipped flowers readily places this herb in the mint family. The flowers of self-heal are arranged in a dense head on the end of the short stems (4–20"). The stamens are hidden under the rounded hood of the upper lip petal. A fringe lines the margin of the lower lip. There are 3 teeth on the upper lobe of the sepals and 2 teeth on the lower.

Bloom Season: May–September.

Habitat/Range: Common and widespread in moist places, from valleys to lower subalpine forests.

Comments: Self-heal, or heal-all, has long been used by herbalists for treating both external and internal wounds. American Indians likewise valued the herb medicinally in caring for a variety of conditions including heart problems, eye sores, and diarrhea.

Self-Heal

Narrow-Leaved Skullcap

NARROW-LEAVED SKULLCAP
Scutellaria angustifolia Pursh
Mint Family (Lamiaceae)

Description: The flowers of narrow-leaved skullcap are in pairs, one each attached in the axils of the opposite leaves. The blue-violet tubular petals are 2-lipped, like snapdragons. Long, flattened white hairs are attached on the palate, or swollen surface of the lower lip. The flowers are ⅞" long or longer. The sepals also form a 2-lipped tube, with a ridged projection across the upper surface.

Bloom Season: May–June.

Habitat/Range: Rocky slopes of dry montane forests.

Comments: Some skullcap species are used by herbalists as a nerve sedative. A specimen of narrow-leaved skullcap was collected by Meriwether Lewis on June 5, 1806, "on the Kooskooskee" or present-day Clearwater River canyon near Kamiah, Idaho.

Siberian Chives

SIBERIAN CHIVES
Allium schoenoprasum L.
Lily Family (Liliaceae)

Description: Chives are perennial herbs growing from clusters of bulbs. The flowers have 3 lilac-colored petals and sepals, which are alike in size and shape. The flowers are arranged in an umbel at the top of the plant, with all the flower stalks attached at a common point, like an umbrella. The flowers begin blooming from the center of the arrangement and progress outward to the perimeter. The leaves are round and hollow, and all parts of the plant have a strong oniony aroma and flavor.

Bloom Season: April–August.

Habitat/Range: Wet meadows, from valleys to subalpine forests.

Comments: Plants in the genus *Allium* (including chives, onions, and garlic) have long been used for food and flavoring. In herbal medicine it is valued for its strongly anti-microbial properties. Wild Siberian chives is the same species that has been cultivated for centuries.

Blue Camas

BLUE CAMAS
Camassia quamash (Pursh) Greene
Lily Family (Liliaceae)

Description: Blue camas flowers are arranged in a raceme with a narrow, leafy bract below each flower. The sepals and petals vary in color from deep purple to pale blue and occasionally white. Each flower has 6 stamens and a single style, which often falls away as the capsule matures. Leaves are linear and arise from an underground bulb. Death camas (*Zigadenus* species) are similar, but can be distinguished by their white to yellow-green flowers with 3 persistent styles and a gland at the base of each petal.

Bloom Season: April–early July.

Habitat/Range: Moist meadows, from valleys to subalpine forests.

Comments: *Camassia* and *quamash* are derived from the names applied to this plant by the Nimi'-pu, or Nez Perce people. On September 20, 1805, William Clark, with an advance party of the Lewis and Clark Expedition, found Nez Perce people busily digging and preparing the blue camas for food near present-day Weippe, Idaho. Clark described in his journals how they gathered immense piles of the camas bulbs and steamed them in pits. At the time, the expedition members were, as Meriwether Lewis wrote, "growing weak for the want of food . . . and have fallen off very much." The friendly Nez Perce shared with them their quamash bulbs and a bread that they made from it, which they called *pas-she-co.*

Purple Trillium

PURPLE TRILLIUM
Trillium petiolatum Pursh
Lily Family (Liliaceae)

Description: Purple trillium has a whorl of 3 large ovate leaves (3–5" in diameter) thrusting upward on conspicuous leaf stalks (petioles) from a short stem, which is often buried in the forest floor. The single, stalkless flower is usually purple but may be red, brown, or yellowish green. At the confluence of the leaf petioles, 3 green sepals form the base of the flower. The much more common white trillium *(T. ovatum)* has a long stem (4–16"), 3 large leaves without petioles, and a stalked flower that is white when fresh, often turning pink or purple with age.

Bloom Season: April–June.

Habitat/Range: Stream banks, meadows, and thickets of moist montane forests.

Comments: *Trillium* is well named, since all of its parts are arranged in threes. The first Western botanical collection of purple trillium was made by Meriwether Lewis on June 15, 1806, near present-day Weippe, Idaho, as the Lewis and Clark Expedition began the return journey over the Lolo Trail. Doubtful of their ability to follow the trail, covered by snowpack 12–15 feet deep, the expedition returned to Weippe Prairie a few days later, waiting there until they could be joined by Nez Perce Indian guides who would show them the way.

DOUGLAS'S WILD HYACINTH
Triteleia grandiflora Lindl.
(also *Brodiaea douglasii* S. Wats.)
Lily Family (Liliaceae)

Description: Wild hyacinth has blue flowers arranged in an umbel on the end of a long stalk. The petals are joined together in a basal tube for about half their length. The leaves are basal, with no leaves on the 8–28" long, slender flower stalk.

Bloom Season: May–July.

Habitat/Range: Grasslands and woodlands, from the valleys to the montane forests.

Comments: *Triteleia* comes from the Greek *trios* (three) and *teleios* (complete). This plant was first discovered and described by Meriwether Lewis on April 17, 1806, near present-day The Dalles, Oregon. Lewis wrote in his journal on that date: "there is a species of hiasinth in these plains the bulb of which the natives eat either boiled baked or dryed in the sun. this bulb is white, not entirely solid, and of a flat form; the bulb of the present year overlays, or crowns that of the last and seems to be pressed close to it. . . . this hiasinth is of a pale blue colour and is a very pretty flower."

Douglas's Wild Hyacinth

BLUE FLAX
Linum lewisii Pursh
Flax Family (Linaceae)

Description: In early summer, the bright blue flowers of blue flax wave above the grasses as if suspended there. Each flower has 5 sepals, 5 petals, 5 stamens, and 5 styles. The styles are considerably longer than the stamens. The leaves are narrow and alternate on the slender stems. The plants are perennial from a woody base and taproot.

Bloom Season: May–July.

Habitat/Range: Grasslands and openings, from valleys to the alpine.

Comments: *Linum lewisii* was named in honor of Meriwether Lewis by Frederick Pursh in his manual *Flora Americae Septentrionalis* (1814). Pursh described the species in this book from a plant collected by Lewis on July 9, 1806, along the Sun River in Montana. The seeds of blue flax were used as food by American Indians both for their flavor and nutritive value. The plants were also used medicinally to treat sore eyes and as a poultice to reduce swellings. The strong fibers of the stems were twisted into fishing line and other cordage.

Blue Flax

Giant Helleborine

CLEARWATER PHLOX
Phlox idahonis Wherry
Phlox Family (Polemoniaceae)

Description: This grandiose phlox stands erect on solitary stems from 20–40" tall. Broad leaves, 3½" long and 1½" wide, are arranged in pairs on opposite sides of the stems. The lower leaves quickly wither and dry up, while the upper ones are persistent. Large, showy, pink to purple flowers are arranged in clusters from the upper leaf axils and the end of the stems.

Bloom Season: June–August.

Habitat/Range: A rare species, restricted to a few meadows in northern Idaho.

Comments: This is the largest and most uncommon phlox in the Northern Rockies. Because of its extreme rarity it is ranked as G1/S1 by the Idaho Conservation Data Center, meaning that it is critically imperiled globally. If this species, or any other rare plant, is encountered in the field, it should be left strictly alone to survive in its natural habitat. Collecting of even a few plants, flowers, or seeds could tip the balance of these rare plants toward extinction.

GIANT HELLEBORINE
Epipactis gigantea Dougl.
Orchid Family (Orchidaceae)

Description: As the name implies, these are large plants, 1–3' tall or more. The numerous leaves clasp the stem. The lowest leaves are oval but quickly become lance shaped up the stem. Several (3–9) flowers occur in a raceme arrangement along the upper part of the stem. The sepals are greenish yellow with purple veins. The petals are similar but are rose with purple veins. The hinged lip is the most colorful petal, having a pink, heart-shaped tip. They reproduce vegetatively from strong underground stems.

Bloom Season: April–early August.

Habitat/Range: Wet soil of seeps and streams, often hot springs. It is rare in the Northern Rockies.

Comments: "Chatterbox" is another common name for this plant. The rapid movement of the hinged lip, with the slightest breeze, resembles the lower jaw of a funny little elf, gabbing away.

Clearwater Phlox

SHOWY JACOB'S LADDER
Polemonium pulcherrimum Hook.
Phlox Family (Polemoniaceae)

Description: Jacob's ladder differs from other members of the phlox family by having an herbaceous, green calyx tube of uniform texture and color. The compound leaves have many definite leaflets arranged pinnately along the main axis. Showy Jacob's ladder has a petal tube that is about as wide as it is long. The plants are usually less than 1' tall, although the variety *calycinum* is often taller (up to 20" high). The plants are covered with glandular hairs.

Bloom Season: May–August.

Habitat/Range: Montane, subalpine forests, and the alpine.

Comments: *Polemonium* is said to have been named either for the Greek philosopher, Polemon, or after the Greek *polemos,* meaning "strife." The glandular hairs of showy Jacob's ladder impart a mildly foul odor in some plants, while others are essentially odorless.

Showy Jacob's Ladder

Columbian Monkshood

COLUMBIAN MONKSHOOD
Aconitum columbianum Nutt.
Buttercup Family (Ranunculaceae)

Description: Monkshood resembles larkspur, but the upper sepal forms a hood that conceals the 2 true petals. The sepals are petal-like and brightly colored from blue to deep purple. Plants are 1–7' tall or taller, with numerous leaves up the flowering stem that are deeply cleft and toothed.

Bloom Season: June–August.

Habitat/Range: Subalpine forests and meadows.

Comments: *Aconitum* comes from the Greek *akoniton* (leopard poison), or possibly from the name Aconis, an ancient city of Bithynia in Asia Minor. *Aconitum* species contain poisonous alkaloids that vary widely in their toxicity; some are deadly poisonous. Columbian monkshood has been blamed for some livestock losses. The main symptoms of poisoning are numbness, and paralysis of the extremities and respiratory system. Trained herbalists have used the plant topically for pain.

Pasqueflower

PASQUEFLOWER

Anemone patens L.
(also *Pulsatilla hirsutissima* [Pursh] Brit.)
Buttercup Family (Ranunculaceae)

Description: Pasqueflower has basal leaves and 3 leafy bracts on the flowering stem, topped by a single, large, purple flower. The flower has many stamens and pistils. Each pistil has a style that persists as a long plumelike beak on the capsule. The leaves have stalks 2–4" long. The blades of the leaves are deeply cut into many long, narrow segments. The entire plant is covered by long, silky, straight hairs. It is often confused with sugarbowls *(Clematis hirsutissima)*, which it resembles. However, sugarbowls has numerous, opposite leaves on the flowering stem and no basal leaves. Pasqueflowers are among the first flowers to announce the coming of spring, with flowers sometimes pushing through the melting snow to bloom.

Bloom Season: March–August.

Habitat/Range: Open slopes and meadows, from the valleys to the alpine.

Comments: *Anemone* is from the Greek *anemos*, "the wind," which employed flowers to herald its coming. Strong winds are common in pasqueflower habitat and the flowers are sometimes called "windflower." It is the floral emblem of South Dakota and Manitoba. American Indians used this plant medicinally and have legends and songs that express their reverence and respect for this plant.

Limestone Columbine

LIMESTONE COLUMBINE
Aquilegia jonesii Parry
Buttercup Family (Ranunculaceae)

Description: The large, purple flowers of limestone columbine seem out of proportion to the small plants they grow on and are truly worth looking for. They are low, ground-hugging plants with leafless stems, seldom more than 4" tall, that bear a single flower (or sometimes 2). The leaves are all basal and densely crowded together near the ground surface. The flowers are quite showy, blue to purple, with short (½" long), straight spurs. It sometimes hybridizes with yellow columbine *(A. flavescens)*, producing a tall plant having large flowers with straight purple spurs and petals, but yellow sepal blades.

Bloom Season: June–July.

Habitat/Range: Limestone soils on alpine and subalpine ridgetops and upper slopes. It has a narrow geographic range along the Rocky Mountain Continental Divide and in island ranges from southern Alberta through Montana to northern Wyoming.

Comments: Most of the wildflowers found in the Northern Rocky Mountains also occur in the adjacent mountain regions of North America in one direction or another. Some are even found in Europe and Asia as well. However, limestone columbine makes its home only here in the high mountains of the Rockies. It is one of our few regional endemics, found nowhere else in the world.

Sugarbowls (flower)

(fruit)

SUGARBOWLS
Clematis hirsutissima Pursh
Buttercup Family (Ranunculaceae)

Description: Sugarbowls is an erect, herbaceous plant, not a twining vine like many other *Clematis* species. Because of its fuzzy plumelike seed heads and hairy, segmented leaves, sugarbowls is often mistaken for the similar pasqueflower *(Anemone patens)*, with which it often occurs. However, sugarbowls has several sets of opposite leaves on its erect stems, while pasqueflower's leaves are basal, with only a single leafy bract on its stem. The deep purple, leathery flower of sugarbowls looks much like an inverted vase; it is also called "vase flower" or "leather flower."

Bloom Season: April–July.

Habitat/Range: Open, dry, grassy areas, in the valleys, dry montane forests, and subalpine forests.

Comments: *Hirsutissima* is from the Latin *hirsut* (hairy) referring to the copious hair that covers this plant. American Indians used sugarbowls as an analgesic for headaches and nasal congestion. It was also applied to the nostrils of fallen horses, acting as a stimulant to bring them to their feet. A lotion of the plant was believed to provide protection from witches. The first scientific botanical specimen of this plant was collected by Meriwether Lewis on May 27, 1806, in the vicinity of present-day Kamiah, Idaho.

Western Virgin's Bower

WESTERN VIRGIN'S BOWER
Clematis occidentalis (Hornem.) DC.
(also *C. columbiana* [Nutt.] T. & G., misapplied)
Buttercup Family (Ranunculaceae)

Description: Western virgin's bower is a vine having compound leaves with only 3 leaflets. The similar Columbia virgin's bower *(C. columbiana)* has 6 or 9 leaflets per compound leaf. Flowers are purple or blue, and large and showy. The stem of the leaf often winds around tree branches or other plants as it climbs, searching for light under the shade of the forest canopy.

Bloom Season: May–July.

Habitat/Range: Shady forests, on cliffs, and in thickets of the montane and subalpine forests.

Comments: *Clematis* is from the Greek *klema*, referring to a plant shoot or vine. *Clematis* species are relatives of buttercups (genus *Ranunculus*), and it is suspected that they may contain similar toxic properties. Shoshone and other American Indians used virgin's bower externally as a poultice to reduce swellings or to bring boils to a head, and for rheumatic pain. Trained herbalists have used the plant as a liniment and internally for migraine headaches, but the amateur should not try this because of the toxic properties.

Low Larkspur

TALL MOUNTAIN LARKSPUR
Delphinium glaucum S. Wats.
Buttercup Family (Ranunculaceae)

Description: Tall mountain larkspur is often 5' tall or more. The flowers are bluish purple to lavender, and usually number 25 or more per stem. The 5 sepals are showy and project forward. The upper sepal has a long projection, or spur, on the back. Below the flowers, the stems are without hairs, but are covered with a fine, white, powdery substance that readily rubs off.

Bloom Season: July–August.

Habitat/Range: Subalpine forests.

Comments: Larkspurs are poisonous plants, causing sickness and death in domestic livestock. Tall larkspur poisoning is responsible for more cattle losses than any other poisonous plant in the Rocky Mountains. It is most toxic before flowering, when the alkaloids are most concentrated. Trained herbalists have used a tincture of larkspur seed externally to kill body lice.

LOW LARKSPUR
Delphinium bicolor Nutt.
Buttercup Family (Ranunculaceae)

Description: Low larkspur plants are usually less than 16" tall, with only a few leaves, which are mostly basal. There are 1–15 rather large, dark blue to purple flowers. Each flower has 5 purple, showy sepals that are widely flaring. The upper sepal has a spur from the back that is longer than the sepal blade. Inside the sepals are 4 smaller petals, less than half the length of the sepals. The pair of lower petals are shallowly lobed, or, more often, merely toothed on the margin. The 3-lobed pistil develops into a dry fruit that splits open when mature.

Bloom Season: May–July.

Habitat/Range: Dry soils in the valleys, dry montane, and subalpine forests.

Comments: *Delphinium* is derived from the Greek *delphin*, or "dolphin," perhaps from a resemblance of the flower to the sea mammal. It is called "larkspur" because the spurred sepal resembles the spur on the foot of a lark.

Tall Mountain Larkspur

MARSH CINQUEFOIL
Potentilla palustris (L.) Scop.
Rose Family (Rosaceae)

Description: Cinquefoils are herbaceous plants of the rose family with compound leaves. The flowers have 10–30 stamens and a style that is smooth and deciduous, or readily broken off. Most cinquefoils have yellow, cream, or white flowers, but those of marsh cinquefoil have purple to deep red flowers, the only exception. The stems of marsh cinquefoil are strongly rhizomatous, creeping along the ground and rooting at the nodes. The pinnately compound leaves have 5–7 leaflets, which are green on the upper surface and white on the lower.

Bloom Season: June–August.

Habitat/Range: Bogs, streams, and ponds, from valleys to the subalpine zone.

Comments: *Palustris* is from the Latin *palus* or *palud* (marsh or swamp), the habitat for these plants. Cinquefoil means "5 leaves," referring to the 5 leaflets commonly found on the compound leaves of these plants.

Marsh Cinquefoil

Wyoming Kittentails

WYOMING KITTENTAILS
Besseya wyomingensis (A. Nels.) Rydb.
Figwort Family (Scrophulariaceae)

Description: The violet to purple color of these flowers comes from the brightly colored filaments of the stamens. Each small flower has 2 hairy sepals and 2 stamens, but no petals. The flowers are densely crowded in a spikelike arrangement on the end of the simple stem. The largest leaves have long petioles that come from the base of the plant. The leaves on the flowering stem are without petioles and get progressively smaller up the stem. The margins of the leaves have fine teeth.

Bloom Season: April–July.

Habitat/Range: Grasslands of the valleys, dry montane forests, and upper subalpine ridges.

Comments: *Besseya* was named in honor of Charles E. Bessey (1845–1915), a professor of botany at the University of Nebraska. It is among the first wildflowers to bloom in the Northern Rockies.

Lewis's Monkeyflower

LEWIS'S MONKEYFLOWER
Mimulus lewisii Pursh
Figwort Family (Scrophulariaceae)

Description: The bright magenta to pink flowers of Lewis's monkeyflower are brilliant along the streams of the Northern Rocky Mountains. Each flower has 2 lips: the upper lip is 2-lobed and the lower lip is 3-lobed. The lower lip is marked with 2 yellow, hairy ridges. The flower stalks (pedicels) originate in the leaf axils and are much longer than the tubular sepals. The sepals have 5 keeled ribs, terminating in sharp teeth about equal in size. These ribs are often reddish tinged. The leaves form pairs attached directly to the main branch. There are coarse teeth on the margin of the leaves. The plants are perennial from underground stems, and quite tall (1–3½').

Bloom Season: July–August.

Habitat/Range: Streamsides in the subalpine and alpine zones.

Comments: *Mimulus* is from the Latin word for a "comic," in reference to the "smiling face" appearance of the flower. This plant was named *lewisii* in honor of Meriwether Lewis of the Lewis and Clark Expedition. Frederick Pursh described and illustrated this species for the first time in *Flora Americae Septentrionalis* in 1814. He credited his knowledge of this plant to a specimen that Lewis collected in August 1805, "on the headsprings of the Missouri, at the foot of Portage Hill," which was probably near Lemhi Pass, in Beaverhead County, Montana. Unfortunately, this specimen has been lost to science.

ALBERTA BEARDTONGUE
Penstemon albertinus Greene
Figwort Family (Scrophulariaceae)

Description: Alberta beardtongue has rather thick and smooth (hairless) leaves with a few small teeth on the margin. The leaves are well developed both at the base and along the stems. The bright blue (or pink) flowers are about ½–¾" long. This species is similar to Wilcox's beardtongue *(P. wilcoxii),* with which it often hybridizes. Alberta beardtongue is distinguished by its smaller size (6–12" tall), smaller and fewer teeth on the leaf margin, somewhat smaller flowers, and denser flower arrangement.

Bloom Season: May–July.

Habitat/Range: Dry, open, and often rocky places from the valleys to the subalpine forests.

Comments: John Macoun (1831–1920) collected the first known botanical specimen of Alberta beardtongue on Sheep Mountain, Alberta.

Alberta Beardtongue

Taper-Leaved Beardtongue

TAPER-LEAVED BEARDTONGUE
Penstemon attenuatus Dougl.
Figwort Family (Scrophulariaceae)

Description: The clustered flowers (⅝–¾" long) vary in color from blue-purple to pink, yellow, or white. The anthers of the fertile stamens are smooth (hairless) and split open full length upon maturity. Yellow hair accents the end of the sterile stamen. Glandular hairs cover the outer surface of the petal tube, sepals, and upper stem. The leaves are lance shaped, mostly smooth on the margin.

Bloom Season: June–August.

Habitat/Range: Valleys to subalpine forests.

Comments: The origin of the word *Penstemon* may be from the Greek *pente,* meaning "five," in reference to the 5 stamens of *Penstemon* (4 fertile and 1 sterile). The sterile stamen of some species has a cluster of hair, or "beard," on the end of the sterile stamen, which may protrude from the mouth of the flower like a "bearded tongue."

Rockvine Beardtongue

ROCKVINE BEARDTONGUE
Penstemon ellipticus Coult. & Fisch.
Figwort Family (Scrophulariaceae)

Description: The flowers of rockvine beard-tongue are deep lavender and seem large and out of proportion to the low-growing plant. The 4 fertile anthers are covered with long, tangled, woolly hair that is visible to the naked eye. The sterile stamen is short and does not extend beyond the lips of the petal. The sepals and upper stems are covered with glandular hairs. The leaves are oval, rounded on the end, and attached with a short petiole. There are fine teeth along the margin of the leaves. The stems are often woody at the base and lie horizontally on the ground, where they root, forming large, dense mats.

Bloom Season: Late June–September.

Habitat/Range: Rocky crevices, talus, and cliffs, in the subalpine forests and the alpine tundra.

Comments: The name *ellipticus* refers to the leaves, which are shaped like an ellipse, that is, egg shaped or oblong with rounded ends.

Shrubby Beardtongue

SHRUBBY BEARDTONGUE
Penstemon fruticosus (Pursh) Greene
Figwort Family (Scrophulariaceae)

Description: Although several *Penstemon* species have woody stems, this one is more shrublike than the others. The plants often form much-branched shrubby colonies 6–16" tall. The leaves are shiny and evergreen; the largest ones occur at the base of the stems and on the flowerless shoots. Large lavender flowers are arranged in a one-sided raceme, with 2 flowers at each node. Inside the petal tube, which is about 1½" long, the 4 fertile stamens have anthers with dense, long, woolly hair. The sterile stamen is shorter than the filaments of the fertile stamens and has a yellow beard toward the tip.

Bloom Season: May–August.

Habitat/Range: Dry montane forests and rocky places in the subalpine forests.

Comments: Shrubby beardtongue was first scientifically described in 1814 by the German botanist Frederick Pursh (1774–1820) in his *Flora Americae Septentrionalis.* The species is illustrated in this early botanical work with an engraving by William Hooker, an early botanical illustrator. The plant was thus described and illustrated from a plant specimen collected by Meriwether Lewis in June of 1806 in northern Idaho along the Lolo Trail during the return journey of the Lewis and Clark Expedition. According to Pursh, the plant was "in great abundance in the pine-forests of the Rocky-mountains."

Lyall's Beardtongue

LYALL'S BEARDTONGUE
Penstemon lyallii A. Gray
Figwort Family (Scrophulariaceae)

Description: Long (1–5"), narrow, and pointed leaves distinguish this plant from other area *Penstemons*. The numerous leaves are deciduous, opposite, and exclusively on the stems (none are basal). The flower arrangement is an open panicle, with short glandular hairs on the upper stems, flower stalks, and sepals. Long, woolly hairs crowd the fertile anthers, while the short, sterile stamen is hairless on the tip. The pale lavender petal tube is up to 1½" long, with two hairy ridges on the palate.

Bloom Season: June–August.

Habitat/Range: Dry, rocky slopes of the montane and subalpine forests to the alpine.

Comments: David Lyall (1817–1895) collected this *Penstemon* in 1862 "between Ft. Colville and the Rocky Mountains." At the time, Lyall was a member of the British Land Boundary Commission surveying the boundary between British Columbia and the United States possessions from the Gulf of Georgia to the summit of the Rocky Mountains. Lyall was a surgeon and naturalist from Scotland who served as a medical officer in the Royal Navy on expeditions to the Antarctic, Arctic, Mediterranean, New Zealand, and western North America. His extensive botanical collections from these expeditions made a major contribution to the understanding of the flora of these regions.

SMALL-FLOWERED BEARDTONGUE
Penstemon procerus Dougl.
Figwort Family (Scrophulariaceae)

Description: Numerous small flowers (³⁄₁₆–³⁄₈" long) are densely crowded in clusters on the slender, smooth stems of this species. Inside the smooth, blue to purple petal tube are 4 fertile stamens with smooth (hairless) anthers and a slightly bearded sterile anther. The plants grow in mats with clusters of stems less than 16" tall with smooth, entire leaves.

Bloom Season: May–August.

Habitat/Range: Widespread, from the valleys to the alpine.

Comments: The genus name *Penstemon* may originate from the Latin *paene,* meaning "almost," and the Greek *stemon,* or "thread." This is in reference to the sterile stamen, which lacks an anther, and therefore is almost (but not quite) a complete stamen. *Procerus* is Latin for "very tall," which this species is not.

Small-Flowered Beardtongue

Lovely Beardtongue

LOVELY BEARDTONGUE
Penstemon venustus Dougl.
Figwort Family (Scrophulariaceae)

Description: Long, white hairs on the upper portion of the filament, just below the horse-shoe-shaped anther (of the fertile stamens), distinguish this species from all other *Penstemon* species in the Northern Rockies. The sterile stamen also has white hair at the expanded, flattened tip. The rather large (¾–1½" long) flowers vary from bright lavender to purple-violet. These are large plants, 1–3' tall, growing in sizeable clusters. Fine teeth, with soft spines from the tip, line the margin of the lance-shaped and smooth leaves.

Bloom Season: May–August.

Habitat/Range: Open, rocky places, from the valleys to the subalpine forests.

Comments: *Venustus* is a Latin term for "beautiful" or "graceful," an appropriate name for this lovely wildflower.

Wilcox's Beardtongue

WILCOX'S BEARDTONGUE
Penstemon wilcoxii Rydb.
Figwort Family (Scrophulariaceae)

Description: These are rather large plants (16–40"), with smooth, tooth-margined leaves that clasp the stem. The bright blue to purple flowers are usually arranged in open panicles but may be more congested. The flower tube is intermediate in length (½–1"), having 4 fertile stamens inside with smooth anthers that split open full length. Yellow hair grows from the tip of the sterile stamen, which is longer than the fertile ones.

Bloom Season: May–July.

Habitat/Range: Valleys, dry montane, and lower subalpine forests.

Comments: Wilcox's beardtongue was named in honor of Earley V. Wilcox, who collected the plant near Kalispell, Montana, in the late 1800s. However, the first botanical specimen of this species was collected by Meriwether Lewis at his "camp on the Kooskooskee May 20, 1806," which is near present-day Kamiah, Idaho, along the Clearwater River. The Lewis and Clark Expedition had camped near the friendly Nez Perce Indians, waiting for the snow to melt sufficiently for safe passage over Lolo Pass.

Cusick's Speedwell

CUSICK'S SPEEDWELL
Veronica cusickii A. Gray
Figwort Family (Scrophulariaceae)

Description: The violet-blue flowers of Cusick's speedwell have 4 sepals, 4 petals, 2 stamens, and a single style. The flowers are wheel shaped: circular and flat, about ⅜–½" wide. The petals are irregular, with the upper one broad and the lower one the narrowest. The filaments are about ¼" long and very conspicuous. The style is even longer (⅜"). The stems are simple, about 6" tall, and terminated by the flower arrangement. Glandular hairs cover the surface of the stems, especially within the flower arrangement. The leaves are egg shaped, smooth, and are arranged in pairs opposite each other on the stem.

Bloom Season: July–early September.

Habitat/Range: Moist, rocky slopes, in meadows, and along stream banks, in the upper subalpine forests and alpine tundra.

Comments: The origin of the name *Veronica* is unknown, but it may honor Saint Veronica, who is said to have offered a cloth to Christ upon which he wiped his face on his way to the crucifixion. Christ's face is said to have left an impression or "portrait" on the cloth. Such an impression is called a "veronica." *Cusickii* honors William Conklin Cusick (1842–1922), who first collected the plant in the alpine region of the Blue Mountains of Oregon.

Climbing Nightshade

CLIMBING NIGHTSHADE
Solanum dulcamara L.
Potato Family (Solanaceae)

Description: Climbing nightshade is an introduced vine, with blue to violet flowers and bright red berries. The petal lobes are much longer than the short tube, and they turn back toward the stem as they mature. The flower arrangement is branched and includes 10–25 flowers. The leaves are egg shaped to heart shaped and sometimes have a pair of lobes at the base. The plants scramble over shrubs and other vegetation for support.

Bloom Season: May–September.

Habitat/Range: Introduced. Moist soils, often along streams in the valleys.

Comments: Climbing nightshade contains poisonous alkaloids causing livestock deaths. Another name for this plant is "bittersweet," and this has led to confusion with an edible "bittersweet" *(Celastrus scandens)*. The bright red berries of climbing nightshade are very attractive and tempting but should not be eaten.

EARLY BLUE VIOLET
Viola adunca Sm.
Violet Family (Violaceae)

Description: The leaves of early blue violet are entire, egg shaped to heart shaped, and have finely rounded teeth on the margin. The leaves appear all basal in the early season, but leafy stems develop later that are up to 4" tall. The lowest petal has a conspicuous hooked spur over half its length. The lateral petals and the style are white bearded. These little blue violets are among the first flowers to announce spring.

Bloom Season: April–August.

Habitat/Range: From the valleys to near timberline.

Comments: *Viola* is from the Latin *violaceous,* for the purple color. *Adunca* is from the Latin word *aduncus,* meaning "hooked" and refers to the hooked spur of the lowest petal. The common garden pansy is also a species of *Viola.* Violets are edible fresh as a salad green or cooked as a potherb. They are rich in vitamins A and C.

Early Blue Violet

PINK FLOWERS

Elk Thistle

*Pink flowers grade into lavender on the blue end
of the spectrum and red on the other. Many
species with pink flowers also have white flower
variations. You may need to check in other sections
of this book if you do not find the flower you are
searching for here.*

Dogbane

DOGBANE
Apocynum androsaemifolium L.
Dogbane Family (Apocynaceae)

Description: A dogbane flower has a pink, bell-shaped petal tube with 5 pointed lobes. The petal tube is more than twice the length of the sepals. The flowers are arranged on the end of the stem and sometimes in the upper leaf axils. The plants are herbaceous and 8–20" tall. The leaves are borne in pairs that droop downward from the stem, opposite each other. When broken, the leaves and stems ooze a white milky sap. The long, narrow pods split open along a suture for seed distribution.

Bloom Season: June–August.

Habitat/Range: Dry soil in the valleys and the dry montane forests.

Comments: *Apocynum* is from two Greek words that mean "away from a dog." *Bane* means poison or death. Dogbane is a poisonous plant, but cases of poisoning are rare. Several chemical resins and glycosides have been isolated from the plant that are of medicinal value in the treatment of congestive heart failure; they increase the force of heart contractions. One of the side effects of ingesting the plant is nausea, and because of this the plant has been used to induce vomiting and is sometimes referred to as "wild ipecac." This is a dangerous plant and not for home use. Strong, supple fibers in the stems of this plant can be twisted into a fine cord for fishing line or other purposes.

Showy Milkweed (flower)

(fruit)

SHOWY MILKWEED
Asclepias speciosa Torr.
Milkweed Family (Asclepiadaceae)

Description: The pink flowers of showy milkweed are striking and very unusual. The 5 pink, lance-shaped petals are turned downward, concealing the 5 sepals. The 5 stamens are joined together and attached to the stigma. Each stamen has a large (½" long), lance-shaped hood that thrusts upward. Within the hood is a horn, attached to the base. The flowers are arranged in large clusters near the top of the plant. The leaves are 4–7" long and opposite on the stem. The plants are 2–4' tall and contain a milky latex.

Bloom Season: May–August.

Habitat/Range: Disturbed soil of streams and roadsides, in the valleys and dry montane forests.

Comments: *Asclepias* was named in honor of Aesculapius, the Greek physician and god of medicine. Various species of milkweed have a history of medicinal use in Europe and North America. Trained herbalists have used showy milkweed to stimulate expectoration, perspiration, and urination to increase expulsion of metabolic waste. The Shoshone Indians of Nevada used the latex of showy milkweed as an antiseptic and healing agent on sores. Other American Indians used the ripe seed to draw out the poison of rattlesnake bites. The plant has been used for food, but it must be prepared properly to render it safe. This and several other species of milkweed have been found to contain various levels of poisonous resinoids, some causing livestock deaths. The "down" in the seedpods makes a fine insulating material.

Spotted Knapweed

SPOTTED KNAPWEED
Centaurea maculosa Lam.
Aster Family (Asteraceae)

Description: The leaves are pinnately compound, with narrow lobes and tiny glandular spots on the surface, hence the name "spotted knapweed." The flower heads have overlapping bracts with vertical lines on the surface, and a dark tip with comblike teeth on the margin. The flower heads consist of pink-purple disk flowers. The plants are mostly perennials with taproots.

Bloom Season: July–September.

Habitat/Range: Introduced noxious weed of disturbed habitats in the valleys and montane forests.

Comments: Spotted knapweed has the competitive advantage over native herbaceous species in the Northern Rockies because it lacks the natural predatory insects and diseases that hold its populations in check in its European homeland. Biological control methods aim to "level the playing field" through the introduction of these natural control agents, and several of them hold some promise in reducing the impact of this aggressive weed.

Elk Thistle

ELK THISTLE
Cirsium scariosum Nutt.
Aster Family (Asteraceae)

Description: The leaf base of elk thistle clasps the stem and does not extend ridgelike down the stem. The leafy bracts around the base of each flower head lack the glandular ridge of certain other species. The tip of the inner bracts of elk thistle is dilated, with a margin that is scarious (thin, parchmentlike) and fringed. Elk thistle is a stout plant, up to 3' (or even 6') tall, with thick, fleshy stems that taper little from the base to the top. The flower color varies from white to somewhat yellow-ish, tan, pink, or lavender. The flower heads are densely clustered on and adjacent to the top of the thick stem. This is a biennial species, growing as a cluster of radiating basal leaves the first year (or years). The second (or subsequent) year the plant sends up the large flowering stem, flowers, and then dies.

Bloom Season: June–August.

Habitat/Range: Moist mountain meadows, from the valleys to the subalpine forests.

Comments: Elk thistle is often called Everts's thistle in Yellowstone National Park. This name honors Truman Everts, a member of the Washburn Expedition that explored what is now Yellowstone National Park in 1870. Everts became separated from the Washburn party and lost his horse and all belongings except for a small knife and opera glass. Enduring snowstorms and the lack of any means to secure better food, Everts subsisted almost exclusively on thistle roots for nearly a month, until rescued (near death at about 50 pounds) by "Yellowstone Jack" Baronett on October 6. This plant and a mountain in Yellowstone National Park are named for Everts, while Yellowstone's Baronett Peak honors his rescuer.

Twinflower

TWINFLOWER
Linnaea borealis L.
Honeysuckle Family (Caprifoliaceae)

Description: Twinflower is a low-growing, evergreen ground cover of the boreal forests. It spreads by horizontal stems on the surface of the organic layer of the forest floor. The small, egg-shaped leaves are in opposite pairs. Each leaf has a few shallow teeth on the margin of the upper half of the leaf. The leafy stems are short (less than 4" long) and bear a pair of pink flowers on the end of slender stalks. The bell-shaped flowers hang downward and are hairy on the inner surface.

Bloom Season: June–September.

Habitat/Range: Widespread in montane and subalpine forests.

Comments: *Linnaea* was named for Carolus Linnaeus (1707–1778) and is said to have been his favorite flower. Linnaeus was professor of medicine and botany at Uppsala University in Sweden from 1742 until his death. In 1753, he wrote *Species Plantarum,* the basis for our present binomial system of naming plants by genus and specific epithet—the scientific name.

COMMON SNOWBERRY
Symphoricarpos albus (L.) Blake
Honeysuckle Family (Caprifoliaceae)

Description: This common forest shrub is easily identified by its opposite, entire (or sometimes irregularly lobed) leaves and round, white berries. It is usually 3' tall or less but may be twice that size. The twigs do not develop terminal buds; instead they die back at the tip of the branches and initiate spring growth from side (lateral) buds. Dense hair lines the inside of the small, bell-shaped flowers, which develop in clusters near the ends of the twigs.

Bloom Season: May–August.

Habitat/Range: Common under the forest canopy, from valleys to lower subalpine forests.

Comments: Snowberry is sometimes confused with Utah honeysuckle, which is distinguished by its large terminal buds, twin flowers, and red berries.

Common Snowberry

MOSS CAMPION
Silene acaulis L.
Pink Family (Caryophyllaceae)

Description: Moss campion is a low, ground-hugging cushion plant. The dense cushions are up to a foot or more in diameter. The plants are usually about 2" tall but may be as much as 6". The bright green leaves are narrow and arise from the base of the plant. The dead leaves from the previous seasons persist for years on the plants. The pink flowers are borne singly on short stalks up to 1½" long but usually much shorter. The sepals are joined together into a tube that conceals the base of the petals, which are entire. The 10 stamens and 3 styles extend well beyond the throat of the flower. Moss campion is often confused with douglasia *(Douglasia montana),* which is distinguished by its stamens and style, which are hidden within the flower tube.

Bloom Season: June–August.

Habitat/Range: Ridges and summits of the upper subalpine forests and alpine.

Comments: Rock gardeners consider this one of the most beautiful and desirable rock garden plants, but please do not take them from the wild.

Moss Campion

Hedge Bindweed

HEDGE BINDWEED
Calystegia sepium (L.) R. Br.
(also *Convolvulus sepium* L.)
Morning-Glory Family (Convolvulaceae)

Description: Hedge bindweed has 1½–2½" large, pale pink to white, funnel-shaped flowers. The flowers occur singly on the ends of 1½–5" long stalks from the leaf axils. A pair of broad, green, leafy bracts at the base of the flower conceals the sepals. The plant is a perennial vine up to 10' long and climbs over other plants for support. The leaves are heart shaped with sharply angled lateral lobes.

Bloom Season: July–August.

Habitat/Range: Introduced; moist soils along river bottoms and ditches in the valleys.

Comments: *Calystegia* comes from the Greek *kalyx* (cup) and *stegos* (cover), in reference to the bracts that cover the sepals (calyx). This beautiful wild morning-glory vine is also called "lady's-nightcap," "bell-bind," and "Rutland beauty." It is closely related to field bindweed, a serious noxious weed.

Kinnikinnick

KINNIKINNICK
Arctostaphylos uva-ursi (L.) Spreng.
Heath Family (Ericaceae)

Description: Kinnikinnick is a forest ground cover. It has somewhat woody, horizontal stems that root and spread along the surface, ,forming large mats. The leathery, evergreen leaves have a smooth margin (no teeth). The flowers are pink, with petals that are fused into an urn shape that hangs downward like a little Oriental lantern. The red berries persist through winter.

Bloom Season: April–June.

Habitat/Range: Widespread from montane forests to alpine.

Comments: *Arctostaphylos* comes from the Greek *arktos* (bear) and *staphyle* (bunch of grapes). *Uva* is Latin for "grape" and *ursi* is Latin for "bear." Both wild animals and humans eat the berries. *Uva-ursi* is an important medicinal herb for treating urinary tract infections and stones, and reducing inflammations. "Kinnikinnick" is from an American Indian word meaning "what you smoke." The tannin in the leaves has been used in tanning hides.

Prince's Pine

PRINCE'S PINE
Chimaphila umbellata (L.) Bart.
Heath Family (Ericaceae)

Description: This deep forest evergreen herb has dark green, leathery leaves that are shiny smooth, toothed on the margin, and arranged in whorls on the stem. Each leaf is 1–3" long, widest above the middle, and tapering to a narrow, pointed base. Several (5–15) pink flowers hang downward from the end of the long (4–12"), slender stems. There are 5 separate sepals and petals, 10 stamens, and a 5-lobed ovary in each flower. The ovary matures into a dry capsule fruit, which is often persistent on the dry stems for a year or more.

Bloom Season: June–August.

Habitat/Range: Moist montane and subalpine forests, often in dense shade.

Comments: One of the original components of root beer, this herb also has a long history of medicinal use. The Salish and Kootenai people used it as an eye medicine and for smoking. Western herbalists rely on its astringent and diuretic properties for kidney ailments. It has also been employed to induce sweating to break a fever. Other common names for this plant include "pipsissewa" and "wintergreen."

Swamp Laurel

SWAMP LAUREL
Kalmia microphylla (Hook.) Heller
(also *Kalmia polifolia* Wang.)
Heath Family (Ericaceae)

Description: Swamp laurel is a low-growing (less than 6" tall) evergreen shrub. The leathery leaves are dark green above and gray-white beneath. The leaf margin is often rolled under but is sometimes flat. The pink flowers are large for the size of the plants and are striking. The petals are fused together to form a shallow floral bowl. Within the flower "bowl" are 10 depressions that the stamens neatly fit within, while in bud. As the flower opens, the stamens spring up from these depressions.

Bloom Season: June–September.

Habitat/Range: Cool bogs, streamsides, and lakeshores of subalpine forests and the alpine tundra.

Comments: *Kalmia* was named for Peter Kalm (1715–1779), a student of Carolus Linnaeus at Uppsala University in Sweden. Swamp laurel is a miniature version of the large flowering laurel shrubs found in the Appalachian Mountains and elsewhere in the world.

Fool's Huckleberry

FOOL'S HUCKLEBERRY
Menziesia ferruginea Smith
Heath Family (Ericaceae)

Description: This medium-tall shrub (3–7') looks like the closely related huckleberries (*Vaccinium* species), but its fruit is a dry capsule, not a berry. The pink to yellowish red flowers are tubular and urn shaped (like huckleberry flowers); however, the ovary is superior, having the petal tube attached to the base of the ovary. In contrast, huckleberry flowers have an inferior ovary, with the petal tube attached near the top of the ovary. Fine teeth line the margin of the egg-shaped leaf of fool's huckleberry, and the small white tip of the midvein protrudes from the leaf tip. A characteristic skunklike odor is produced by glands on the foliage and young stems.

Bloom Season: May–August.

Habitat/Range: Widespread in moist montane and subalpine forests.

Comments: *Menziesia* was named in honor of Archibald Menzies (1754–1842), who collected this plant while serving as a physician and naturalist with the Vancouver Expedition to western North America from 1790 to 1795. *Ferruginea* is from the Latin *ferruginus* (iron rust), referring to the rusty cast to the otherwise green leaves. Fool's huckleberry is also known as "mock azalea" and "rusty menziesia." This is one of the most abundant shrubs in the Northern Rockies, forming extensive and dense communities that can impede foot travel, especially on steep slopes.

Red Mountain Heather

RED MOUNTAIN HEATHER
Phyllodoce empetriformis (Sm.) D. Don
Heath Family (Ericaceae)

Description: Red mountain heather is a low shrub with red, bell-shaped flowers protruding from near the tips of the low branches. The closely spaced evergreen leaves resemble the needles of a fir tree. The similar moss-heather (*Cassiope* species), which is also found in the Northern Rocky Mountains, has 4-ranked, scalelike leaves and white flowers. The closely related yellow mountain heather *(P. glanduliflora)* has yellow to greenish white, urn-shaped flowers and sepals with glandular hairs. Red and yellow mountain heathers are often found together and hybridize, producing offspring with pale pink flowers.

Bloom Season: July–August.

Habitat/Range: Alpine and upper subalpine zones.

Comments: *Phyllodoce* is from the Greek name for a sea nymph. It is called "heather" because it resembles the true heather (*Calluna* species) of Scotland and other European countries.

DWARF HUCKLEBERRY
Vaccinium cespitosum Michx.
Heath Family (Ericaceae)

Description: Leaves that are widest above the middle and taper toward the base are a key identifying trait of dwarf huckleberry. These dwarf shrubs are low (6–12" tall) with round, brownish twigs. Narrowly urn-shaped flowers, about half as wide as they are long, further distinguish this species. The fruit is a round blue berry with a whitish coating.

Bloom Season: May–July.

Habitat/Range: Mountain meadows and forested swales from the moist montane to the subalpine forests. Dwarf huckleberry has an affinity for low-lying, concave terrain where cold air and moisture collect.

Comments: Dwarf huckleberry is most often confused with the similarly short grouse huckleberry *(V. scoparium),* which differs by having green twigs, globe-shaped flowers, and red berries.

Dwarf Huckleberry

Big Huckleberry

BIG HUCKLEBERRY
Vaccinium membranaceum Dougl. ex Hook.
    and Torr.
Heath Family (Ericaceae)

Description: The large (½–⅜" wide), dark purple and juicy berries of this species make huckleberry picking worthwhile. Often taller (1–4' or more) than most *Vaccinium* species in the Rockies, big huckleberry has alternate, egg-shaped leaves with a pointed tip. The leaves of the similar globe huckleberry *(V. globulare)* are rounded on the tip. Fine teeth line the leaf margin. Thin ridges are found on the surface of the young twigs, while the older twigs have shredding, gray bark. The yellowish pink, urn-shaped flowers hang downward singly from the axils of the leaves.

Bloom Season: April–June.

Habitat/Range: Widespread in montane and subalpine forests.

Comments: This plant is food for black bears and grizzlies, and the availability of huckleberries from year to year is a major determinant in the condition of bears going into hibernation. When huckleberry crops are short, bears are more likely to seek other food sources near human development, endangering both the human inhabitants and themselves. With the increasing popularity of wild collected huckleberries for the commercial candy and jam market, some conservationists worry that the competition between bears and humans may accelerate. Fortunately, scientists are at work trying to solve the various problems with cultivating our western huckleberries for the commercial berry market.

Grouse Huckleberry

GROUSE HUCKLEBERRY
Vaccinium scoparium Lieberg ex Cov.
Heath Family (Ericaceae)

Description: Grouse huckleberry is a low shrub (less than 1' high) with numerous, broomlike stems. It often grows in large mats that cover the forest floor. The stems are green and strongly angled in cross section. The small (less than ⅝" long) leaves are lance shaped, with fine teeth on the margin. The pink flower petals are joined together into an urn-shaped tube that hangs downward. The small (less than ³⁄₁₆" in diameter), bright red berries are tart and very delicious.

Bloom Season: May–August.

Habitat/Range: Widespread in subalpine forests.

Comments: *Vaccinium* is the Latin name for blueberry. Other common names applied to plants in the genus include "bilberry," "cranberry," and "whortleberry." Herbalists value *Vaccinium* species for their acidic, astringent properties. They use the herbs in treating diarrhea, ulcers, gum and skin inflammation, urinary tract infections, certain cases of diabetes, and eye problems.

Fitweed Corydalis

FITWEED CORYDALIS
Corydalis caseana A. Gray
Fumitory Family (Fumariaceae)

Description: The unusual flowers of this plant have 4 pink petals in 2 pairs. The outer pair of petals are "hooded." The upper one has a narrow spur, about ½" long, that serves as a vessel for the nectar to attract pollinating insects. The inner pair of petals are joined together at their tip and enclose the stamen and pistil. There are many flowers (50–200) arranged in a simple or compound raceme on the end of the branches. The plants are perennial and quite tall, reaching 2–6' high or higher. The foliage has a gray-green appearance as a result of a glaucous coating (a fine, white powdery substance on the surface, which readily rubs off).

Bloom Season: June–August.

Habitat/Range: Beside streams in moist montane and subalpine forests. An uncommon species found in the Idaho portion of the Northern Rockies.

Comments: *Corydalis* comes from the Greek name for the "crested lark," probably because the spur of the flower resembles the spur on the head of the lark. The flowers are usually pollinated by bumblebees with long tongues that can reach to the nectar in the flower spur. The plants are rich in alkaloids that are toxic to sheep and cattle and have caused livestock deaths. "Fitweed" refers to the symptoms (convulsive spasms, bleating, and bawling) that livestock endure when poisoned by eating this plant.

Steer's Head

STEER'S HEAD
Dicentra uniflora Kell.
Fumitory Family (Fumariaceae)

Description: These distinctive flowers actually do look like a steer's head. Arising from the plant base are flower stalks 2–4" long that have solitary flowers on the ends. The pinkish and purple-tipped flowers are heart shaped at the base, forming the steer's head proper, while the outer petals are spreading and recurved to form the steer's horns. The leaves are all compound and basal, with leaflets in threes that are again deeply divided.

Bloom Season: February–June.

Habitat/Range: Valleys to subalpine forests in well-drained soil.

Comments: Steer's head is closely related to the much larger cultivated garden flowers bleeding heart *(D. formosa)* and Dutchman's breeches *(D. cucullaria)*. With its small flowers and brief flowering period, steer's head is an inconspicuous and seldom-noticed wildflower, best left in its natural, wild habitat.

SILVERLEAF PHACELIA
Phacelia hastata Dougl. ex Lehm.
Waterleaf Family (Hydrophyllaceae)

Description: This plant has fine, silvery hairs that loosely cover the leaves, giving them a sheen. The leaves are usually entire, but sometimes they have a pair of narrow lobes near the base. The plants have several stems that rise up to 20" from the branched, woody rootstock. The flowers are arranged in compact, spiraled clusters, like a snail shell. The petals are pink to dull white to lavender. The stamens are hairy near the middle and protrude well beyond the flower petals.

Bloom Season: May–August.

Habitat/Range: Open, dry places, from the valleys to the alpine zone.

Comments: *Phacelia* comes from the Greek *phakelos* (fascicle), which refers to the compact flower arrangement. This species was first described to botanical science from a specimen collected by David Douglas (1798–1834) "on the barren plains of the Columbia." Douglas was a Scottish botanist and early explorer.

Silverleaf Phacelia

NETTLELEAF HORSEMINT
Agastache urticifolia (Benth.) Kuntze
Mint Family (Lamiaceae)

Description: Nettleleaf horsemint has square stems, opposite leaves, and 2-lobed flowers typical of the mint family. It is distinguished from its close relatives by a combination of the following characteristics: the style and stamens extend well beyond the petal tube; it has 4 stamens arranged in pairs, with one pair extending much farther from the tube than the other pair; the plants are large and coarse, 1–5' tall; and the lower leaf surface is smooth or only sparsely covered with long hairs.

Bloom Season: June–August.

Habitat/Range: Valleys to subalpine forests.

Comments: *Urticifolia* means that the foliage *(folia)* looks like that of nettle *(Urtica),* with its similar opposite, lance-shaped, toothed leaves. Species of *Agastache* have been used by American Indians for treating indigestion, colds, coughs, and fevers. Modern herbalists use it to induce sweating and for its astringent, sedative properties.

Nettleleaf Horsemint

Wild Bergamot

WILD BERGAMOT
Monarda fistulosa L.
Mint Family (Lamiaceae)

Description: The strong, minty aroma is the first thing noticed about this herbaceous plant. It is about 1–2' tall, with the square stems, opposite leaves, and 2-lipped flowers that characterize most mints. The narrow upper lip of the flower is long and arches over the lower, down-turned lip. Two stamens and the single style extend just beyond the upper lip.

Bloom Season: June–September.

Habitat/Range: Valleys and dry montane forests.

Comments: It is also called "bee balm" and "Oswego tea," for the soothing tea that is brewed from the leaves and flowers. American Indians used this herbal tea for stomachaches and externally for skin eruptions. It was also used as an aromatic hair rinse and was reported to have been used ceremonially in the sun dance. Herbalists use the plant to induce sweating and for its antiseptic and anesthetic properties. A leaf chewed and placed against the gum often deadens the pain of a sore tooth.

Nodding Onion

NODDING ONION
Allium cernuum Roth
Lily Family (Liliaceae)

Description: The flower heads of this small herb bend downward. The flowers are arranged in a simple umbel, with the individual flower stalks coming together at a common point on the end of a leafless stem 4–20" tall. The 6 pinkish tepals (petals and petal-like sepals) are separate all the way to the base. The 6 stamens and the style extend well beyond the tepals. Flat to concave in cross section, the numerous leaves are solid, not hollow like garden onions. The entire plant has a distinctly oniony aroma.

Bloom Season: June–July.

Habitat/Range: Widespread in the valleys, dry montane forests, and dry parks in the moist montane and subalpine forests.

Comments: *Allium* is the classical name for garlic. All true onion and garlic species fall in this genus. *Cernuum* means "drooping" or "nodding." Nodding onion and other *Allium* species are edible, and useful for flavoring foods.

Douglas's Onion

DOUGLAS'S ONION
Allium douglasii Hook.
Lily Family (Liliaceae)

Description: Douglas's onion has only 2 basal leaves, which are often broad, flat, and recurved or sickle shaped, but they may also be narrow, channeled, and not recurved. The single, leafless flower stalk is round in cross section and 8–12" long, extending above the basal leaves. Arranged in an umbel on the top of the flower stalk are numerous pink flowers, with 6 entire tepals (petals and petal-like sepals). The 6 stamens are as long or longer than the tepals.

Bloom Season: May–July.

Habitat/Range: Restricted to valleys of eastern Washington, northern Idaho, and western Montana.

Comments: *Allium douglasii* is named in honor of David Douglas (1798–1834), a Scottish plant collector who contributed much to the early botanical exploration of northwestern America. Twenty-seven species of native onions occur in the Pacific Northwest. Some are rare endemics, while others are common. All onion species are both edible and valuable medicinal herbs. However, digging their bulbs for food kills them. If tempted to sample onions when out in the backcountry, try eating just the leaves, sort of like chives. Gather them carefully so as not to remove all the leaves of any one plant.

Mountain Hollyhock

MOUNTAIN HOLLYHOCK
Iliamna rivularis (Dougl.) Greene
Mallow Family (Malvaceae)

Description: Like all mallows, mountain hollyhock has flowers with many stamens that are joined together by their filaments to form a tube. The numerous anthers are free from the tube, while the styles run through the tube, exiting above. Mountain hollyhock has large pink petals (greater than ¾" long). The leaves are 2–6" long, with 3–7 toothed lobes, resembling maple or grape leaves. It is among the largest herbaceous plants in the Northern Rockies, often growing 3–6' tall or more.

Bloom Season: June–August.

Habitat/Range: Moist, disturbed openings, from the valleys to the subalpine zone.

Comments: *Rivularis* is Latin for "brook-loving." Mountain hollyhock likes the moist soil near streams. It is particularly abundant after a forest fire.

Elkhorns

ELKHORNS
Clarkia pulchella Pursh
Evening Primrose Family (Onagraceae)

Description: This bright and showy annual has pink flowers with 4 petals; each petal branching into 3 distinctive lobes. The branching of these petal lobes is reminiscent of the branching of an elk's antlers, hence the name. Eight stamens are included in each flower, 4 fertile ones that produce pollen, and 4 smaller sterile ones. The stigma has 4 white, petal-like lobes that mimic a tiny flower. Numerous narrow, linear leaves line the slender 4–20"-tall stems. Turned downward while the flowers are in bud, the stems turn upward as they bloom. The plants often grow as winter annuals, germinating with the fall moisture and overwintering close to the ground. In the spring and early summer they grow rapidly, flower, produce seed, and die.

Bloom Season: May–June.

Habitat/Range: Valleys and dry montane forests.

Comments: Elkhorns was collected by Meriwether Lewis near present-day Kamiah, Idaho. Lewis wrote on his plant label: "A beautiful plant from the Kooskooskee and Clark's River, June 1, 1806." When this plant specimen was examined in London by the German botanist Frederick Pursh, he found it to be so unique and new to botanical science that it did not fit any genus that was currently known. Thus, he named the new genus *Clarkia*, in honor of William Clark (1770–1838). Other common names include "pink fairies," "beautiful Clarkia," "ragged robin," and "deer horn."

Fireweed

FIREWEED
Epilobium angustifolium L.
Evening Primrose Family (Onagraceae)

Description: Fireweed has numerous (15 or more), showy, pink to purple flowers on the end of its usually unbranched stem. The sepals and petals (about ½–¾" long) are attached to the top of the long, narrow ovary, which resembles a stout flower stalk. The long style of fireweed extends out beyond the stamens and ends in a prominent, 4-cleft stigma. The leaves are narrow and long (4–6"). Fireweed plants grow from 3–9' tall.

Bloom Season: June–September.

Habitat/Range: Disturbed soils, from the valleys to the upper subalpine forests.

Comments: Fireweed is especially abundant on moist soils after a forest fire. Because the seed is distributed readily by the wind, fireweed often spreads rapidly, becoming the dominant species for the first few years following a forest fire. It has a reputation as a nutritious, wild edible plant and as an astringent and anti-inflammatory herb. The herb is useful in treating diarrhea, hemorrhoids, and other conditions.

COMMON WILLOWHERB
Epilobium ciliatum Raf.
(also *Epilobium glandulosum* Lehm.)
Evening Primrose Family (Onagraceae)

Description: This small (2–36" tall), perennial willowherb has glandular hairs on the ovaries and upper stems. The leaves are less than 5" long and often clasp the stem at the base. Small (about ¼" long) pink to rosy-purple petals are notched at the tip. The 4 sepals, 4 petals, and 8 stamens are attached at the end of the long, stalklike ovaries that arise in the axils of the upper leaves. The stigmas are entire, not lobed as in fireweed and dwarf fireweed. Small, bulblike, scaly shoots are attached to the slender underground stems.

Bloom Season: June–August.

Habitat/Range: Streamsides and seeps of the moist montane and subalpine forests.

Comments: Willowherbs and fireweeds (*Epilobium* species) have seeds with a tuft of long hairs on their tips that carry them aloft in the wind to germinate and colonize new locations.

Common Willowherb

Dwarf Fireweed

DWARF FIREWEED
Epilobium latifolium L.
Evening Primrose Family (Onagraceae)

Description: Superficially similar to fireweed *(E. angustifolium),* dwarf fireweed is a smaller plant (2–16" tall), with leaves that are much shorter (1–3" long), and with larger flowers, having petals as much as 1" long. The sepals and bright, pink-purple petals of dwarf fireweed are attached to the top of the ovary. The style is shorter than the stamens, and the stigma has 4 lobes.

Bloom Season: June–September.

Habitat/Range: Gravel bars along streams and in talus, from the montane forests to the alpine.

Comments: *Epilobium* is derived from the Greek *epi-* (upon) and *lobos* (pod), referring to the inferior ovary with the sepals and petals attached to the top. The vitamin-rich dwarf fireweed plants are eaten by Eskimos, raw or cooked, and often mixed with seal oil and blubber.

Fairy Slipper

FAIRY SLIPPER
Calypso bulbosa (L.) Oakes
Orchid Family (Orchidaceae)

Description: Fairy slipper is most often confused with lady's slippers (*Cypripedium* species) and was initially placed in that genus by Linnaeus in 1753. Both have flowers with an inflated saclike lip petal. However, fairy slipper has a single anther and a single, egg-shaped basal leaf, while lady's slippers have 2 anthers and 2 or more leaves, often attached to the flowering stem. The lip of fairy slipper has a flat apron with 3 short rows of white or yellow hairs on its surface and 2 short spurs near the tip.

Bloom Season: May–July.

Habitat/Range: Cool, coniferous forests and bogs of the montane and subalpine zones. There are two varieties of fairy slipper in North America. The variety *occidentalis* (illustrated) has sparse white hair on the apron and is most common in the Northern Rockies. The variety *americana* (with dense, yellow hair on the lip apron) is more common in the Central and Southern Rockies.

Comments: *Calypso* is named for the legendary sea nymph of Homer's *Odyssey,* perhaps because of the secluded haunts of this orchid. Fairy slipper and other orchids have a very specialized reproductive ecology, requiring exacting habitat conditions. The human development of wild forests has caused a decline of these sensitive wildflowers. We can help by protecting fairy slipper habitat from disturbance and by not picking or collecting these precious gems of the forests.

NARROW-LEAVED COLLOMIA
Collomia linearis Nutt.
Phlox Family (Polemoniaceae)

Description: Although small in stature (4–24" tall), this little annual is often noticed because of its showy display of bright pink flowers. The slender petal tube flares to form 5 short lobes less than ⅛" long. The paperlike and sharply pointed sepals are persistent on the plant in fruit, long after the petals fall away. Narrow, lance-shaped leaves are arranged alternately on the generally unbranched slender stems.

Bloom Season: May–August.

Habitat/Range: Dry, disturbed places, from the valleys to the lower subalpine forests.

Comments: Narrow-leaved collomia often grows in little communities of annuals that include blue-eyed Mary *(Collinsia parviflora)*. These two annual herbs were collected on April 17, 1806, by Meriwether Lewis at Rock Fort Camp near what is now The Dalles, Oregon.

Narrow-Leaved Collomia

Showy Phlox

SHOWY PHLOX
Phlox speciosa Pursh
Phlox Family (Polemoniaceae)

Description: The distinctive notch in the petals of showy phlox quickly distinguishes it from other *Phlox* species in the Northern Rockies. It is an erect plant 6–20" tall with narrow leaves up to 2¾" long, and somewhat woody lower stems. Flower color varies from pink to white. The flower tube is about ½" long, or only slightly longer than the sepals. The very short style is shorter than the stigma.

Bloom Season: April–June.

Habitat/Range: Dry areas in the valleys and dry montane forests.

Comments: This beautiful wildflower adorns the woods in spring with bright patches of pink. Meriwether Lewis collected the first known botanical specimen of showy phlox on May 7, 1806, along the Clearwater River. The similar long-leaved phlox *(P. longifolia)* was used medicinally by American Indians for treating a variety of conditions including colds, stomachache, sore eyes, anemia, and diarrhea.

Bitterroot

BITTERROOT
Lewisia rediviva Pursh
Purslane Family (Portulacaceae)

Description: When in full, glorious bloom the bitterroot is unmistakable. However, in its vegetative state it is inconspicuous: a basal rosette of small leaves (2" tall or less) growing close to the ground. The leaves first appear with the fall rains. They are narrow and succulent, almost round in cross section. The leaves resume growth in early spring, during flower bud development, but wither by the time the flowers are fully opened. The flowers are large and very beautiful. They have 5–9 sepals and 12–18 petals. Both sepals and petals are showy and vary in color from deep pink to rose or sometimes white.

Bloom Season: May–July.

Habitat/Range: Dry, exposed slopes and poorly developed soils, in sagebrush in the valleys and up into the dry, open montane forests.

Comments: *Lewisia* was named in honor of Meriwether Lewis, who collected a specimen of bitterroot on July 1, 1806, near the present town of Lolo, Montana, during the Lewis and Clark Expedition. Lewis attached a note to the specimen, stating, "The Indians eat the root of this Near Clark's R." (now the Bitterroot River, named in honor of the plant). As noted by Lewis, the bitterroot was an important food plant of many American Indian tribes. Legends associated with the bitterroot attest to the importance of this plant in their culture. Still important in our culture today, it is the floral emblem of Montana.

Jeffrey's Shooting Star

JEFFREY'S SHOOTING STAR
Dodecatheon jeffreyi van Houtte
Primrose Family (Primulaceae)

Description: Shooting stars are easily recognized by their flamelike petals, swept back away from the sharp-pointed tip, looking much like a rocket. The stamens converge around the style, forming the darkly colored tip of the rocket. When examined with a 10x hand lens, the stigma appears relatively thick and headlike, at least twice the thickness of the style, and the filaments are less than ¹⁄₁₆" long. The plants grow in large clumps, up to 2' tall, with smooth basal leaves (2–16" long) that are widest above the middle and gradually taper to a narrow petiole. Several (3–20) flowers are arranged in a simple umbel on the end of the slender flower stalk.

Bloom Season: June–August.

Habitat/Range: Wet meadows and along streams of the moist montane and subalpine forests to timberline.

Comments: A specimen of a shooting star, reported to be *D. jeffreyi*, was collected by Meriwether Lewis "in the narrows of the Columbia" (now The Dalles–Celilo Falls area) on April 16, 1806, as the members of the Lewis and Clark Expedition were ascending the Columbia River on their return voyage to St. Louis.

Woodland Shooting Star

WOODLAND SHOOTING STAR
Dodecatheon pulchellum (Raf.) Merrill
Primrose Family (Primulaceae)

Description: This common shooting star has stems less than 16" tall. Its smooth leaves are all basal and mostly less than 8" long. The stigma is less than twice as thick as the style and is not headlike, as in Jeffrey's shooting star. The filaments are more than ⅟₁₆" in length, forming a narrow, yellow band between the petal tube and the dark anthers. A close look (with a 10x hand lens) at the base of the dark anthers just above the filament will reveal subtle, lengthwise wrinkles, or it may be smooth. There are 1–25 flowers arranged in a simple umbel on the end of the flower stalk. Woodland shooting star is often confused with prairie shooting star *(D. conjugens),* which can be distinguished by its shorter filaments (less than ⅟₁₆") and crosswise wrinkles on the base of the anthers.

Bloom Season: April–August.

Habitat/Range: Widespread from the valleys to timberline.

Comments: The name *Dodecatheon* is from the Greek *dodeka-* (twelve) and *theos* (god) because this plant was said to be protected by the 12 Greek gods. *Pulchellum* comes from the Latin *pulchellus,* meaning "small and beautiful," a fitting name for this charming plant.

Mountain Douglasia

MOUNTAIN DOUGLASIA
Douglasia montana Gray
Primrose Family (Primulaceae)

Description: Mountain douglasia is a ground-hugging cushion plant. The small linear to lance-shaped leaves form mats of basal rosettes. The flowering stems are leafless, each with a single, showy flower. The sepals are tubular with 5 keeled and pointed lobes. The pink to violet flower is wheel shaped, with a short petal tube and wide, horizontally flaring limbs.

Bloom Season: March–April (valleys); June–July (alpine).

Habitat/Range: Open, dry exposures in the valleys, upper subalpine forests, and alpine.

Comments: *Douglasia* was named in honor of David Douglas (1798–1834), an early plant collector in northwestern America, employed by Britain's Royal Horticultural Society. The pink-flowered cushions of *Douglasia* are sometimes mistaken for a common companion, moss campion *(Silene acaulis)*. However, the stamens and style of *Douglasia* are hidden within the petal tube, while the stamens and style of moss campion protrude far beyond the flaring petals.

Western Meadowrue (female flowers)

(male flowers)

WESTERN MEADOWRUE
Thalictrum occidentale A. Gray
Buttercup Family (Ranunculaceae)

Description: At first glance, western mead-owrue leaves look just like columbine leaves (*Aquilegia* species). However, columbines in the Northern Rocky Mountains have leaves that are twice ternate (3 x 3), with a total of 9 leaflets per compound leaf. Western meadow-rue leaves are at least 3 times ternate (3 x 3 x 3), with a total of 27 leaflets (or more) per leaf. In addition, most of the leaves of our columbines originate from the plant base, with only a few reduced leaves on the flowering stem. Western meadowrue has most of its leaves up on the main stems, with seldom any from the base. Meadowrue lacks the colorful, showy flowers of columbine. Instead, it has rather inconspicuous unisexual flowers, with the female and male flowers occurring on sep-arate plants. The flowers lack petals, consist-ing only of the greenish sepals, tinged with purple, and either pistils or stamens. The male flowers look like wind chimes, the anthers quivering with the slightest breeze on the ends of the delicate, flexible filaments.

Bloom Season: May–August.

Habitat/Range: Cool, moist woods, from the montane to subalpine forest.

Comments: American Indians have used this plant variously as a medicine in treating headaches, nasal congestion, and other com-plaints; as a love charm in seeking the affec-tion of a lover; and as a stimulant to horses, placed in their nostrils to increase endurance. Meadowrue is among the plants being inves-tigated for naturally occurring bioagents in cancer chemotherapy research.

Woods Rose

WOODS ROSE
Rosa woodsii Lindl.
Rose Family (Rosaceae)

Description: Woods rose has stout (often curved) prickles just below the stipules, where the leaves are attached to the stem, and much smaller prickles on the internodes between the leaves. The compound leaves have 5–9 leaflets with coarse teeth. The flowers are clustered on the ends of the lateral branches. The sepals are ⅜–¾" long, while the petals are ½–1" long. The styles are persistent on the mature red fruit.

Bloom Season: May–July.

Habitat/Range: Moist areas in the valleys and montane forests.

Comments: "Wild rose" is the floral emblem of Alberta, North Dakota, and New York. People around the world have used roses for food, medicine, and cosmetics. The hips are an excellent source of vitamin C and make a fine tea, syrup, or jam. American Indians used woods rose as a beverage, a cure for colds, to stimulate urination, to treat diarrhea, and as a dressing for wounds.

SUBALPINE SPIRAEA
Spiraea splendens Baum. ex Koch
(also *Spiraea densiflora* Nutt. ex T. & G.)
Rose Family (Rosaceae)

Description: Subalpine spiraea is a low shrub, less than 40" tall. It has alternately arranged, toothed leaves and a flat-topped flower arrangement much like the common white spiraea *(S. betulifolia)*. However, subalpine spi-raea has bright pink to rose-red flowers, while white spiraea has white flowers.

Bloom Season: June–August.

Habitat/Range: Along streams, in moist montane to upper subalpine forests.

Comments: *Spiraea* comes from a Greek word meaning "coil" or "wreath." Herbalists value the medicinal properties of some *Spiraea* species for relieving pain and inflammation. Although it shares aspirin's analgesic qualities, *Spiraea* is soothing to the mucus membranes of the stomach and digestive tract. American Indians used various *Spiraea* species to treat diarrhea and wounds.

Subalpine Spiraea

Split-Leaved Indian Paintbrush

SPLIT-LEAVED INDIAN PAINTBRUSH
Castilleja rhexifolia Rydb.
Figwort Family (Scrophulariaceae)

Description: This Indian paintbrush of the subalpine meadows is mostly 6–12" tall. The bracts and sepals are a brilliant rose-pink or magenta. The upper petal segment (galea) is shorter than the petal tube but much longer than the short, green lower lip. The petal tube extends well beyond the sepals. The leaves are lance shaped and usually entire (not lobed). The bracts, below each flower, normally have a pair of short lateral lobes. This species is most often confused with scarlet Indian paintbrush *(C. miniata)*, which is a taller plant (mostly greater than 12" tall), with deeply cut bracts and scarlet flowers.

Bloom Season: June–August.

Habitat/Range: Meadows of the subalpine forests and alpine tundra.

Comments: *Rhexifolia* means "split-leaved," probably in reference to the lobed leafy bracts or to the occasional lobed leaf. It seems an inappropriate name, since the leaves are normally entire, or uncut. The species was named from a specimen collected by two prominent botanists, Per Axel Rydberg and Ernst Bessey, on Cedar Mountain in Madison County, Montana, on July 16, 1897. At the time, Rydberg and Bessey were collecting plant specimens on the first official botanical field trip for the New York Botanical Garden. This is the most common high-mountain Indian paintbrush of the Northern Rocky Mountains. It seems to gather the bright alpine sunlight and glow, as if from its own inner fire.

Thin-Leaved Owl's Clover

THIN-LEAVED OWL'S CLOVER

Orthocarpus tenuifolius (Pursh) Benth.
Figwort Family (Scrophulariaceae)

Description: Owl's clovers (*Orthocarpus* species) look a lot like paintbrushes (*Castilleja* species). However, paintbrushes are mostly perennials whose flowers have an upper lip that is much longer than the lower lip, while owl's clovers are all annuals having an upper floral lip that is only slightly if at all longer than the lower. The upper floral lip of thin-leaved owl's clover is slightly longer than the lower lip, and it is hooked at the tip. Bright and showy, pink-purple bracts are attached at the base of the yellow flowers and partially conceal them. These small, annual plants are 4–12" tall. The lower leaves are narrow and entire, while the upper leaves have 1 or 2 pairs of slender lobes.

Bloom Season: May–August.

Habitat/Range: Valleys, dry montane, and subalpine forests.

Comments: The first botanical specimen of thin-leaved owl's clover was collected on July 1, 1806 "on the banks of Clark's R.," now known as the Bitterroot River, near present-day Lolo, Montana. Here the Lewis and Clark Expedition was camped at "Travellers Rest," recuperating from its exhausting journey over the Bitterroot Mountains.

Elephant's Head

ELEPHANT'S HEAD
Pedicularis groenlandica Retz.
Figwort Family (Scrophulariaceae)

Description: The individual flowers of this plant are shaped like the head of a little pink elephant, complete with a long, curved trunk and large, drooping ears. The resemblance is amazing! The elephant's trunk is the upturned beak (to ½" long) of the upper flower petal. The leaves are fernlike, with individual leaf segments arranged opposite each other along the main leaf axis.

Bloom Season: June–August.

Habitat/Range: Wet meadows and stream banks in montane and subalpine forests.

Comments: Elephant's head and other species of *Pedicularis* are used by herbalists as sedative herbs. The wet meadow habitat of elephant's head is rich in floral diversity, and the fragile ecological balance of wet meadow habitat is more vulnerable to disturbance than the adjacent uplands. It deserves special care.

Red and Orange Flowers

Scarlet Gilia

You may also need to check the blue/purple and pink sections of this book if the flower you are searching for is not found here.

Orange Mountain Dandelion

ORANGE MOUNTAIN DANDELION
Agoseris aurantiaca (Hook.) Greene
Aster Family (Asteraceae)

Description: The flower color of orange mountain dandelion distinguishes it from the yellow common dandelion *(Taraxacum officinale).* The outer bracts of common dandelion are much shorter than the inner bracts, and they turn backward away from the flower head, while the bracts of *Agoseris* species are all similar in size and project forward. A slender projection from the end of the single-seeded fruit (achene) of orange mountain dandelion connects it with the pappus, which is the "parachute" that carries the achene aloft in the wind.

Bloom Season: June–August.

Habitat/Range: Valleys to subalpine.

Comments: *Agoseris* is named for the Greek *aix* (goat) and *seris* (chicory). Mountain dandelions are native plants and thus do not deserve the scornful reputation of the introduced common dandelion.

ROSY PUSSYTOES
Antennaria microphylla Rydb.
Aster Family (Asteraceae)

Description: Rosy pussytoes is a low, mat-forming perennial that spreads by trailing stems. The leaves are gray, equally woolly-hairy on both surfaces, and spatula shaped. The basal leaves are larger than the sparse leaves on the slender stem. Surrounding the flower heads are several series of overlapping bracts, which are dry, thin, and translucent. The color of the bracts varies from white to rosy red. They lack the basal dark spot of tall pussytoes.

Bloom Season: June–August.

Habitat/Range: Valleys to the lower subalpine forests.

Comments: *Microphylla* refers to the bracts, or phyllaries, that surround the flower heads, which are smaller in rosy pussytoes than in most other species of *Antennaria*. According to herbalists, pussytoes is a mild astringent herb, useful in quieting simple intestinal and liver inflammations.

Rosy Pussytoes

Trumpet Honeysuckle

TRUMPET HONEYSUCKLE
Lonicera ciliosa (Pursh) Poir ex DC.
Honeysuckle Family (Caprifoliaceae)

Description: A twining vine with clusters of orange flowers, trumpet honeysuckle brightens the woods with splashes of color. The broadly egg-shaped leaves are arranged opposite on the hollow stems. Below the flower arrangement, the uppermost leaves are joined together at their bases into a single bractlike leaf, which appears as if the stem passes through the center. With a flower tube 3 to 4 times as long as the flaring lips, the flowers are trumpet shaped. Inside, the flower tube is lined with dense hair.

Bloom Season: May–July.

Habitat/Range: Valleys, montane forests, and the lower subalpine forests.

Comments: *Ciliosa* refers to the cilia, or short hairs, that line the margin of the leaves. The sweet nectar at the base of the flower tube attracts hummingbirds and butterflies. This lovely plant was collected by Meriwether Lewis twice in northern Idaho in June 1806: on June 5, while camped along the Kooskooskee (Clearwater) River, and again on June 16, along Hungry Creek, as the Lewis and Clark Expedition began the first of two attempts to ascend and traverse the Lolo Trail back to present-day Montana that spring.

Mountain-Lover

MOUNTAIN-LOVER
Pachistima myrsinites (Pursh) Raf.
Staff Tree Family (Celastraceae)

Description: Mountain-lover is a low shrub, usually less than 2' tall. The glossy, evergreen leaves are arranged in pairs opposite each other on the stems. The leaves have fine teeth along the margin. The shiny evergreen leaves could be mistaken for those of kinnikinnick or twinflower. However, kinnikinnick has leaves that are arranged alternately and are smooth on the margin, and twinflower has a pair of showy white to pink flowers. Mountain-lover flowers are small and inconspicuous, but they have 4 lovely, maroon petals.

Bloom Season: May–June.

Habitat/Range: Montane and subalpine forests.

Comments: Mountain-lover is a fine ornamental shrub, being shade tolerant and easily grown. *Pachistima* comes from Greek words meaning "thick stigma." This genus name is sometimes spelled *Paxistima* or *Pachystima*. *Myrsinites* comes from the Greek word for myrrh, which the aroma of the flowers resembles.

STRAWBERRY BLITE
Chenopodium capitatum (L.) Asch.
Goosefoot Family (Chenopodiaceae)

Description: Strawberry blite is distinctive with its triangular or arrowhead-shaped leaves. The tiny, bright red flowers are arranged in dense, fleshy clusters. These red floral clusters are attached to the end of the branches and in the leaf axils. When they are pressed between the fingers, a red juice is rendered, much like an overripe strawberry.

Bloom Season: June–August.

Habitat/Range: Valleys to subalpine forests; especially after forest fires.

Comments: *Chenopodium* is Greek for "goose foot," in reference to the shape of the leaves. The leaves of strawberry blite and the related lamb's quarter *(C. album)* are edible and rich in vitamins and minerals. This species is a fine potherb, tasting much like spinach. It is high in oxalic acid, however; if eaten in excess, it can interfere with calcium absorption and form a precipitate of calcium oxalate that may interfere with kidney function.

Strawberry Blite

Pinedrops

PINEDROPS
Pterospora andromedea Nutt.
Heath Family (Ericaceae)

Description: The tall yellowish orange stems of pinedrops stand like stoic sentinels of the forest floor, unbranched and leafless. The live stems are 12–40" tall, fleshy, and covered with glandular hairs. The dried stalks of dead plants remain standing for a year or more. The plants grow singly or in clusters but are seldom abundant. They have no need for chlorophyll for food production. They are nourished by fungi, which they parasitize for nutrients. The fungi obtain these nutrients in turn from live trees or from decaying organic matter in the soil. The upper half of the stem supports a raceme of yellowish flowers that hang downward from recurved pedicels (bent-back flower stalks). The petals are united into an urn-shaped tube with 5 small, spreading lobes at the apex.

Bloom Season: June–August.

Habitat/Range: Montane and subalpine forests.

Comments: *Pterospora* means "winged-seed." In Greek mythology Andromeda was the daughter of Cassiopeia and Cepheus, the queen and king of Ethiopia. To punish the boastful Cassiopeia, the sea nymphs had Andromeda chained to a rock at the edge of the sea, where she could be attacked by Cetus, the whale. However, Perseus intervened and turned Cetus into stone by showing him the head of Medusa, thus saving the distressed Andromeda. In autumn's night sky, Andromeda is a constellation that lies near Cassiopeia and Cetus, with Perseus nearby.

Swamp Currant

SWAMP CURRANT
Ribes lacustre (Pers.) Poir.
Currant Family (Grossulariaceae)

Description: This is a spiny shrub 3–5' tall, with black to purple berries that are covered with gland-tipped hairs. There is a distinct joint on the stalk of the berry (and the flower). The berries (and flowers) hang downward in racemes of 3–15. Each flower is saucer shaped, or shallowly cup shaped, and reddish in color, deepening to purplish with age. The distinctly 3–5-lobed leaves have a deeply double-toothed margin.

Bloom Season: April–July.

Habitat/Range: Widespread along streams and seeps from the moist montane and subalpine forests to the alpine.

Comments: *Lacustre* is derived from the Latin *lacus* (lake) or *lacustris* (inhabiting lakes), a good name for this water-loving shrub. The berries are edible and were a food source for Native American people. However, the strong flavor imparted by the gland-tipped hairs makes them objectionable to the palate of some.

Wood Lily

WOOD LILY
Lilium philadelphicum L.
(also *Lilium umbellatum* Pursh)
Lily Family (Liliaceae)

Description: Wood lily is among the largest and showiest of the wildflowers in the Northern Rocky Mountains. The 6 bright orange to brick-red flower petals are 2–3" long and up to ¼" wide, tapering to a long, narrow basal segment. The lower ⅓ of the petal blades is purple spotted. The stamens are also purple. The stems are erect and about 1–2' tall or taller. The long, narrow leaves are usually arranged alternately, except the uppermost leaves, which form a whorl below the flower. There is usually only 1 flower per stem, but sometimes up to 3.

Bloom Season: June–August.

Habitat/Range: Clay-loam soils (derived from limestone or other alkaline rocks) in meadows, grasslands, and open woodlands, from the prairies, valleys, and foothills into the montane forests, often in aspen groves.

Comments: Wood lily was collected by Meriwether Lewis near the Mandan villages of present-day North Dakota, where the Lewis and Clark Expedition spent the winter of 1804–1805. The native Dakota people used this plant to treat spider bites, chewing or pulverizing the flowers before applying them to the bites. This was said to relieve the inflammation and swelling immediately.

Striped Coralroot

STRIPED CORALROOT
Corallorhiza striata Lindl.
Orchid Family (Orchidaceae)

Description: Coralroot orchids have no green leaves in which to conduct photosynthesis. They obtain their nutrients and energy by parasitizing fungi, which in turn obtain these substances from live plants or rotting organic matter on the forest floor. The leaves are reduced to tubular sheaths that enclose and conceal the purple stem below. Flowers are borne in an unbranched raceme along the upper half of the stem. The sepals and petals are yellowish pink with prominent reddish brown to purple stripes.

Bloom Season: June–July.

Habitat/Range: Montane and subalpine forests.

Comments: Coralroots are named for their many branched underground stems that look like branches of sea coral. They have no true roots. The coralroots are highly evolved organisms, dependent for germination and survival on the fungi in the humus layer of the forest floor.

Scarlet Gilia

SCARLET GILIA
Ipomopsis aggregata (Pursh) Grant
(also *Gilia aggregata* [Pursh] Spreng.)
Phlox Family (Polemoniaceae)

Description: Scarlet gilia is normally a biennial, growing the first year as a low, leafy rosette. The second year it sends up an 8–40"-tall leafy flowering stem, completes its life cycle, and dies. The leaves have many narrow, pinnately arranged segments and a skunklike odor when crushed. The flower petals are joined into a slender tube about ½–¾" long that abruptly expands (like a trumpet) into 5 sharply pointed lobes. The plants have many showy flowers that vary in color from scarlet to pale pink, speckled with white.

Bloom Season: April–August.

Habitat/Range: Dry, open forests of the valleys and dry montane forests.

Comments: The name *Ipomopsis* comes from Greek words meaning "striking appearance." It was formerly included in the genus *Gilia* but is now distinguished as a separate genus having well-developed leaves on the flowering stem and trumpet-shaped flowers. An important medicinal plant for American Indians, gilia was used to treat spider bites, fevers, constipation, aches and pains, itching, and venereal diseases. It was also used by the Salish people as a cleanser for the hair and face.

Red Columbine

RED COLUMBINE
Aquilegia formosa Fisch.
Buttercup Family (Ranunculaceae)

Description: Red columbine is among the most showy of the Northern Rockies wildflowers. The 5 red sepals and 5 yellow petal blades (with straight red spurs) are unmistakable. The numerous stamens extend well beyond the petal blades. Like many columbines, the leaves are mostly basal and compound, with 3 sets of 3 leaflets each. The stem leaves are reduced in size and have only 3 leaflets each. Plants vary in size from 8–28".

Bloom Season: May–August.

Habitat/Range: Meadows within dry and moist montane to subalpine forests, but usually at lower elevations than the similar yellow columbine *(A. flavescens).*

Comments: The sweet nectar in the spurs of columbine species attracts hummingbirds and is also relished by children. Some Native American people considered red columbine as a love charm and good luck charm. To impart its pleasant aroma, the plant was used as a hair wash, and the seeds were rubbed on the body and clothing. It was also used medicinally to treat rheumatic joints, colds and coughs, stomachaches, sores, bee stings, and head lice. To increase stamina in racing, the root was rubbed on the legs of both horses and people.

Nootka Rose

NOOTKA ROSE
Rosa nutkana Presl
Rose Family (Rosaceae)

Description: Nootka rose is similar to the common woods rose *(R. woodsii),* but differs from it by having larger flowers, which are often solitary on the branches, and by its tendency to grow in wooded areas at higher elevations in the mountains. The sepals of Nootka rose are ½–1½" long, while the petals are 1–1½" long. Flower color varies from pink to deep rose. The familiar rose hip fruit is purplish, with long persistent sepals. The stems have large, stout prickles at the nodes below the leaf attachment and often somewhat smaller ones on the internodes between leaves.

Bloom Season: May–July.

Habitat/Range: Moist, wooded areas, from the montane to the lower subalpine forests.

Comments: Nootka rose was widely used by many American Indian tribes for healing, food, fiber, and many other uses. It was applied to help heal eye sores, bee stings, and sore throats, and to treat vomiting, diarrhea, and swellings. The rose hips were used for food, and a tealike beverage was brewed from the hips and branches. The petals were used for making a cosmetic.

Harsh Paintbrush

HARSH PAINTBRUSH
Castilleja hispida Benth.
Figwort Family (Scrophulariaceae)

Description: Upper leaves with 1–3 pairs of lateral lobes; and the long, straight hairs on the stems and foliage distinguish harsh paintbrush from most other bright red or scarlet paintbrushes. The stems are clustered, 8–24" tall, and usually unbranched. The central, terminal lobe of the leaf is much broader than the lateral lobes.

Bloom Season: April–June.

Habitat/Range: Grassy slopes and forest openings in the valleys and dry montane forests.

Comments: *Hispida* refers to the straight, bristly hairs that cover the herbage of this paintbrush. Various species of paintbrush were utilized by American Indians for dye and decorations, a component in games, and for medicine. The nectar was often sucked from the flowers as a refreshing treat.

Scarlet Paintbrush

SCARLET PAINTBRUSH
Castilleja miniata Dougl.
Figwort Family (Scrophulariaceae)

Description: Scarlet paintbrush is rather tall as paintbrushes go, reaching a height of about 1–3'. The leaves are all entire (not lobed) and narrowly lance shaped. The brightly colored bracts are lance shaped and deeply divided into 1 or 2 pairs of lateral lobes, beginning from the middle of the bract or lower. Both bracts and sepals are bright red, scarlet, or crimson to red-orange. The upper lip petal is rather long (½–¾") and extends well beyond the sepals and bracts. In the Central Rocky Mountains scarlet paintbrush often hybridizes with split-leaved paintbrush *(C. rhexifolia)* and other species, resulting in intermediates that complicate identification even for professional botanists.

Bloom Season: July–August.

Habitat/Range: Widespread, from the valleys to the subalpine forests.

Comments: Paintbrushes are partially parasitic plants, deriving some of their nutrients and water from nearby host plants. The paintbrush plant attaches to the roots of a host plant by means of a short side branch of a root, which is formed specifically for that purpose. The paintbrush exerts a negative pressure on the host's tissues, pulling water and nutrients into its own roots and stems. During a drought, paintbrushes will often appear healthier than their withered neighbors, which are doubly stressed.

YELLOW FLOWERS

Mountain Goldenpea

This section includes flowers from a bright, golden yellow to a pale, cream color. Some flowers have mixed colors, such as yellow and red, or yellow and white; if the predominant color is yellow, they are included here. Many species with yellow flowers also have green or orange flower variations. You may need to check those sections of this book if the flower you are searching for is not found here.

Western Poison Ivy

WESTERN POISON IVY

Toxicodendron rydbergii (Small ex Rydb.) Greene
(also *Rhus rydbergii* Small)
Sumac Family (Anacardiaceae)

Description: Western poison ivy is a low shrub (less than 5' tall), without the climbing habit or aerial roots of the more eastern poison ivy vine *(T. radicans)*. The stems are hairy and stand upright. The compound leaf has 3 smooth, green leaflets that turn bright red in the fall. The leaf margin has a few irregular teeth. The flowers are small and cream colored with purplish veins. The fruit is a round, cream-colored, berrylike drupe. The cluster of "berries" remains on the plants through the winter.

Bloom Season: May–June.

Habitat/Range: Along streams in the valleys and dry montane forests.

Comments: The name *Toxicodendron* is from the Greek *toxikos* (poisonous) and *dendron* (tree). The well-known itchy rash that results from handling these plants comes from a poison in the resin ducts throughout the plant. Firefighters have been infected by breathing the ash of burning plants.

Yellow Angelica

YELLOW ANGELICA
Angelica dawsonii Wats.
Parsley Family (Apiaceae)

Description: Yellow flowers ·clustered in a single compound umbel are unique features of yellow angelica, easily separating it from the several umbeled, white-to-pink-flowered *Angelica* species in the Rocky Mountains. Well-developed leafy bracts are positioned just below the junction of the primary radiating branches (rays) of the flowering umbel. These bracts are sharply toothed on the margin and often as long as the rays themselves. They are stout plants, 1–4' tall, with pinnately compound leaves that have a toothed margin.

Bloom Season: June–August.

Habitat/Range: Streams and wet slopes, from valleys to subalpine forests. The range of this species is essentially restricted to the Northern Rockies, barely crossing the eastern boundary with the Central Rockies.

Comments: Yellow angelica was named from a specimen collected by David Lyall (1817–1895) along the boundary between Canada and the United States. Lyall was a surgeon and naturalist of the British navy, who was employed at the time (starting in 1858) in a boundary survey party. A species, believed to be yellow angelica, was twice collected by Meriwether Lewis: the first near Lost Trail Pass, between Montana and Idaho, and the second in Idaho along the Lolo Trail near Hungry Creek. American Indians value this plant for its healing powers. Herbalists rely on species of *Angelica* as a digestive aid, for reducing gas, to promote sweating when there is fever, and to loosen phlegm in cases of bronchitis.

Cous Biscuit-Root

COUS BISCUIT-ROOT
Lomatium cous (Wats.) Coult. & Rose
Parsley Family (Apiaceae)

Description: Cous biscuit-root is a low plant (less than 14" tall) with compound leaves that are finely dissected into many small segments. The plants are usually smooth (hairless). The leaves tend to wither and turn yellow as the fruit matures. The flowers are yellow and are arranged in compound umbels, typical of the parsley family. A whorl of well-developed leafy bracts is present at the common point where the individual flower stalks join together. These bracts are relatively large and broadly egg shaped or spatula shaped, the key to correct identification. There are no leafy bracts at the point where the rays join the main stem. The rays are of various lengths; some long, some short. The fruit has a narrow, thin margin (lateral wing), which is typical of the genus *Lomatium*.

Bloom Season: April–June.

Habitat/Range: Open slopes, from the valleys and dry montane forests to subalpine parks and alpine turf.

Comments: According to the Lewis and Clark journals, "cous" or "cows" is the "Chopunnish" (Nez Perce) Indian name for this plant, while the Walla Walla people referred to the plant as "shappellel." Meriwether Lewis collected a specimen of the plant on April 29, 1806, near what we now call the Walla Walla River, in Washington. On the specimen's label, his description reads: "An umbelliferous plant of the root of which the Wallowallows make a kind of bread." This plant was among the most important food plants of the native peoples of the region, and it was mentioned often as a food and trade item in the Lewis and Clark journals. On May 10, 1806, in the Chopunnish village of "Broken Arm," William Clark wrote in his journal, "the noise of their women pounding the cows root remind me of a nail factory."

Fern-Leaved Desert Parsley

FERN-LEAVED DESERT PARSLEY
Lomatium dissectum (Nutt.) Math. & Const.
Parsley Family (Apiaceae)

Description: Also called "giant lomatium," this is a large plant with several stout, smooth (hairless) stems up to 5' or more tall. The large leaves (4–12") are divided into many lacelike ultimate segments up to about ⅜" long. The leaf surface often has short, bristly hairs that are rough to the touch. Compound umbels of yellow (or purple) flowers are arranged on the ends of the stems. The fruit is strongly flattened on the back and has a corky, thick-winged margin.

Bloom Season: April–June.

Habitat/Range: Dry, rocky places, in valleys, dry montane, and subalpine forests.

Comments: Meriwether Lewis collected a specimen of fern-leaved desert parsley on June 10, 1806, near present-day Kamiah, Idaho. The label on the specimen states: "A great horse medicine among the natives." The medicinal value has been rediscovered by modern herbalists, who value it especially for treating respiratory infections.

Nine-Leaf Biscuit-Root

NINE-LEAF BISCUIT-ROOT
Lomatium triternatum (Pursh) Coult. & Rose
Parsley Family (Apiaceae)

Description: This common herb (8–38" tall) is called "nine-leaf biscuit-root" because the compound leaves are often in 3 sets of 3 leaflets each. These ultimate leaf segments are usually quite long (up to 8") and narrow (less than ³⁄₁₆" wide). Fine hair normally covers the surface of the stems and foliage. The tiny yellow flowers occur in clusters, arranged in compound umbels. Just below the junction of the individual flower stalks are a few slender, leafy bracts, while no bracts occur at the junction of the main radiating branches (rays) of the flower arrangement. The ovary matures into a narrow, winged fruit.

Bloom Season: May–July.

Habitat/Range: Open slopes, from the valleys to the subalpine forests.

Comments: A specimen of this biscuit-root was collected by Meriwether Lewis on May 6, 1806, in Idaho, along the Clearwater River between the Potlatch River and Pine Creek. In 1814 Frederick Pursh described this specimen in his book *Flora Americae Septentrionalis:* "The fusiform root of this species is one of the grateful vegetables of the Indians: they use it baked or roasted."

Skunk-Cabbage

SKUNK CABBAGE
Lysichiton americanus Hultén & St. John
Arum Family (Araceae)

Description: In bloom, the bright yellow hood of skunk cabbage, enclosing a spike of tiny yellow flowers, is unmistakable in the Northern Rockies. These unique flowers are in full bloom as the leaves of this plant are just emerging from the wet earth. The ornate yellow hood is a bract, called a "spathe" in the arum family, while the thick, fleshy flower stalk is referred to as a "spadix." Hundreds of minute yellow flowers are embedded in the spadix. Although inconspicuous when the flowers first bloom, the exceptionally large leaves (16–60"), like elephant's ears, rapidly become the dominant feature of the plant.

Bloom Season: April–July.

Habitat/Range: Low-elevation swamps and bogs of the moist montane forest.

Comments: *Lysichiton* comes from the Greek *lysis* (loosening) and *chiton* (tunic), referring to the yellow hood. It is called "skunk cabbage" because of its unpleasant aroma. American Indians used the large leaves to line their cooking pits and as a food wrapping. The plants are said to be edible when fully cooked. Taro, the staple food of the Polynesians, is in the arum family and also must be properly cooked before eating. If not removed by proper cooking, poisonous compounds (oxalates) in these plants may impair kidney function, with potentially fatal results. These compounds are also very sharp, biting or burning the mouth and throat if eaten raw. The large leaves of the poisonous false hellebore (*Veratrum* species) have been mistaken for skunk cabbage and eaten, causing severe sickness and death.

Mountain Arnica

MOUNTAIN ARNICA
Arnica latifolia Bong.
Aster Family (Asteraceae)

Description: Mountain arnica leaves are opposite and lance shaped. The leaves on the stem are without leaf stalks (petioles). The middle leaves on the stem are commonly as large as those lower down. The flower heads consist of yellow rays surrounding a yellow disk. The sunflower-like fruit is smooth (without hair), at least on the lower half of the pod. The similar heart-leaved arnica *(A. cordifolia)* has heart-shaped stem leaves with petioles, and the fruit is covered with short hair.

Bloom Season: June–July.

Habitat/Range: Moist woods from the dry montane forests to timberline.

Comments: Some American Indians value *Arnica* species as a love charm and for its medicinal value in healing bruises and reducing swellings. Herbalists prepare a liniment from *Arnica* as a counterirritant for improving circulation to speed the healing of injuries, especially sprains, sore muscles, and strained joints.

SEEP-SPRING ARNICA
Arnica longifolia DC. Eat.
Aster Family (Asteraceae)

Description: Seep-spring arnica spreads by underground stems and forms dense colonies, often to the exclusion of other plant species. The leafy stems are 1–3' tall. Some stems are topped by several flower heads, while many other stems are without flowers. The leaves are in 5–7 pairs arranged opposite each other on the stem, with no true basal leaves. The foliage is covered with short hairs, rough to the touch, and sometimes with a glandular secretion. The leafy bracts that ring the base of the flower head are sharply pointed.

Bloom Season: July–September.

Habitat/Range: Moist openings, from the subalpine zone to timberline.

Comments: Several species of *Arnica* have long been used by herbalists in the external treatment of injuries and joint inflammation. They are believed to be effective in fighting bacteria and increasing circulation to speed healing. Taken internally, however, arnica has been known to cause severe gastroenteritis.

Seep-Spring Arnica

Hairy Arnica

HAIRY ARNICA
Arnica mollis Hook.
Aster Family (Asteraceae)

Description: Hairy arnica plants are similar in size, creeping habit, and wet habitat to seep-spring arnica. However, hairy arnica has fewer pairs of stem leaves (3–4) and larger heads, with the disk sometimes up to 1½" wide. The leaves of hairy arnica are more than 2" wide and thus broader than those of seep-spring arnica. The lower leaves of hairy arnica are usually the largest. The entire plant is covered with short, glandular hairs. The flower heads are solitary, and both ray and disk flowers are yellow.

Bloom Season: July–early September.

Habitat/Range: Along streams, seeps, and springs of the upper montane and subalpine zones to timberline.

Comments: In the Rocky Mountains, hairy arnica often shares its streamside habitat with monkeyflowers (*Mimulus* species) and columbines (*Aquilegia* species) in showy riparian gardens.

Arrow-Leaved Balsamroot

ARROW-LEAVED BALSAMROOT

Balsamorhiza sagittata (Pursh) Nutt.
Aster Family (Asteraceae)

Description: Arrow-leaved balsamroot is most often confused with mule's-ears (*Wyethia* species). However, arrow-leaved balsamroot has well-developed leaves that originate at the base of the plant and very small, reduced, ones (if any) on the flowering stem. Mule's-ears have large, well-developed leaves on the flowering stem. The leaves and bracts of arrow-leaved balsamroot appear silvery due to dense, white, feltlike hair that covers the plant surface, especially early in the season. The leaves are large (up to 12" long and 6" wide) and shaped like giant arrowheads. The yellow flower heads are solitary on the long stems and resemble sunflowers.

Bloom Season: April–July.

Habitat/Range: Dry soil of grasslands in the valleys and the dry montane forests.

Comments: *Balsamorhiza* (balsamroot) is named for the sap in its large woody root, which has the aroma and texture of balsam fir pitch. American Indians used the root for treating various diseases, swellings, and insect bites, and as a fumigant. They also relied on all parts of the plant for food. The seeds were ground into flour and made into a kind of bread. Meriwether Lewis collected a specimen of balsamroot on April 14, 1806, near present-day White Salmon, Washington. The specimen label and journal entries for that day document the native people gathering "parcels of the Stems" and eating the stems of balsamroot "without any preparation." Modern herbalists rely on the plant to fight infections, loosen phlegm, and boost the immune system.

Rubber Rabbitbrush

RUBBER RABBITBRUSH
Chrysothamnus nauseosus (Pall.) Britt.
Aster Family (Asteraceae)

Description: Rubber rabbitbrush is a medium-sized woody shrub, 1–5' tall. The flower heads have only disk flowers: about 5 tiny yellow flowers per head. The bracts surrounding the base of each flower head are arranged in 5 vertical ranks, overlapping like shingles on a roof. The stems and twigs are covered with a fine, white, feltlike hair. The leaves are narrow (⅛"), linear, and 1–3" long.

Bloom Season: August–October.

Habitat/Range: Dry, open places in valleys and the dry montane forests.

Comments: The name *Chrysothamnus* is derived from the Greek roots *chrys-* (golden yellow) and *thamnos* (bush). *Nauseosus* implies that the plant produces sickness or nausea. Rabbits often hide under its cover to conceal themselves from the watchful eyes of eagles soaring overhead. The Shoshone people of Nevada used the plant to stop diarrhea and as a remedy for coughs and colds. The Cheyenne used it to relieve itching and treat smallpox.

Oregon Sunshine

OREGON SUNSHINE
Eriophyllum lanatum (Pursh) Forbes
(also *Actinella lanata* Pursh)
Aster Family (Asteraceae)

Description: Oregon sunshine is a perennial, herbaceous plant 4–24" tall. The stems and foliage are covered with densely matted, soft, woolly hair that gives the plant a grayish appearance. The leaves may be entire, lobed, or deeply cleft into several narrow segments. The flower heads have bright, golden yellow ray and disk flowers. The woolly bracts that surround the base of each flower head are all about the same size. They form a single vertical row, but they overlap horizontally.

Bloom Season: May–August.

Habitat/Range: Open, dry places, from valleys to the alpine.

Comments: *Eriophyllum* was derived from the Greek *erion* (wool) and *phyllon* (foliage). *Lanatum* is from the Latin *lanatus* (woolly). Meriwether Lewis collected a specimen of this species on June 6, 1806, along the high uplands of the "Kooskooskee" (Clearwater) River, near "Camp Chopunnish," or present-day Kamiah, Idaho.

Blanketflower

BLANKETFLOWER
Gaillardia aristata Pursh
Aster Family (Asteraceae)

Description: Blanketflower has multicolored flower heads. The showy ray flowers (on the outer margin of the flower head) are yellow, becoming purplish toward the base. The disk flowers (in the center of the flower head) are purple to brownish purple and covered with woolly hair. The tips of the ray petals are deeply divided into 3 prominent lobes. The leafy bracts (around the base of the flower head) taper to a long point. The stems, leaves, and bracts are covered with long, loose hairs. The shape of the leaf is variable, from entire to toothed and deeply cut into lobes.

Bloom Season: May–September.

Habitat/Range: Dry soil of the valleys and dry montane forests.

Comments: *Gaillardia* was named in honor of the French botanist Gaillard de Marentonneau. The name *aristata* comes from the Latin *arista* (awn, bristle) in reference to the bristles on the single-seeded fruit (achene). The species was first named and described to science by Frederick Pursh in 1814, from a specimen collected by Meriwether Lewis on July 7, 1806. On that day Lewis and nine men of the Lewis and Clark Expedition crossed the Continental Divide on the return trip to the Great Falls of the Missouri. American Indian people used blanketflower medicinally for intestinal infections, skin disorders, kidney problems, as an eyewash, and for preparing nose drops.

Hound's-Tongue Hawkweed

HOUND'S-TONGUE HAWKWEED
Hieracium cynoglossoides Arv.-Touv.
Aster Family (Asteraceae)

Description: Hound's-tongue hawkweed's foliage and stems are covered with bristly hairs from top to bottom, but often less so on the bracts of the flower heads. When broken the plants exude a milky juice. The yellow flowers are arranged in heads and consist only of single-petaled ray flowers with tan, fine, hairlike sepals (pappus). The bracts around the base of the flower head have both glands and sparse bristly hairs on the surface. Western hawkweed *(H. albertinum)* is similar, but it is more densely hairy on the flower head bracts and lacks the glands.

Bloom Season: June–August.

Habitat/Range: Dry, open places in the valleys, dry montane forests, and upper subalpine forests.

Comments: *Hieracium* is derived from the Greek *hierax* (hawk). The Okanagan-Colville Indians brewed the leaves and roots to make a tea and a tonic. Various other American Indians valued hawkweeds for luck in hunting and for treating diarrhea.

Pineapple Weed

PINEAPPLE WEED
Matricaria matricarioides (Less.) Porter
(also *Matricaria discoidea* DC.)
Aster Family (Asteraceae)

Description: This little annual is more likely to be noticed because of its pleasant pineapple aroma than its inconspicuous flowers. The flower disk is conical and yellowish green, with only disk flowers (no showy ray flowers). The bracts around the base of the flower head have a thin, translucent margin. The plants are 2–12" tall, with numerous leaves that are divided into fine, short, linear segments.

Bloom Season: May–August.

Habitat/Range: Disturbed places in valleys and dry montane forests.

Comments: *Matricaria* is from the Latin *mater* (womb). The name *matricaria* was given by early herbalists to plants of gynecological value. This plant is related to German chamomile *(M. recutita)* and may have similar properties. Herbalists use chamomile for indigestion, insomnia, tension, insect bites, and eczema. Meriwether Lewis collected a specimen of this plant along the "Kooskoosky" (Clearwater) River of Idaho in the spring of 1806 while among the Nez Perce Indians. Several Indian tribes used pineapple weed for colds, upset stomach, as an aid at childbirth, and to relieve menstrual cramps. They also used it to help preserve meat. Its fragrant flower heads were used to line babies' cradles or were strung as a necklace.

Woolly Groundsel

WOOLLY GROUNDSEL
Senecio canus Hook.
Aster Family (Asteraceae)

Description: These small plants (4–12") are covered with dense, tangled, white hairs (like wool). The larger leaves are clustered at the plant base or on the lower portion of the stems. On the upper stems the leaves get progressively smaller. Several flower heads (6–15) are arranged on the ends of the stems. A single, uniform row of bracts, with darkened tips, lines the base of the flower heads. Each head has yellow ray flowers surrounding a yellow disk.

Bloom Season: May–August.

Habitat/Range: Dry, open, rocky places, from valleys to the alpine zone.

Comments: *Senecio* is from the Latin *senex* (old man), perhaps for the gray beardlike hair that covers some species, including this one. Poisonous alkaloids are known to occur in some *Senecios*. Other common names for groundsels include "butterweed" and "ragwort."

TALL BUTTERWEED
Senecio serra Hook.
Aster Family (Asteraceae)

Description: The stems of tall butterweed are 2–6' tall and crowded with leaves. The leaves are 3–6" long, about 1" wide, and lance shaped. Fine, sharp teeth (like a saw) line the margin of the leaf. The abundant yellow flower heads are crowded on the top of the stems. Leafy bracts surround the base of each small flower head, forming a single row of uniform length, touching at the margins but not overlapping. There are often a few shorter bracts, irregularly spaced, in a second outer whorl. The pointed tip of each bract is often black or at least darker than the body.

Bloom Season: June–September.

Habitat/Range: Moist openings, from the valleys to the subalpine forests.

Comments: There are 50 or more species of *Senecio* in North America. At least 7 of them contain toxic alkaloids that are poisonous if eaten, causing acute liver damage to livestock and humans. Species of *Senecio* have also caused cell mutations, birth defects, and liver tumors when consumed.

Tall Butterweed

ARROW-LEAVED GROUNDSEL
Senecio triangularis Hook.
Aster Family (Asteraceae)

Description: The triangular or arrowhead-shaped leaves of this plant are toothed on the margin and taper to a sharp point. These leaves are numerous and well developed on the full length of the tall (1–5') plants. A flat-topped cluster of yellow flower heads is arranged on the ends of the stems. At the base of each flower head is a single row of 8–13 narrow, pointed bracts of equal size and a few, scattered smaller bracts. The yellow ray flowers are few (5–8), surrounding a yellow disk.

Bloom Season: June–September.

Habitat/Range: Stream banks and moist slopes, from the moist montane and subalpine forests to timberline, and occasionally in the valleys.

Comments: *Triangularis* refers to the triangular shape of the leaves, the key identifying feature. This plant is an indicator of moist habitats.

Arrow-Leaved Groundsel

Meadow Goldenrod

MEADOW GOLDENROD
Solidago canadensis L.
Aster Family (Asteraceae)

Description: Meadow goldenrod is 1–6' tall or taller. The stems have dense, short hairs throughout, or at least above the middle of the plant. The lance-shaped leaves are 2–6" long and less than 1" wide, and they are well distributed on the stems (not basal). The leaf margin is often toothed. There are 3 main nerves or veins from the base of the leaf. Numerous small, yellow flower heads crowd the ends of the stems. Surrounding the base of each flower head are long, thin overlapping bracts of varying lengths.

Bloom Season: July–October.

Habitat/Range: Streams and moist places, from the valleys to subalpine forests.

Comments: The Omaha Indians correlated the blooming of goldenrod with the ripening of corn. The plants often develop large, round insect galls on their stems. These galls have been used by some American Indians to make a tea for kidney problems.

Common Tansy

COMMON TANSY
Tanacetum vulgare L.
Aster Family (Asteraceae)

Description: Common tansy often grows in dense communities (1–5' tall) along the roadsides, often to the exclusion of other plants. The fernlike foliage consists of pinnately arranged leaflets that are deeply lobed and toothed. The numerous, flat, disk-shaped flower heads, without ray flowers, are in a corymb-like arrangement on the ends of the stems. Glandular dots on the leaves give the plants a rather strong, peculiar odor.

Bloom Season: August–October.

Habitat/Range: Introduced noxious weed found on roadsides and disturbed places, most often in the valleys and montane forests.

Comments: *Vulgare* means "common." Herbalists have long valued this plant for expelling worms from the digestive tract. Externally it is useful in treating scabies. It has also been used as a bitter tonic to stimulate digestion and menstruation. It is not an herb to experiment with, though, as it could be dangerously poisonous.

Creeping Oregon Grape

CREEPING OREGON GRAPE
Berberis repens Lindl.
(also *Mahonia repens* [Lindl.] G. Don)
Barberry Family (Berberidaceae)

Description: Creeping Oregon grape is a low shrub, about 1' tall, with distinctive hollylike evergreen leaves. Its "creeping" habit—spreading by runners or horizontal stems below the soil surface—makes it resistant to damage by fire. The leaves are less than twice as long as broad, with small spines on the margin. The bright yellow flowers give way to a grapelike cluster of purple berries with a whitish coating. In the fall, some of the leaves often turn bright red, orange, or bronze.

Bloom Season: April–June.

Habitat/Range: Dry slopes, from valleys to the lower subalpine forests.

Comments: The tart berries make a refreshing lemonade-like drink and fine jelly or wine. The yellow inner bark was used widely by American Indians as a yellow dye and as a medicine with many applications. It was believed to be especially useful for easing child delivery, healing wounds, fighting infections, and treating venereal disease and kidney problems. The alkaloid berberine, isolated from the yellow sap, has been shown to have antibiotic activity against a broad spectrum of bacteria and protozoa. Modern herbalists use the herb for fevers, inflammations, infections, indigestion, and liver and gallbladder disorders.

Western Stoneseed

WESTERN STONESEED
Lithospermum ruderale Dougl. ex Lehm.
Borage Family (Boraginaceae)

Description: Western stoneseed is an erect herbaceous plant with a cluster of vertical stems from a woody taproot. Numerous narrow, lance-shaped to linear leaves, 1–4" long, are arranged alternately on the stems. The largest leaves are on the upper stems, and they get progressively smaller downward. Long, spreading, and rather stiff hairs cover the stems. Clusters of yellowish flowers arise from the upper leaf axils, with a small leafy bract at the base of each flower. Inside the trumpet-shaped flowers the style runs down between the 4 distinct parts of the ovary, where it attaches to the enlarged receptacle. These 4 ovary segments ripen into smooth and very hard, bony nutlets.

Bloom Season: May–July.

Habitat/Range: Open, dry places, from the valleys to the lower subalpine forests.

Comments: *Lithospermum* is derived from the Greek *lithos* (stone) and *sperma* (seed), referring to the plant's hard, bony nutlets. Shoshone Indians have used the roots as a remedy for diarrhea and as a contraceptive. Long-term use is said to induce permanent sterility. Modern pharmacological research has verified the contraceptive properties of this plant.

Rough Wallflower

ROUGH WALLFLOWER
Erysimum capitatum (Dougl. ex Hook) E. Greene
(also *Erysimum asperum* [Nutt.] DC.)
Mustard Family (Brassicaceae)

Description: This is an erect plant, 8–40" tall, often with a single stem but sometimes having a few branches. A cluster of spreading or radiating leaves grows from the base of the plant, while numerous alternate leaves also line the stems. The margin of the leaves varies widely from entire to toothed. A cluster of bright yellow to orange flowers is arranged in a raceme on the end of the stem. The flowers are rather large, each with 4 petals as much as 1" long. The fruit is a long, narrow pod, 1–4" long, which reaches upward.

Bloom Season: May–July.

Habitat/Range: Dry places, from valleys to timberline.

Comments: Wallflowers and other members of the mustard family have long been used medicinally in a mustard plaster poultice for relief of bronchial congestion. Left on too long, the poultice can cause serious skin blistering.

Bearberry Honeysuckle

BEARBERRY HONEYSUCKLE
Lonicera involucrata (Rich.) Banks ex Spreng.
Honeysuckle Family (Caprifoliaceae)

Description: Bearberry honeysuckle is a medium-sized shrub (2–6' tall or taller) with opposite, entire leaves. The yellow flowers occur in pairs from the leaf axils. Immediately underneath the twin flowers are 2 sets of conspicuous, green- to purple-tinged leafy bracts. As the fruit develops, the bracts enlarge and deepen in color. The mature fruits are pairs of round, black berries with large purplish red bracts just beneath.

Bloom Season: April–August.

Habitat/Range: Streamsides and moist woods, from the valleys to subalpine forests.

Comments: *Lonicera* is named in honor of Adam Lonitzer (1528–1586), a German botanist. The name *involucrata* refers to the prominent bracts or involucre of bearberry honeysuckle. Utah honeysuckle *(L. utahensis)* is also common in the Rocky Mountains. It lacks the prominent bracts of bearberry honeysuckle, has bright red twin berries, and its leaves have a rounded tip.

Common St. John's Wort

COMMON ST. JOHN'S WORT
Hypericum perforatum L.
St. John's Wort Family (Clusiaceae)

Description: Common St. John's wort is a perennial, herbaceous plant 1–3' tall that spreads with creeping horizontal stems. The leaves are opposite, much longer than wide, and tend to taper toward the base. The surface of the leaf has tiny glandular dots, like pinpricks. Crushing the leaves yields a red pigment. The plant has bright yellow flowers clustered on the ends of the stems. The sepals are narrow, 3–5 times longer than wide. The margin of the petals is lined with dots similar to those on the leaves. The numerous stamens have purple-tipped anthers. There are 3 styles on the ovary, which matures into a 3-beaked capsule.

Bloom Season: June–July.

Habitat/Range: Introduced noxious weed of disturbed places, from valleys to montane forests.

Comments: The name *perforatum* refers to the pinhole dots, or perforations, on the leaves and the margin of the petals. Western St. John's wort *(H. formosum)* is a related species that is native to the Northern Rocky Mountains at high elevations. It has much broader leaves and sepals than common St. John's wort. Herbalists value St. John's wort for treating depression. It is also used to treat gastritis, ulcers, abrasions, and burns. The main active ingredient, hypericin, can cause photosensitivity and dermatitis in animals, including humans. Livestock feeding on the foliage have developed severe skin lesions, sometimes causing death.

Lance-Leaved Stonecrop

SILVERBERRY
Elaeagnus commutata Bernh.
Oleaster Family (Elaeagnaceae)

Description: Silverberry is a 3–12'-tall shrub with silvery leaves and fruit. The numerous stems are flexible, like a willow, and without thorns. Leaves are 1½–3 times as long as wide. The surfaces of the leaves and fruit are covered with small star-shaped scales, visible with a hand lens. The dry, berrylike fruit is round to egg shaped, rather large (½" long), and remains through the winter. The flowers consist of 4 yellow sepals (there are no true petals), 4 stamens, and a pistil. The flowers emit a pleasant lemony fragrance when in bloom.

Bloom Season: May–July.

Habitat/Range: Valleys and dry montane forests.

Comments: *Elaeagnus* comes from the Greek *elaia* (olive) and *agnos* (willow). Russian olive *(E. angustifolia)* is a closely related species introduced from Europe; it is a thorny tree (up to 30' tall) with narrow leaves that are 3–8 times as long as wide. Planted for windbreaks on farmland, Russian olive often escapes and has been gradually crowding out the native vegetation along streams.

LANCE-LEAVED STONECROP
Sedum lanceolatum Torr.
Stonecrop Family (Crassulaceae)

Description: Lance-leaved stonecrop is a small (less than 12" tall), herbaceous plant with succulent leaves that are round in cross section. The leaves are lance shaped, tapering from midlength to the tip. At the base of the plants there are short, sterile shoots that are densely crowded with clusters of radiating basal leaves. The leaves on the flowering stem are alternately arranged and often fall off by the time of flowering. The flowers are like yellow stars, with 5 sepals and 5 sharply pointed petals.

Bloom Season: June–August.

Habitat/Range: Dry, rocky and gravelly soils, in valleys to the alpine.

Comments: The name *Sedum* is derived from the Latin *sedere* (to sit), probably because of its low-growing habit. Native peoples in the Arctic eat the rose-colored stonecrop that grows there. Some edible plant enthusiasts also relish the juicy leaves of lance-leaved stonecrop, although others find it unpalatable.

Silverberry

Russet Buffaloberry (flowers)

(berries)

RUSSET BUFFALOBERRY
Shepherdia canadensis (L.) Nutt.
Oleaster Family (Elaeagnaceae)

Description: This is a medium, deciduous shrub (3–6' tall or taller), without the thorns of the related silver buffaloberry *(S. argentea)*. The upper surface of the leaves is green, while the lower surface is covered with brownish scales and star-shaped hairs. The flowers are unisexual and rather inconspicuous, with 4 yellowish sepals and no petals. Male and female flowers appear on separate plants (dioecious). Bright red berries decorate the shrubs in late summer and fall.

Bloom Season: May–early July.

Habitat/Range: Valleys to subalpine forests.

Comments: Other common names include "soapberry," "bitter buffaloberry," "bearberry," and "soopolallie." Bears relish the berries. American Indians use a stick to whip the berries with water into a foamy mixture, like whipped cream, which they enjoy eating. It is an acquired taste, though, because the bitterness of the berries is at first rather repulsive. The foam is from the bitter chemical saponins in the berries. Both food and medicine, the berries are used to treat a wide range of ailments from indigestion to the flu.

Yellow Mountain Heather

YELLOW MOUNTAIN HEATHER

Phyllodoce glanduliflora (Hook.) Coville
Heath Family (Ericaceae)

Description: Yellow mountain heather is a dwarf, woody shrub, 4–16" tall, with evergreen leaves that look like coniferous fir needles. The plants often form mats that appear to be coniferous krummholz. The flowers are narrowly contracted at the mouth, like an urn or pitcher. The outer surfaces of the sepals, petals, and young stems are densely covered with short glandular hairs. The fruit is a capsule that splits open along the lines of the partitions.

Bloom Season: July–August.

Habitat/Range: Upper subalpine forest ridges and the alpine.

Comments: *Phyllodoce* is from the Greek name for a sea nymph. Yellow mountain heather often hybridizes with the closely related red mountain heather *(P. empetriformis),* producing plants with pink flowers and sparse glandular hairs on the sepals.

YELLOW SWEETVETCH

Hedysarum sulphurescens Rydb.
Pea Family (Fabaceae)

Description: Yellow sweetvetch develops several leafy stems, 1–2' tall, from a thick rootstock. The leaves are pinnately compound, with numerous pairs of oval leaflets. The pale yellow flowers are arranged in a raceme of 20–100 flowers that hang downward from the main flower stalk. The irregular flowers have 5 petals: a banner, 2 wings, and a keel. The wing petals are much shorter than the large keel petal. The fruit is a pod, constricted between the seeds, with up to 4 segments.

Bloom Season: June–August.

Habitat/Range: Open areas in montane and subalpine forests.

Comments: Yellow sweetvetch is most likely to be confused with yellow-flowered species of locoweed (*Astragalus* species) or crazyweed (*Oxytropis* species), which also have pinnately compound leaves. However, the wing petals of locoweed and crazyweed are as long as (or even longer than) the keel petal, and the pods are not constricted between the seeds.

Yellow Sweetvetch

SILKY CRAZYWEED
Oxytropis sericea Nutt.
Bean Family (Fabaceae)

Description: Silky crazyweed leaves are pinnately compound, with 5–10 pairs of leaflets having soft, silky hairs. The numerous (10–30) flowers are arranged in a raceme on the end of a leafless stem 4–10" long. Flower color varies from yellow to white. The wings are longer than the keel petal, concealing it. The keel petal is abruptly contracted into a thin, often purple-tipped point. The fruit has a thick, fleshy wall that hardens into a bony pod.

Bloom Season: May–July.

Habitat/Range: Dry, open areas, from valleys to subalpine forests.

Comments: The name *Oxytropis* comes from the Greek *oxys* (sharp) and *tropis* (keel). The sharp beak on the end of the keel petal of the flower separates *Oxytropis* from locoweed (*Astragalus* species). Foraging on silky crazyweed may cause livestock to develop symptoms of loco poisoning: emaciation, trembling of the head, difficulty eating and drinking, listlessness, and death.

Silky Crazyweed

Mountain Goldenpea

MOUNTAIN GOLDENPEA
Thermopsis montana Nutt.
(also *T. rhombifolia* [Nutt. ex Pursh] Richardson, var. *montana*)
Bean Family (Fabaceae)

Description: Mountain goldenpea is usually 2–3' tall, with many bright yellow, pea-family flowers arranged in a raceme on the flowering stem. The pods are straight, erect, and several times longer than the sepals. Silky hair covers the surface of the narrow pods. The leaf consists of 3 large leaflets, each as much as 4" long. Two rather large leaflike stipules are attached at the base of the leaf stalk.

Bloom Season: May–August.

Habitat/Range: Wet meadows to well-drained slopes, from valleys to the lower subalpine forests.

Comments: Also known as "false lupine." There have been some reports of livestock and human poisoning attributed to this plant. A similar species, round-leaved goldenpea (*T. rhombifolia* var. *rhombifolia*), is distinguished by its shorter stature (mostly less than 14" tall), shorter leaves, and curved pods.

Hop Clover

GOLDEN SMOKE
Corydalis aurea Willd.
Fumitory Family (Fumariaceae)

Description: Golden smoke germinates in the fall and overwinters as a seedling. In the spring it grows rapidly, flowers, and then dies by the end of the growing season. The foliage consists of compound leaves with many small, linear segments. The leaves appear smoky green because they are covered with a fine, white, powdery substance, which rubs off. The flowers are yellow and quite showy. There are 4 petals, the outer 2 hooded and crested, and the inner 2 joined together at the tip. A long spur, containing nectar, extends backward from the upper (outer) petal.

Bloom Season: May–July.

Habitat/Range: Disturbed places, especially after a forest fire, in valleys and montane forests.

Comments: *Corydalis* comes from the Greek *korydallis* (crested lark). Golden smoke is suspected of being poisonous to livestock, like its close relative fitweed *(C. caseana)*. In clinical trials, drugs from some species of *Corydalis* show promise in treating cardiac arrhythmia and venereal disease.

HOP CLOVER
Trifolium aureum Pollich
(also *Trifolium agrarium* L.)
Bean Family (Fabaceae)

Description: This yellow-flowered clover from Europe is well established in the Northern Rockies. It is an annual, 8–20" tall. The rather broad flower heads (⅜" wide or wider) arise from the leaf axils on flower stalks that are longer than the leaves. At the base of the leaf are narrow stipules that are joined to the leaf stalk for at least half of their length. The individual flowers hang downward in dense heads. The dominant feature of the flower is the flared banner petal, which is much longer than the wing and keel petals. The lower 3 sepals are twice the length of the 2 upper ones.

Bloom Season: June–September.

Habitat/Range: Introduced in disturbed places, in valleys to subalpine forests.

Comments: *Agrarium* is from the Latin *agrarius* (land; field), possibly because this aggressive annual is a weed in agricultural areas and other disturbed places in Europe and elsewhere.

Golden Smoke

Glacier Lily

GLACIER LILY
Erythronium grandiflorum Pursh
Lily Family (Liliaceae)

Description: Glacier lily is easily recognized by its few (2–4) large, showy, yellow (or white) flowers, with 6 tepals (petals and petal-like sepals) that are abruptly bent backward toward the base. The 6 protruding stamens may have white, yellow, red, or purple anthers. The style is tipped with 3 stigma lobes. There are 2 parallel-veined (unmottled) leaves, 4–8" long, near the base of the stem. The white-flowered glacier lilies of southeastern Washington and adjacent Idaho are the variety *candidum*.

Bloom Season: March–August.

Habitat/Range: Valleys, montane, and subalpine forests to timberline.

Comments: *Erythronium* comes from the Greek *erythros* (red), referring to the red flowers of some species. Glacier lily is also known as "adder's tongue," "trout lily," "fawn lily," and "dogtooth violet." Glacier lilies bloom as the snow melts in the mountains, following the snow line as it recedes up the slopes. These flowers are so lovely that it can be tempting to plant them in the garden. However, those who have tried have usually failed. It is best to enjoy glacier lilies in their wild habitat. In the spring of 1806, Meriwether Lewis made two separate collections of this plant; once along the Clearwater River (May 8), and again along Eldorado Creek (June 15), where his journal entry states, "the dogtooth violet is just in blume."

Yellow Bell

YELLOW BELL
Fritillaria pudica (Pursh) Spreng.
Lily Family (Liliaceae)

Description: Yellow bell is a small (4–12"
tall), perennial, herbaceous plant with erect
stems and leaves that develop from a cluster of
bulblets. There are 2–8 leaves on the stem.
The leaves are about 4" long and narrowly linear in shape. The flowers are yellow to orange
when they first bloom, but fade to red or purple as they age. Most plants have but a single
flower, but occasionally plants are seen with 2
or 3. The flowers hang downward like a bell.
Each flower consists of 6 tepals (the petals and
sepals are similar) and the more or less concealed stamen and style within. The fruit is a
cylindrical to globe-shaped pod.

Bloom Season: March–June.

Habitat/Range: Open areas, in valleys and
montane forests.

Comments: "The bulb is the shape of a bis-
cuit which the natives eat." Thus wrote Meriwether Lewis on the label of his specimen of
yellow bell, collected on May 8, 1806, near the
Kooskooskee (Clearwater) River in Idaho.
The Salish-Kootenai Indians of Montana are
said to have mixed yellow bell bulbs with
those of the bitterroot, which were ready for
digging at the same time. The green seedpods
are also known to be edible fresh or boiled.
With the decline of wild habitats where these
lovely plants can be seen, it is best to leave
them for others to enjoy.

Blazing Star

BLAZING STAR
Mentzelia laevicaulis (Dougl.) T. & G.
Blazing Star Family (Loasaceae)

Description: The spectacular flowers of this plant are large (up to 6" in diameter) and lemon yellow. Each flower has 5 lance-shaped petals and numerous yellow stamens. Appearing like a set of narrow petals that alternate with the larger (true) petals, the 5 outer stamens have expanded, showy filaments. The fruit is a capsule up to 1½" long. Harsh, barbed hairs cover the stems and foliage of these plants, which are 9–40" tall. The leaves have a deeply wavy margin. Because they are night blooming, closing during the heat of day, the flowers are best viewed at dawn.

Bloom Season: July–September.

Habitat/Range: Dry, disturbed soil, in the valleys and dry montane forests.

Comments: *Mentzelia* is named in honor of the German botanist Christian Mentzel (1622–1701). The Dakota and Cheyenne people are said to have used blazing star medicinally to treat fevers, earache, rheumatism, arthritis, mumps, measles, and smallpox.

Indian Pond Lily

INDIAN POND LILY
Nuphar polysepalum Engelm.
Water-Lily Family (Nymphaeaceae)

Description: We are all familiar with pond lilies, whose leaves float on the surface of ponds and lakes. The leaves of Indian pond lily are broadly heart shaped and 4–16" long. The stem reaches as much as 6' down to the roots in the mud. The flowers are bright yellow and quite large, 3–5" in diameter. There are numerous red to purple stamens. Up to 25 lines radiate from the center of the unusually broad stigma, which is about 1" wide. The fruit is cylindrical, about 3" long, and filled with pelletlike seeds.

Bloom Season: May–August.

Habitat/Range: Aquatic; rooted in the muddy bottoms of lakes, ponds, and sluggish streams from the valleys to the subalpine forests.

Comments: *Nuphar* is derived from an Arabic name for pond lily. Dr. Ferdinand V. Hayden made the initial scientific botanical collection of Indian pond lily from a small lake between the Henry's Fork and Snake River Fork of the Columbia River, on June 20, 1860, while on the expedition led by Captain William F. Raynolds and guided by mountain man Jim Bridger. The seeds of Indian pond lily were a staple food of the Klamath Indians, who roasted and ground them into a meal. The roots are edible, too, but only as an emergency food; those who are less hungry find their flavor disagreeable.

Long-Leaved Evening Primrose

LONG-LEAVED EVENING PRIMROSE

Camissonia subacaulis (Pursh) Raven
(also *Oenothera heterantha* Nutt.)
Evening Primrose Family (Onagraceae)

Description: The 2–12"-long leaves of this low plant are all basal, without a leafy stem. The leaves are widest well above the middle, tapering to a narrow basal portion at the petiole (the leaf stem). Some leaves have a few small lobes below the middle of the blade. The flowers are technically stemless, with the ovary attached directly to the leaf axil. Look carefully; the petals and other floral parts are attached to the top of a very slender projection of the ovary, which appears to be a flower stalk. The flowers are short-lived, blooming in the morning and wilting later that same day. The 4 yellow petals are about as wide as they are long. The 4 narrow sepals turn back away from the petals.

Bloom Season: May–July.

Habitat/Range: Moist meadows, from valleys to subalpine forests.

Comments: *Camissonia* is named in honor of the German poet and botanist Ludolf Adelbert von Chamisso (1781–1838), who visited California in 1816. Another German, botanist Frederick Pursh, named this plant *Jussieua subacaulis* in 1814, from a specimen collected by Meriwether Lewis from "moist ground on the Quamash flats June 14, 1806," a place today known as Weippe Prairie, Idaho.

Yellow Evening Primrose

YELLOW EVENING PRIMROSE

Oenothera villosa Thunb.
(also *O. strigosa* Mkze. & Bush)
Evening Primrose Family (Onagraceae)

Description: These are biennials (or short-lived perennials), growing the first year as a basal rosette. In the second year, a tall stem (1–5') shoots upward, crowned with a spike of light yellow flowers. Dense hairs cover the foliage and stems. The flowers are stalkless, with the ovary attached in the axils of leafy bracts. What appears to be a flower stalk is actually a floral tube, a slender projection of the ovary. Joined at the top of this floral tube are the sepals, petals, and stamens. The fruit is a narrow capsule (about 1–2" long) that splits open at the summit to distribute the numerous seeds.

Bloom Season: June–August.

Habitat/Range: Meadows and stream banks, in valleys and montane forests.

Comments: *Villosa* refers to the long, silky, straight hairs that cover these plants. *Strigosa* further describes these hairs as being pressed flat and all pointing in the same direction.

Yellow Lady's Slipper

YELLOW LADY'S SLIPPER
Cypripedium calceolus L.
Orchid Family (Orchidaceae)

Description: The distinctly orchid flower of yellow lady's slipper has a large, yellow lip petal, inflated like a pouch. Purplish dots decorate the mouth, or opening of the pouch. A triangular sterile stamen, also yellow with purple dots, hangs down into the pouch opening, pointing the way for insects to enter. The sepals and petals, surrounding the lip, are purplish brown. The lateral petals are long, narrow, and twisted, making up to 3 complete turns. The leaves are broad, taper to a point, and have prominent parallel veins. The stems are 8–16" tall, with 3 or 4 alternate leaves and a leafy bract below the solitary flower (or pair of flowers).

Bloom Season: May–June.

Habitat/Range: Wetlands in the valleys and montane forests. It is a rare species in the Northern Rockies, with small, widely separated populations.

Comments: The Orchidaceae is one of the largest plant families, with about 500 genera and 1,500 species worldwide, mostly in tropical forests. *Cypripedium* is named from the Greek *kypris* (Venus) and *pes* (foot), referring to the moccasin-shaped lip. Yellow lady's slipper and other western terrestrial orchids have very specialized habitat and soil requirements, requiring specific soil microorganisms for germination and growth. Because they are rare, and their requirements cannot be duplicated in the garden, they should never be transplanted.

Clustered Broomrape

CLUSTERED BROOMRAPE
Orobanche fasciculata Nutt.
Broomrape Family (Orobanchaceae)

Description: This strange parasitic plant is often overlooked. The stout main plant stems are 2–7" long but appear much shorter because about ⅔ of their length are buried in the soil. The plants are root parasites, attaching themselves to the roots of various species, especially sagebrush *(Artemisia* species). Since they get their nutrients from the host plant, they have no need for photosynthesis. Hence, the leaves are vestigial: small and bractlike, without chlorophyll. There are 4–10 flower stalks (pedicels) attached to each stem where the bractlike leaves join (in the leaf axils). Each pedicel bears a single flower, which is yellowish to dull red with purple lines. The petal tube is curved and funnel shaped with 5 lobes. The sepals are likewise tubular with lobes about the same length as the tube, or shorter.

Bloom Season: April–August.

Habitat/Range: Valleys and dry montane forests.

Comments: *Orobanche* comes from the Greek *orobos* (vetch) and *anchein* (to choke). It is interesting to note how people have applied human values and judgments in naming these parasitic plants, giving the impression that they are plants of violence, raping or strangling their hosts. Nevada Indians were reported to use broomrape plants for both food and medicine.

Yellow Buckwheat

YELLOW BUCKWHEAT
Eriogonum flavum Nutt.
Buckwheat Family (Polygonaceae)

Description: Forming large, flat mats up to 12" wide, the leaves of this plant are green and less hairy on the upper surface, and grayish with dense woolly hair beneath. The woolly flowering stems are 2–12" tall, with an umbel flower arrangement. A whorl of leaflike bracts radiates from just below the common junction of the rays (branches) of the umbels. The individual flowers are on long, slender flower stalks attached within a cuplike bract with 4 or 5 erect to slightly spreading lobes. The bright yellow tepals (petals and petal-like sepals) are woolly on the back surface.

Bloom Season: June–August.

Habitat/Range: Dry, open, rocky places, from mountain valleys to the alpine zone.

Comments: *Eriogonum* comes from the Greek roots *erion* (wool) and *gony* (knee), probably because of the woolly hair on the stems. *Flavum* means "yellow." Various American Indian tribes used buckwheat species for treating colds, tuberculosis, rheumatism, stomach trouble, diarrhea, bleeding, sore eyes, and as a diuretic.

Yellow Columbine

YELLOW COLUMBINE
Aquilegia flavescens S. Wats.
Buttercup Family (Ranunculaceae)

Description: Columbine flowers are easily identified by their 5 showy, spurred petals and 5 showy, petal-like sepals. The spurs of yellow columbine are curved inward but not hooked. The sepals are yellow, often tinged with pink (or entirely pink in the variety *miniana*). The petals have cream-colored blades and yellow spurs. The leaves are mostly basal and compound, with 3 sets of 3 (that is, 9) leaflets per leaf. Leaves and/or leafy bracts on the flowering stem are much reduced, both in size and in the number of leaflets. The stems are 8–30" tall.

Bloom Season: June–early August.

Habitat/Range: Moist mountain meadows, streams, and canyon bottoms, from montane and subalpine forests to the alpine.

Comments: The derivation of *Aquilegia* is disputed. Some say it is derived from the Latin *aqua* (water) and *legere* (to draw), possibly because of its affinity for streamside habitats. Others believe that it is derived from the Latin *aquila* (eagle), because of the resemblance of the spurs to the talons of an eagle. Columbine is from the Latin *columbinus* (dovelike). If the spurs are viewed as the heads of 5 doves, and the petal blades as their wings, then a columbine flower does resemble 5 doves taking flight. Thus, the columbine can be seen as a symbol of war (the eagle) or of peace (the dove).

Subalpine Buttercup

SUBALPINE BUTTERCUP
Ranunculus eschscholtzii Schlecht.
Buttercup Family (Ranunculaceae)

Description: Subalpine buttercup is a low-growing plant, with stems only 2–8" tall. It has smooth, shiny green leaves with 3 deep lobes. The leaf segments are sometimes lobed again once or twice. Most of the leaves are basal, with the few leaves and/or leafy bracts on the flowering stem reduced in size. The flowering stems are smooth (hairless), with 1–3 flowers each. The flowers usually have 5 sepals and 5 petals. A smooth nectary scale lies at the base of the bright yellow petals. Stamens and pistils are numerous.

Bloom Season: June–August.

Habitat/Range: Meadows in subalpine forests and alpine tundra.

Comments: *Ranunculus* is from the Latin *rana* (frog) and *-unculus* (little), likely referring to the wet habitat of many species. Buttercups have acrid juice that can blister or even ulcerate the skin, especially the mucous membranes. Clinical trials have shown the juice to be active against a broad spectrum of bacteria.

Straightbeak Buttercup

STRAIGHTBEAK BUTTERCUP

Ranunculus orthorhynchus Hook.
Buttercup Family (Ranunculaceae)

Description: This is usually an erect plant, 8–24" tall, although sometimes the stems lie horizontally. Dense hair covers the stems, leaf stalks, and sepals. Most of the leaves are basal and pinnately compound, with numerous segments. The leaves on the flowering stems are more deeply divided into narrower segments than the basal leaves. The sepals are turned downward away from the 5 yellow petals. Looking at the single-seeded fruit with a hand lens reveals that it is very flat and thin (¼ as thick as broad), smooth (hairless), and has a rather long (⅛") straight beak.

Bloom Season: April–August.

Habitat/Range: Moist meadows, from valleys to subalpine forests.

Comments: *Orthorhynchus* is from the Greek *orthos* (straight) and *rhynchos* (beak; snout) referring to the straight beak of the fruit. Species of buttercup have been used in folk herbal medicine to treat abrasions, toothache, rheumatism, hemorrhoids, and perineal tears.

Globeflower

GLOBEFLOWER
Trollius albiflorus (A. Gray) Rydb.
(also *Trollius laxus* Salisb. var. *albiflorus* A. Gray)
Buttercup Family (Ranunculaceae)

Description: Pale yellow as they begin to open, the petal-like sepals of globeflower are white to cream colored when in full flower. Numerous bright yellow stamens and green pistils accent the center of the flowers. The flowering stems are smooth (hairless), with 1–3 alternately arranged leaves having short stalks that flare out at the base, clasping the stems. The basal leaves have long leaf stalks (2–10" long). All the leaves are deeply divided into several segments, which are in turn lobed and toothed. The plants are 4–16" tall.

Bloom Season: May–August.

Habitat/Range: Wet meadows, from montane forests to the alpine zone.

Comments: *Trollius* comes from the German *trollblume* (globeflower). Globeflower is often confused with marsh marigold *(Caltha leptosepala)*, with which it often coexists. However, the leaves of marsh marigold are heart shaped and not divided into segments. Globeflower has acrid juice that can blister the skin, like its close relatives the buttercups. The closely related spreading globeflower *(T. laxus)* of eastern North America was used by American Indians to treat fungal infections of the mouth.

Yellow Mountain Avens

YELLOW MOUNTAIN AVENS
Dryas drummondii Richards.
Rose Family (Rosaceae)

Description: Yellow mountain avens establishes easily on raw gravel, often forming circular mats several feet in diameter. The leaves are green on the upper surface and white-woolly beneath, with a wavy margin and a wedge-shaped base. Individual yellow flowers rise above the leafy mats on hairy, leafless stalks that are up to 8" long. The many pistils of the flower mature into a cluster of single-seeded dry fruits with showy plumelike styles that are more dramatic than the flowers. Without the flowers, the similar white mountain avens *(D. octopetala)* may be distinguished by its heart-shaped or rounded leaf base.

Bloom Season: May–July.

Habitat/Range: Along gravelly streams in the valleys, in rocky ridges of the upper subalpine forest, and on the alpine fellfield.

Comments: In Greek mythology a dryad *(Dryas)* is a nymph living in a tree. "Avens" is a common name for several herbs in the rose family, especially those in the genus *Geum.*

LARGE-LEAVED AVENS
Geum macrophyllum Willd.
Rose Family (Rosaceae)

Description: Large-leaved avens has basal leaves up to 12" long. The terminal segment of these basal leaves is several times larger than the lateral lobes below it. The flowering stems are as much as 2' tall. The leaves on the stem are much smaller than the basal ones and have leafy stipules at their base. The flowers have sepals that turn back toward the flower stalk as the petals fully open.

Bloom Season: April–August.

Habitat/Range: Stream banks and moist woods, from the valleys to the subalpine forests.

Comments: *Geum* species are highly astringent herbs, valued by herbalists for treating diarrhea, dysentery, and inflamed mucous membranes, as in sore throat and gingivitis. Some American Indian tribes likewise used the herb for coughs, diarrhea, and toothaches.

Large-Leaved Avens

Shrubby Cinquefoil

SHRUBBY CINQUEFOIL

Pentaphylloides fruticosa (L.) Schwarz
(also *Potentilla fruticosa* L.)
Rose Family (Rosaceae)

Description: This low (1–3' high) shrub, with yellow flowers, is popular in ornamental landscaping. The leaves are compound, with 5 pinnately arranged leaflets. The leaves and stipules are clothed in long, silky hairs that give them a bluish green hue. Shredding, reddish brown bark hangs loosely from the stems. Individual flowers grow from the leaf axils along the stem, while groups of 3–7 flowers are arranged at the tip. The flowers have 5 petals and numerous stamens and pistils.

Bloom Season: June–August.

Habitat/Range: Wet meadows to dry rocky slopes, from valleys to the alpine.

Comments: *Pentaphylloides* is derived from the Greek *penta-* (five) and *phylloides* (like leaves) for the foliage with 5 leaflets. This genus of shrubs was separated from *Potentilla*, which now includes only herbaceous species. Herbalists value the plant for treating inflammatory conditions. Meriwether Lewis collected a specimen of this low shrub on July 6, 1806, near present-day Ovando, Montana.

Common Silverweed

COMMON SILVERWEED
Potentilla anserina L.
(also *Argentina anserina* [L.] Rydb.)
Rose Family (Rosaceae)

Description: Silverweed spreads by long, red runners on the surface of the ground that root at the nodes, like strawberry plants do. Pinnately compound leaves, with numerous coarsely toothed leaflets, occur at intervals on the runners. The upper surface of the leaves is often dark green, while the lower surface is covered with white silky hair; or sometimes both surfaces are silky white. Yellow flowers arise singly on leafless stalks up to 4" long that originate in the leaf axils.

Bloom Season: May–August.

Habitat/Range: Wet meadows, from valleys to the montane forests.

Comments: Meriwether Lewis collected a specimen of this plant on March 13, 1806, while the Lewis and Clark Expedition was spending the winter at Fort Clatsop, in present-day Oregon. Lewis's specimen label states: "The roots are eat by the natives, & taste like Sweet Potatoes, grows in marshy ground." It was a principal food source of the Okanagan Indians. The runners were used as cordage to hold leggings in place. American Indians also used the plant medicinally to treat diarrhea, skin sores, and stomach problems.

Sticky Cinquefoil

STICKY CINQUEFOIL
Potentilla glandulosa Lindl.
Rose Family (Rosaceae)

Description: Glandular hairs, which exude an aromatic fluid, cover the leaves and stems of this perennial herb. The stems are usually 16" or less high, with a rather open-branching flower arrangement. The basal leaves are compound, with 5–9 toothed leaflets pinnately arranged. The leaves on the stems are few and much smaller than the basal leaves. The flowers are deep yellow to creamy white. The style is attached to the ovary below the middle. The similar tall cinquefoil *(P. arguta)* has erect stems greater than 16" long, with a narrow, compact flower arrangement.

Bloom Season: June–August.

Habitat/Range: Meadows, from valleys to the subalpine forests.

Comments: *Potentilla* is from the Latin *potens* (powerful), probably because of the potent medicinal properties of some of the herbs in this genus. *Potentilla* has a high tannin content, making it very astringent and anti-inflammatory. Herbalists use it to treat diarrhea and various sores and inflammatory conditions of the intestinal tract and mucous membranes.

Bitterbrush

BITTERBRUSH
Purshia tridentata (Pursh) DC.
Rose Family (Rosaceae)

Description: This woody shrub is densely and rigidly branched and is usually 3–6' tall. However, treelike forms over 12' in height are found in some areas. The leaves are wedge shaped with 3 lobes, like big sagebrush, but without the pungent sagebrush aroma. The upper leaf surface is green, while dense hair on the lower surface gives it a gray cast. The leaf margin is rolled under to the lower leaf surface. The yellow flowers are highly fragrant, emitting a strong, pleasant perfume to attract pollinating insects. The flowers have 5 sepals, 5 petals, numerous stamens, and a single pistil.

Bloom Season: April–June.

Habitat/Range: Dry slopes of the valleys and montane forests.

Comments: Bitterbrush was first described by Frederick Pursh (1774–1820), from a specimen collected by Meriwether Lewis near present-day Ovando, Montana. The label accompanying Lewis's specimen reads: "A shrub common to the open prairie of the knobs, July 6, 1806." Pursh named the species *Tigarea tridentata,* placing it into an existing genus. Later botanists created a new genus, naming it in Pursh's honor, *Purshia.* Bitterbrush is a nutritious browse plant, highly sought after by both wild ungulates (deer, elk, etc.) and domestic livestock. "Antelope brush" is another common name.

Creeping Sibbaldia

CREEPING SIBBALDIA
Sibbaldia procumbens L.
Rose Family (Rosaceae)

Description: This is a ground-hugging plant that forms cushions in the alpine turf. The leaves are compound, with 3 leaflets each, like clover or strawberry leaves. However, creeping sibbaldia leaves are uniquely wedge shaped, with 3 teeth on the apex. The flowering stems are 1–4" tall, with 2–15 flowers arranged on the end. The tiny flower parts are attached to a shallow, cuplike hypanthium. The 5 yellow, spatula-shaped petals are only half the length of the 5 sepals.

Bloom Season: June–August.

Habitat/Range: Moist areas in subalpine and alpine zones.

Comments: *Sibbaldia* is named in honor of Sir Robert Sibbald (1641–1722), professor of medicine at Edinburgh. *Procumbens* refers to the prostrate growth form of the plant. Because *Sibbaldia* is a late snowbank indicator, Scandinavian engineers use it in road design, to point out areas to avoid.

Sulphur Paintbrush

SULPHUR PAINTBRUSH
Castilleja sulphurea Rydb.
Figwort Family (Scrophulariaceae)

Description: Sulphur paintbrush has broad, yellow bracts that largely conceal the inconspicuous flowers, which can be seen peeking over the top of the showy bracts. The bracts often (but not always) have a pair of short, lateral lobes. The leaves are entire (without lobes) and are shaped like a narrow lance, tapering from the base to the tip. The plants are 8–24" tall.

Bloom Season: June–September.

Habitat/Range: Subalpine meadows and on open slopes up to timberline.

Comments: Except for the yellow flower color, sulphur paintbrush looks very much like the closely related split-leaved paintbrush *(C. rhexifolia)*, which has rose-purple flowers and grows in the same habitat. The yellow western paintbrush *(C. occidentalis)* may be a dwarf alpine form of sulphur paintbrush. They are almost identical, but western paintbrush is 8" or less tall.

BUTTER AND EGGS
Linaria vulgaris Hill
Figwort Family (Scrophulariaceae)

Description: The showy, snapdragon-like flowers of butter and eggs thrust upward on spikelike racemes on the ends of 8–32" tall, erect stems. The numerous, linear leaves are often narrower at the base. The yellow, tubular flowers are tinged with orange on the well-developed, hair-lined "mouth." A straight spur, about as long as the rest of the flower, protrudes from the base.

Bloom Season: June–September.

Habitat/Range: Introduced noxious weed of disturbed places, from valleys to subalpine forests.

Comments: *Linaria* is derived from the Latin *Linum* (flax), because of the vegetative resemblance of butter and eggs to the common cultivated flax *(Linum usitatissimum)*. Like many of our troublesome weeds, butter and eggs came to us from a foreign land, and here it lacks the biological controls that kept it in balance at home. Herbalists view this plant as a medicinal herb and use it to treat hepatitis and other liver problems.

Butter and Eggs

YELLOW MONKEYFLOWER
Mimulus guttatus DC.
Figwort Family (Scrophulariaceae)

Description: The blossoms of yellow monkeyflower often line the edges of streams. The plants may grow as annuals or as perennials that spread by creeping stems above the soil surface. They are highly variable in size, sometimes trailing along the ground as low as 2", and sometimes growing up to 3' tall. The leaves are broad, more or less egg shaped, and coarsely toothed. The green sepal tube is ridged and irregularly toothed, with the upper tooth the longest. The yellow petal tube spreads back into 5 irregular lobes: 2 upper and 3 lower. The inner surface of the flaring throat of the flower is covered with hair and marked with maroon dots.

Bloom Season: March–September.

Habitat/Range: Water's edge; valleys to subalpine forests.

Comments: *Mimulus* comes from the Latin *mimus*, likening it to a mimic actor. *Guttatus* is a Latin word meaning "spotted," referring to the small maroon dots on the flower's mouth.

Yellow Monkeyflower

NARROW-LEAVED COW WHEAT
Melampyrum lineare Desr.
Figwort Family (Scrophulariaceae)

Description: This is a small (4–12") annual herbaceous plant with long, narrow leaves. The tubular flowers arise on short flower stalks from the axils of the leaves, which are opposite. The upper lip of the flower forms a hood that is about the same length as the 3-lobed lower lip. The white to pinkish flower tube is highlighted by the bright yellow "mouth" of the inner lower lips.

Bloom Season: June–August.

Habitat/Range: Meadows and woods in montane and subalpine forests.

Comments: *Melampyrum* comes from the Greek *melas* (black) and *pyros* (wheat) in reference to the black seeds of this plant.

Narrow-Leaved Cow Wheat

Yellow Owl's Clover

YELLOW OWL'S CLOVER
Orthocarpus luteus Nutt.
Figwort Family (Scrophulariaceae)

Description: Owl's clovers resemble miniature Indian paintbrushes (*Castilleja* species), to which they are closely related. However, paintbrushes are mostly perennials, and the upper lip of the flower tube is usually much longer than the lower lip. Owl's clovers (*Orthocarpus* species) are all annuals, and both upper and lower lips of the flower tube are of about equal length. Yellow owl's clover has glandular hairs on the sepals and bracts. The bract, below each flower, is divided above the middle into 3 pointed lobes. The leaves are mostly entire, narrow, and pointed, but the upper ones are 3-lobed like the bracts.

Bloom Season: July–August.

Habitat/Range: Dry soils, in valleys to montane forests, often in sagebrush communities or open woodlands.

Comments: *Orthocarpus* comes from the Greek *orthos* (straight) and *karpos* (fruit), referring to the straight capsule of owl's clovers. *Luteus* is Latin for "yellow." The botanist Thomas Nuttall (1786–1859) collected the initial specimen of yellow owl's clover, from which the species was first described, "on the plains of the Missouri, near Ft. Mandan," while he traveled with the American Fur Company up the Missouri River in 1811. He described the species in his book *Genera of North American Plants* in 1818.

Bracted Lousewort

BRACTED LOUSEWORT
Pedicularis bracteosa Benth.
Figwort Family (Scrophulariaceae)

Description: Bracted lousewort is sometimes called "fernleaf." The leaves are divided into many long, narrow, toothed segments, like the leaves of many ferns. The leaves are attached well up on the stems, usually without any true basal leaves. The numerous flowers are arranged, spikelike, on the ends of the 1–3'-tall, erect, unbranched stems. Each flower arises from the axil of a leafy bract. The flowers are irregular, divided into upper and lower segments. The long upper segment is shaped like a hood or helmet, while the lower segment has 3 small lobes. Color varies from yellow to red or purple.

Bloom Season: Late June–early August.

Habitat/Range: Meadows of montane and subalpine forests.

Comments: *Bracteosa* refers to the conspicuous leafy bracts below each flower. Louseworts are partially parasitic plants, deriving part of their nutrients from host plants through a root graft. The plants are used by herbalists as a sedative and muscle relaxant.

Yellow Beardtongue

YELLOW BEARDTONGUE
Penstemon confertus Dougl.
Figwort Family (Scrophulariaceae)

Description: The flowers of yellow beard-tongue are arranged in several layers, each consisting of numerous flowers in crowded clusters that are widely spaced on the stem. Each flower has 1 sterile and 4 fertile stamens, all hidden within the petal tube. The sterile stamen is bearded on the tip. The anthers of the fertile stamens are purple and smooth (hairless) and split open full length for pollen dissemination. Individual flowers are small (½" or less). The plants are 8–20" tall and smooth (hairless). The basal leaves are oval with rounded ends, while the leaves on the stem are lance shaped, tapering to a point.

Bloom Season: May–August.

Habitat/Range: Meadows and open woods, from the valleys to the lower subalpine forests.

Comments: *Confertus* is from the Latin *confert* (dense; crowded), in reference to the crowded clusters of flowers. A similar species, pale yellow beardtongue *(P. flavescens)*, grows in the Bitterroot Mountains of the Northern Rockies. It has larger flowers (½–⅝" long) that are concentrated in a large terminal cluster, with 1–3 smaller clusters below.

Stream Violet

STREAM VIOLET
Viola glabella Nutt.
Violet Family (Violaceae)

Description: The stems of stream violet are 2–12" long and are naked or leafless on the lower ⅔ of their length, bearing leaves and flowers only on the upper ⅓. These stem leaves, and the leaves from the base, are heart shaped with a pointed tip and minute teeth on the margin. The leaf stalks of the basal leaves are 4–8" long. Both front and back surfaces of the petals are yellow. Purplish lines, like pencil marks, decorate the inner surface of the lower 3 petals, while fine hair trims the lateral petals and style head.

Bloom Season: April–July.

Habitat/Range: Streams and damp woods of the moist montane and subalpine forests.

Comments: Violets are nutritious, edible herbs, high in vitamins A and C. They may be eaten raw or cooked. Some American Indians ate the leaves and stems, mixed with other herbs, parboiled, and fried. Violets are grown in vegetable gardens in Europe and North America; it is a versatile plant used as a potherb, in salads, to thicken soup, flavor vinegar, and to brew a delicious tea. Because of its slimy texture, violets have been used as a substitute for okra in thickening gumbo in the South.

Round-Leaved Violet

ROUND-LEAVED VIOLET
Viola orbiculata Geyer
Violet Family (Violaceae)

Description: This small violet (seldom over 2" tall) has leaves and flowers nearly full length on its stems. The leaves are quite round in outline with a subtle, heart-shaped base and fine teeth on the margin. The petals are lemon yellow to gold in color; all 5 petals have purple lines, and the 2 lateral ones have yellow hair. The end of the style is also covered with short hair.

Bloom Season: May–August.

Habitat/Range: Shady woods, from the moist montane forests to timberline.

Comments: Violets are both edible and medicinal herbs. American Indians made a poultice of the leaves for headache and for treating boils and wounds. They also took it internally for diarrhea, colds, nasal congestion, and heart problems. Both Chinese and Western herbalists likewise have used violets for centuries in a variety of medicinal applications. As an expectorant, violets are used for reducing upper respiratory phlegm in bronchitis, coughs, and colds. It is an anti-inflammatory herb said to be useful for various skin conditions and treating urinary infections. The herb was once called "heartsease" for its use as a love potion.

Yellow Mountain Violet

YELLOW MOUNTAIN VIOLET
Viola purpurea Kell.
Violet Family (Violaceae)

Description: The pansylike flowers of yellow mountain violet have brown-purple lines. The upper petals are purple on the back. The flowers sometimes fade to a brownish purple color as they age. These are small plants, usually less than 6" tall. They are sometimes called "goosefoot violet" because of the leaf shape; they are longer than broad (1½" long and 1" wide), with a few coarse, shallow lobes ("goose toes"). The leaves are often purplish, at least on the coarse veins.

Bloom Season: May–August.

Habitat/Range: Both dry and moist habitats, from the valleys to timberline.

Comments: The similar yellow prairie violet *(V. nuttallii)* is distinguished by having oval or lance-shaped leaf blades (up to 4" long) that lack the lobes, coarse veins, and purplish color of yellow mountain violet.

WHITE FLOWERS

Mockorange

This section is for pure white and cream-colored flowers, although many flowers vary from white to very pale green or very pale yellow. Other white flowers fade to pink, lavender, or some other color as they age. If you cannot find the flowers you are looking for here, you may want to check the other sections.

Arrowhead

ARROWHEAD
Sagittaria cuneata Sheld.
Water-Plantain Family (Alismataceae)

Description: This is an aquatic plant, rooted in the mud, with distinctive leaves shaped like arrowheads. The leaves originate from the plant base, often underwater, and emerge above the water's surface. Flowers are found in groups of 3 along the leafless stem. Each flower has 3 greenish sepals and 3 white petals. The flowers are unisexual, with female (seed-bearing) flowers on the lower portion of each stem, and the male (pollen-producing) flowers on the upper stem.

Bloom Season: June–September.

Habitat/Range: Ponds, streams, and swamps, in valleys and moist montane forests.

Comments: The arrowhead was known as *wapato* by American Indians of western Washington and Oregon and was a major food source for them. On March 29, 1806, soon after starting the return journey up the Columbia River from Fort Clatsop, Meriwether Lewis noted in his journal, "the wappetoe furnishes the principal article of traffic with these people . . . the natives of the Sea coast . . . will dispose of their most valuable articles to obtain this root"; and William Clark wrote, "they Collect great quantities of pappato, which the womin collect by getting into the water, Sometimes to their necks holding by a Small canoe and with their feet loosen the wappato or bulb of the root from the bottom from the fibers, and it imedeately rises to the top of the water, they Collect & throw them into the Canoe."

Lyall's Angelica

LYALL'S ANGELICA
Angelica arguta Nutt.
Parsley Family (Apiaceae)

Description: Lyall's angelica is a large, perennial, herbaceous plant 1–6' tall. The leaves are twice compound, with 11–23 leaflets per leaf. Each leaflet is about 2–5" long. The lateral leaf veins are directed to the end of the tooth on the leaf margin. The numerous white (or pinkish) flowers are densely arranged in the compound umbels. The fruit is flattened dorsally, that is, on the back, parallel to the joint between the 2 segments. The ribs on the margin and the back of the fruit are elongated into obvious "wings," with the marginal wings much broader than the ones on the back. The fruit is smooth (hairless).

Bloom Season: June–August.

Habitat/Range: Streamsides, lakeshores, and wet meadows in the montane and subalpine forests.

Comments: *Angelica* is named from the Latin *angelus* (angel), because of the beneficial qualities of the herb. *Arguta* means "sharp-toothed," descriptive of the sharp teeth on the leaf margin. This species is named for David Lyall, a British botanist and geologist who collected the plant while working on the boundary survey between Canada and the western United States in the 1880s. *Angelica* species have long been prized by herbalists for improving digestion, reducing gas, and loosening phlegm in bronchitis. They also promote sweating and urination for eliminating toxins. Unfortunately, *Angelica* is so similar in both appearance and habitat to the poisonous water hemlock (*Cicuta* species), that it is dangerous for novice herbalists to use.

Water Hemlock

WATER HEMLOCK
Cicuta maculata L.
Cicuta douglasii (DC.) Coult. and Rose
Parsley Family (Apiaceae)

Description: The primary lateral veins of the leaf of water hemlock are most often directed to the notch between the teeth, best seen by holding a leaflet up to the light. This venation is unique, separating water hemlock from other parsley family plants in the Rocky Mountains. The fruit is round or broadly oval, with ribs that are nearly equal in size and not expanded or winged. Flower and leaf characteristics are similar to *Angelica* species. Two similar species of water hemlock (*C. maculata* and *C. douglasii*) occur in the Northern Rockies. They differ mainly in subtle fruit characteristics, and are treated as one here.

Bloom Season: June–August.

Habitat/Range: Streamsides, wet meadows, and other marshy places in the valleys and moist montane forests.

Comments: Water hemlock has the reputation of being the most violently poisonous plant in the northern temperate zone. Many human and livestock fatalities have resulted from ingesting even small portions of the plant, especially the root. The poisonous compound in water hemlock, cicutoxin, acts on the central nervous system, causing violent convulsions, interspersed with periods of relaxation. Death usually occurs from 15 minutes to 8 hours after ingesting a lethal dose. Accidental poisonings happen most frequently because water hemlock is mistaken for edible members of the parsley family, which it resembles in both appearance and odor. One should never experiment with eating wild food plants without verifying the plant identification with an expert.

Poison Hemlock

POISON HEMLOCK
Conium maculatum L.
Parsley Family (Apiaceae)

Description: Poison hemlock often grows 4–9' tall, with leaves that are finely dissected into numerous small segments, like carrot or parsley leaves. Its purple-spotted stems are the key distinguishing characteristic. It is a biennial, growing as a low, leafy plant the first year. In the second growing season, the plant rapidly shoots upward on tall flowering stems. The white flowers are arranged in compound umbels on the end of the stems and the leaf axils. The fruit is round or broadly oval, with ribs that are nearly equal in size and somewhat wavy. The plants die at the end of the season in which they flower and fruit, leaving tall, straw-colored stalks that often persist throughout the winter.

Bloom Season: May–September.

Habitat/Range: Introduced weed, in disturbed areas.

Comments: This is the hemlock that was used to put Socrates to death in 399 B.C. Symptoms of poisoning appear as soon as 12 minutes after ingestion. At first it acts as a stimulant, causing nervousness and trembling. This is soon followed by slowed heartbeat, paralysis and coldness of the legs and arms, and finally death by respiratory failure. In Africa the poison has been used on darts and arrows. Poisoning of humans often occurs because of the resemblance of the foliage to parsley, or the seeds to anise or caraway. Sampling of wild food plants is a dangerous, potentially lethal activity.

Cow Parsnip

VERTICILLATE-UMBEL LOVAGE

Ligusticum verticillatum (Geyer) Coult. & Rose
Parsley Family (Apiaceae)

Description: The whorled arrangement of its flowering stems, from the opposite uppermost leaves, distinguishes verticillate-umbel lovage from related species. It has compound leaves with numerous large leaflets (up to 3¼" by 2") that are cut into lobes. The stems are up to 6' tall. The fruit is oblong, rounded in cross section, with thin, winglike ribs in parallel lines on the surface. The similar Canby's lovage *(L. canbyi)* is distinguished by its smaller size (less than 4' tall) and smaller leaflets (2" by ⅞" or less).

Bloom Season: May–August.

Habitat/Range: Moist slopes, streamsides, moist montane and subalpine forests.

Comments: Verticillate-umbel lovage was first collected for science by Carl Andreas Geyer (1809–1853) on the lands of the Nez Perce Indians. Lovage species were used medicinally for coughs and colds and other ailments by various Indian tribes.

COW PARSNIP

Heracleum lanatum Michx.
Parsley Family (Apiaceae)

Description: Cow parsnip leaves comprise 3 very large leaflets that are 4–12" long and equally wide. The leaflets are palmately lobed and have a double-toothed margin. The plant is 3–6' tall and covered with long, silky, straight hairs. Cow parsnip's large umbels of white flowers are as much as 8" across, and the rays are as much as 4" long. The fruit is strongly flattened on the back, parallel to the joint between the fruit segments.

Bloom Season: June–August.

Habitat/Range: Stream bottoms and seeps, in valleys, montane forests, and lower subalpine forests.

Comments: These plants are rich in minerals and relished by grazing animals. In herbal medicine the plants were long used to treat epilepsy. Cow parsnip is known to contain compounds that cause photodermatitis in humans, causing a sunburnlike rash when one is exposed to both the plant and ultraviolet radiation.

Verticillate-Umbel Lovage

Yampah

YAMPAH
Perideridia montana (Blank) Dorn
(also *Perideridia gairdneri* [H. & A.] Math.)
Parsley Family (Apiaceae)

Description: The leaves of yampah are compound with 3–5 long, narrow, linear segments. The leaves begin to wilt and dry as the flowers fade and the fruit appears. The white flowers are arranged in compound umbels on top of slender stems 1–4' tall. The fruit is round and scarcely (if at all) flattened. Yampah looks very similar to bulb-bearing water hemlock *(Cicuta bulbifera)*, a highly poisonous plant. However, *C. bulbifera* has tiny bulbs in the axils of some of the upper leaves, and it usually grows adjacent to water or on marshy ground.

Bloom Season: July–August.

Habitat/Range: Meadows and open forests, from the valleys to the subalpine forests.

Comments: Yampah was among the most important food plants of the American Indians within its range. On August 26, 1805, while among the Shoshone Indians near present-day Lemhi Pass in Idaho and Montana, Meriwether Lewis wrote in his journal: "I observe the indian women collecting the root of a species of fennel which grows in the moist grounds and feeding their poor starved children; (the root) is white firm and crisp in its present state, when dryed and pounded it makes a fine white meal." A detailed, clear botanical description of the yampah is included in this portion of the journal. Because of the similarity to poisonous bulb-bearing water hemlock, extreme caution is advised.

Trail Plant

TRAIL PLANT
Adenocaulon bicolor Hook.
Aster Family (Asteraceae)

Description: Triangular to heart-shaped leaves, green on the upper surface and white beneath, distinguishes trail plant. These leaves are up to 6" wide, have rather long leaf stalks, and are arranged alternately at the base of the stem. Small, white flower heads are arranged in a panicle on the end of the slender stems. The stems are up to 3' tall and covered with tiny, stalked glands. Although requiring a hand lens to see, the flowers have some unique characteristics. All are unisexual disk flowers without pappus; the outer flowers are female, and the inner ones are male with an undivided style.

Bloom Season: June–September.

Habitat/Range: Damp, shady woods, from moist montane to lower subalpine forests.

Comments: *Adenocaulon* is derived from the Greek *adeno-* (gland) and *kaulos* (stem), acknowledging the glandular stems of this plant. *Bicolor* refers to the two-toned leaves, green above and white below. A person or an animal walking through these plants would tend to leave an obvious trail of the white, upturned leaves, hence the common names "trail plant" or "pathfinder." A poultice was prepared from this plant and applied to boils and sores by some American Indians in the state of Washington.

YARROW
Achillea millefolium L.
Aster Family (Asteraceae)

Description: This common plant is easily recognized by its lacy, fernlike leaves and its distinctive aroma. It is a herbaceous plant 8–24" tall. The leaves are evenly distributed along the stem, but the largest leaves are on the lower portion, and they get progressively smaller up the stem. The numerous flower heads are in a flat-topped arrangement on the end of the stems. The flower petals are normally white.

Bloom Season: April–October.

Habitat/Range: Dry to moist areas, from valleys to the alpine summits.

Comments: *Achillea* is named for Achilles, the Greek warrior and hero of Homer's *Iliad*. An herb used to treat the wounds of soldiers during the Trojan War, yarrow has been used for medicinal purposes throughout history. It is especially useful in stopping bleeding. The herb has also been used to promote urination and sweating, as a digestive aid, for treating colds and flu, and to alleviate menstrual disorders.

Yarrow

Pearly Everlasting

PEARLY EVERLASTING
Anaphalis margaritacea (L.) Benth. & Hook.
Aster Family (Asteraceae)

Description: This plant is often confused with pussytoes *(Antennaria)*. However, pussytoes has well-developed basal leaves, while those on its stems get progressively smaller upward. In contrast, pearly everlasting lacks basal leaves; instead, it has leaves of about the same size equally distributed along the stems. The underside of the leaf of pearly everlasting is covered with dense, white hair. The top of the leaf is green and smooth or only thinly hairy. It is an upright plant, with stems 8–36" tall. The heads have bracts around the margin that are pearly white.

Bloom Season: July–October.

Habitat/Range: Disturbed places and forest openings; the valleys to the subalpine forests.

Comments: The persistent white bracts that surround the numerous flower heads make long-lasting dry floral arrangements, hence the common name.

Tall Pussytoes

TALL PUSSYTOES
Antennaria anaphaloides Rydb.
Aster Family (Asteraceae)

Description: This is a large (for pussytoes), upright plant, 8–20" tall, resembling pearly everlasting. However, tall pussytoes is distinguished by its large, well-developed basal leaves and the smaller stem leaves that are reduced in size progressively upward on the stem. The surfaces of the leaves are equally woolly-hairy on both sides. The unisexual flower heads consist of tiny disk flowers only, with no showy rays. The bracts around the margin of the heads are white, thin, and translucent, often with a basal dark spot.

Bloom Season: June–August.

Habitat/Range: Foothills and montane forests.

Comments: *Antennaria* is named for the resemblance of the modified sepals (pappus) of the male flowers to the antennae of a small insect. American Indians used pussytoes for various medicinal purposes ranging from rattlesnake bites to coughs.

WOODS PUSSYTOES
Antennaria racemosa Hook.
Aster Family (Asteraceae)

Description: A mat-forming ground cover of the shady forest floor, woods pussytoes reproduces vegetatively by runners, like a strawberry plant. The upper leaf surface is green and rather smooth, while the underside is white and densely woolly-hairy. Upper stems are densely set with glands on the surface, lacking the woolly hair of the lower stems. The main flowering stems are 4–24" tall. The unisexual flower heads occur in open raceme or panicle-like arrangements on the end of long stalks. Male and female flowers are on separate plants. The lower bracts around the base of the heads are greenish, while the upper ones are colorless or reddish brown.

Bloom Season: May–August.

Habitat/Range: Cool, shaded woods, in valleys, montane, and subalpine forests.

Comments: *Racemosa* refers to the raceme-like arrangement of the flower heads. Herbalists value pussytoes for treating liver inflammation and upper intestinal irritations.

Woods Pussytoes

ENGELMANN'S ASTER
Aster engelmannii (Eat.) A. Gray
Aster Family (Asteraceae)

Description: The flower head consists of 8–13 showy white (or pale pink) ray flowers surrounding the numerous golden yellow disk flowers. The bracts around the base of the flower head overlap like roof shingles. Each bract has a strong midvein and is often keeled like the bottom of a boat. The plants are rather large, often 2–4' tall. The leaves midway on the stem are the largest, while the lowest leaves are much smaller. The leaves are lance shaped and average about 3" in length and 1" in width.

Bloom Season: July–September.

Habitat/Range: Moist montane and subalpine forests.

Comments: Engelmann's aster is named in honor of the famous St. Louis botanist, physician, and meteorologist, George Engelmann (1809–1884). In the mid-1840s, he and the Harvard botanist Asa Gray promoted western plant collection by providing equipment and instruction to explorers and analyzing the specimens they brought back.

Engelmann's Aster

HOOKER'S THISTLE
Cirsium hookerianum Nutt.
Aster Family (Asteraceae)

Description: Hooker's thistle has an unbranched stem, 16–32" tall, having a congested cluster of creamy white flower heads. The bracts surrounding the heads are narrow and long-tapering. Cobwebby silky hair covers the bracts, stems, and leaves. The leaves are rather narrow (less than 1½" wide).

Bloom Season: July–August.

Habitat/Range: Stream bottoms and open slopes, from the valleys through the montane and subalpine forests to timberline.

Comments: Hooker's thistle is named in honor of Sir William Jackson Hooker (1785–1865), the prestigious botanist who wrote *Flora Borealis-Americana* (1833–1840), was the founder and editor of the *Journal of Botany*, and was the editor of *Botanical Magazine*. Hooker also directed the Kew Herbarium and Botanical Gardens in England from 1841 until his death. Thistles were a food source for American Indians; the roots were dug and cooked, or dried for later use.

Hooker's Thistle

Cut-Leaved Daisy

CUT-LEAVED DAISY
Erigeron compositus Pursh
Aster Family (Asteraceae)

Description: The basal leaves of this daisy consist of many narrow, branching segments, with 1–4 groups of 3 leaflets each. The few leaves on the stems are small and often unbranched. The stem seldom exceeds 10" in height and has a single flower head. The flower head usually consists of white rays surrounding a yellow disk. Sometimes the rays are pink or blue, but occasionally there are no ray flowers at all. The bracts around the base of the flower head are in a single row, and they have glands and spreading hairs.

Bloom Season: May–August.

Habitat/Range: Thin, poorly developed soils, from the valleys to the alpine summits.

Comments: *Compositus* is a Latin word meaning "compound," of many parts, referring to the compound, many-divided leaves of cut-leaved daisy. The leaf is the distinguishing feature of this species. In 1806 Meriwether Lewis collected a specimen of cut-leaved daisy near present-day Kamiah, Idaho, while the Lewis and Clark Expedition was waiting for the snow to melt sufficiently for safe passage over Lolo Pass.

ARROW-LEAVED COLTSFOOT

Petasites sagittatus (Banks) Gray
Aster Family (Asteraceae)

Description: Arrow-leaved coltsfoot has flower heads with whitish disk flowers that bloom before the leaves emerge. Later, the large, arrowhead-shaped basal leaves develop to a length of up to 12". White, woolly hair covers the underside of the leaves. Instead of true leaves on the stem, it has a series of overlapping bracts with parallel veins.

Bloom Season: April–June.

Habitat/Range: Wetlands of the montane and subalpine forests.

Comments: *Petasites* is derived from the Greek *petasos,* a type of "broad-brimmed hat." Species of *Petasites* have long been used in herbal medicine for treating coughs, asthma, and intestinal colic. It is also an effective diuretic. The fresh leaves have been applied to external wounds to reduce pain and inflammation.

Arrow-Leaved Coltsfoot

Fern-Leaved Candytuft

FERN-LEAVED CANDYTUFT

Smelowskia calycina (Steph.) C. A. Mey.
Mustard Family (Brassicaceae)

Description: This perennial alpine plant is covered with feltlike, soft, dense, light gray hair. Some of the hairs are long and straight while others are shorter and branched. The plants grow in leafy mats on the ground, with flowering stems that reach up to 8" tall. The plant has compound leaves with 5–9 narrow, pinnately arranged leaf segments. The flowers have 4 white petals, often with a purplish tinge. The fruit is a narrow pod (silique), more than 4 times as long as wide.

Bloom Season: May–August.

Habitat/Range: Ridges and open rocky places of the upper subalpine forests and the alpine fellfield.

Comments: *Smelowskia* was named for the Russian botanist Timotheus Smelowsky (1770–1815). The feltlike leaf surface and low-growing habit help it to endure the harsh alpine wind.

Utah Honeysuckle

UTAH HONEYSUCKLE
Lonicera utahensis Wats.
Honeysuckle Family (Caprifoliaceae)

Description: This is a common forest shrub (3–6' tall) having opposite, egg-shaped leaves (about 2" by 1") that are rounded on the ends. The opposite branching twigs have stout buds with purplish (white-lined) bud scales, especially on the twig ends. Pale yellowish white flowers are arranged in pairs in the leaf axils. A small spur extends from one side at the base of each flower. As the season progresses, the flowers are replaced by bright red twin berries. Utah honeysuckle is often mistaken for common snowberry *(Symphoricarpos albus)* but the latter is distinguished by having clusters of flowers that are replaced by white berries. Snowberry also lacks buds on the twig ends and instead dies back at the tip, initiating new growth from side buds.

Bloom Season: May–July.

Habitat/Range: Wooded slopes, from the valleys to the upper subalpine forests.

Comments: *Lonicera* is named in honor of the German botanist, Adam Lonitzer (1528–1586). Often called "red twinberry," this plant's fruit is juicy and mild in flavor. American Indians ate the berries and used the plant for medicine and good luck. On September 2, 1805, while the Lewis and Clark Expedition was traveling along the North Fork Salmon River in Idaho, Meriwether Lewis collected a plant specimen that appears to be Utah honeysuckle. The specimen today resides in the herbarium at the Academy of Natural Sciences in Philadelphia.

Blue Elderberry

BLUE ELDERBERRY
Sambucus cerulea Raf.
Honeysuckle Family (Caprifoliaceae)

Description: Blue elderberry's creamy white flowers are arranged in flat-topped clusters. It is a tall shrub (6–12' or more), sometimes appearing treelike. The opposite, branching, woody stems are stout and filled with spongy pith in the center. The pinnately compound leaves consist of 5–9 large leaflets, 2–6" long. Pale, powdery blue berries easily distinguish blue elderberry in late summer and fall, often persisting on the shrub after the leaves drop.

Bloom Season: May–July.

Habitat/Range: Streams and open forests of the valleys and montane forests.

Comments: Blue elderberries are delicious, whether eaten fresh or prepared as jelly, syrup, or wine. However, the berries of elderberry should not be eaten until fully ripe. The unripe berries, leaves, and stems contain cyanogenic glycosides capable of releasing hydrocyanic acid and causing cyanide poisoning. Children have been poisoned by placing whistles or peashooters made from the fresh, green stems into their mouths. The plants were widely used by American Indians for food, medicine, musical instruments, and fire making.

Black Elderberry

BLACK ELDERBERRY
Sambucus racemosa L.
Honeysuckle Family (Caprifoliaceae)

Description: Black elderberry has white to cream-colored flowers arranged in pyramid-shaped clusters. It is a sprawling shrub 3–6' tall with opposite branching. The stout stems have spongy, reddish brown pith that looks like Styrofoam. The pinnately compound leaves have 5 (or 7) large leaflets 2–7" long. In late summer the dense clusters of dark purple to black, shiny berries are relished by bears.

Bloom Season: May–July.

Habitat/Range: Streams and open forests of the montane and subalpine forests, especially after a disturbance such as fire.

Comments: Elderberry syrup is well known. However, black elderberry often has a disagreeable taste, and it is not recommended for consumption. The powder-blue berries of blue elderberry *(S. cerulea)* are much more palatable. Herbalists value elderberry for its many medicinal uses: the leaves as an ointment for bruises, wounds, and tumors; and the flowers for colds, flu, and upper respiratory infections, especially sinusitis. It is believed to be especially helpful for reducing phlegm that results from respiratory inflammations.

Highbush Cranberry

HIGHBUSH CRANBERRY
Viburnum edule (Michx.) Raf.
Honeysuckle Family (Caprifoliaceae)

Description: A sprawling shrub, 2–8' tall, highbush cranberry is most attractive in the fall, when it is decorated with brilliant foliage and clusters of red berries. Arranged opposite on the stems, the leaves are broadly U-shaped at the base and have 3 widely spaced lobes at the tip. The leaf margin is sharply toothed. Two small glands arise on the leaf base on opposite sides of the leaf stalk. The outer scales of the winter buds are fused at the base, and they often remain, hanging curiously, like a collar around the twig bases, after spring growth begins. Clusters of white flowers (and later the berries) are arranged on short shoots above a pair of leaves.

Bloom Season: May–July.

Habitat/Range: Streams and swamps of the moist montane and subalpine forests.

Comments: *Edule* means "edible." The acidic and tart highbush cranberries are best consumed after a frost, when sugar content is highest. American Indians not only relished the berries, they also valued the leaves, buds, and bark for treating colds, coughs, sore throat, dysentery, and tuberculosis.

Field Chickweed

FIELD CHICKWEED
Cerastium arvense L.
Pink Family (Caryophyllaceae)

Description: Field chickweed has stems 2–20" tall. Leaves are arranged opposite each other on the stem. Clusters of secondary leaves are often crowded in the axils of the larger leaves. The flowers have 5 styles, 10 stamens, and 5 white, 2-lobed petals that are about twice as long as the 5 sepals. The lance-shaped bracts below the flowers have a thin, membranelike margin.

Bloom Season: April–August.

Habitat/Range: Dry, open places, from the valleys to the alpine zone.

Comments: Field chickweed is most often confused with sandwort (*Arenaria* species) and chickweed (*Stellaria* species). However, the flowers of these two genera usually have only 3 styles. Also, the petals of *Arenaria* species are entire (unlobed), and those of *Stellaria* species are more deeply lobed, appearing to be 10 separate petals.

PARRY'S CAMPION
Silene parryi (Wats.) Hitch. & Mag.
Pink Family (Caryophyllaceae)

Description: There are usually 3 styles on the ovary of Parry's campion, but sometimes there are 4 or 5. The flower has 10 stamens and 5 white petals that are often greenish or purple tinged. The blade of each petal has 4 lobes. The tubular, fused portion of the sepals has 10 prominent purple nerves and 5 teeth. Glandular hairs cover the surface of the sepals and the upper part of the foliage. The leaves are mostly basal, with only 2 or 3 pairs of leaves on the flowering stem.

Bloom Season: July–August.

Habitat/Range: Open, rocky slopes of the dry montane forests to above timberline.

Comments: Parry's campion was named in honor of Charles C. Parry (1823–1890), a British American botanist and explorer. Parry worked on the Mexican Boundary Survey from 1849 to 1852 as a geologist and botanist. Many plants that he collected are named for him, including Parry's primrose *(Primula parryi)*.

Parry's Campion

Bunchberry

BUNCHBERRY
Cornus canadensis L.
Dogwood Family (Cornaceae)

Description: This lovely, low-growing plant of the deep woods has 4 large, white bracts that are often mistaken for the petals. Upon a closer look (with a 10x hand lens), it is apparent that the bracts surround a cluster of tiny flowers, each with 4 petals and 4 stamens. The plants spread on underground stems. There are 4–7 leaves arranged in a whorl (originating from a common point on the stem). The lateral leaf veins are conspicuous, pinnately arranged, and bend to run parallel with the leaf margin. The fruit is a cluster of bright, coral red berries.

Bloom Season: June–August.

Habitat/Range: Moist, shady woods of the montane and subalpine forests.

Comments: *Cornus* is from a Latin word meaning "horn" or "antler." This may refer to the hard wood of some species. However, ornamental knobs on the ends of ancient manuscript cylinders were also called "cornus," suggesting the resemblance with the berry clusters of this plant. The berries of bunchberry are edible, being mild and delicate in taste. The plant has been used medicinally as a poultice to treat burns, insect bites, and other skin afflictions. A specimen of bunchberry in flower was collected by Meriwether Lewis on June 16, 1806, along the Lolo Trail in Idaho. On that day the Lewis and Clark Expedition traversed from Eldorado Creek to Hungry Creek, in the direction of Lolo Pass.

Pacific Flowering Dogwood

PACIFIC FLOWERING DOGWOOD

Cornus nuttallii Aud.
Dogwood Family (Cornaceae)

Description: The large, showy flower arrangement of this rare, treelike shrub is unmistakable. It is actually the 4–7 petal-like floral bracts that attract attention. These large (1–3" long) bracts, greenish white and purple tipped, surround a rounded cluster of tiny, rather unexciting flowers. This flower cluster develops into a dense bunch of bright red berries. Oppositely arranged on the branches, the leaves (up to 4" long) have pinnate lateral veins that bend to run parallel to the leaf margin. This stately shrub is commonly 6–30' tall, with treelike individuals up to 60' tall.

Bloom Season: April–June.

Habitat/Range: Streams and damp woods of the moist montane forests. Within the Northern Rockies, Pacific flowering dogwood is known only from the Lochsa and Selway Rivers in Idaho, where it is among the rarest of plants in the state. It is more common from coastal British Columbia to southern California west of the Casade and Sierra summits.

Comments: Dogwood anthracnose *(Discula destructiva)*, an introduced fungal disease, has reduced the Idaho population of Pacific flowering dogwood to less than 5 percent of its original size, according to USDA Forest Service scientists. Perhaps the best hope for the survival of the species lies with any genetic resistance that may reside within the surviving shrubs. For this reason Pacific flowering dogwood should be left undisturbed in its natural habitat whenever it is encountered.

Red Osier Dogwood

RED OSIER DOGWOOD
Cornus sericea L.
(also *Cornus stolonifera* Michx.)
Dogwood Family (Cornaceae)

Description: Often called "red willow," red
osier dogwood and its bright, reddish purple
twigs are common along streams throughout
the Rockies. This many-stemmed shrub
spreads vegetatively when stems take root as
they are bent down (perhaps by the snow or a
flood) and make contact with the soil, a
process known as layering. The egg-shaped
leaves are 1½–4½" long, with lateral veins that
run parallel to the leaf margin. Greenish white
flowers appear in flat-topped cymes on the
end of the twigs, without the showy bracts of
bunchberry. As the season progresses, the tiny
flowers are replaced by white or bluish white
berries.

Bloom Season: May–July.

Habitat/Range: Along streams and ponds
and on seepy slopes, from the valleys to the
subalpine forests.

Comments: This species was important to
American Indians for food, medicine, basket-
making, dye, and "tobacco." The berries were
eaten, and a wide variety of conditions were
treated with the bark, including wounds and
bleeding, sore eyes, diarrhea, headache, and
nasal congestion. However, it was primarily
used for smoking; the inner bark and sometimes the leaves were commonly used, often in
combination with other herbs.

Merten's Moss Heather

MERTEN'S MOSS HEATHER
Cassiope mertensiana (Bong.) G. Don
Heath Family (Ericaceae)

Description: The foliage of Merten's moss heather has small, scalelike leaves. These are arranged in an opposite pattern, are distinctly 4-ranked, and overlap to completely conceal the stems. The leaves are smooth (hairless) or sometimes have a fringe of short hair on the margin only. The foliage forms low mats on the ground. A cluster of white flowers is arranged near the tips of the branches, which are up to 12" tall. The bell-shaped white flowers, with reddish sepals, hang downward.

Bloom Season: July–August.

Habitat/Range: Open, rocky slopes of the alpine tundra and subalpine forests.

Comments: *Cassiope* is named for Cassiopeia, in Greek mythology, the queen of Ethiopia and the wife of King Cepheus. She was vain and boastful, claiming to be more beautiful than the sea nymphs. This angered the sea nymphs, who had Neptune, king of the sea, send a whale to punish her. Only the sacrifice of Cassiopeia's daughter, Princess Andromeda, would save the kingdom. Just as the whale was about to attack poor Andromeda, Perseus intervened to save her. In the night sky, the constellation Cassiopeia looks like a W in the Milky Way and is often called the "the lady in the chair."

Trapper's Tea

TRAPPER'S TEA
Ledum glandulosum Nutt.
Heath Family (Ericaceae)

Description: Trapper's tea is an evergreen shrub, usually about 3' tall. The leaves are egg shaped and shiny, dark green on the upper surface, and light green to white on the lower surface. The foliage of trapper's tea has a fragrant aroma when crushed. The twigs are covered with glandular dots and minute hair. The flowers are arranged in open clusters on the ends of the stems. The 5 petals are distinct to the base, not joined together like many other flowers in the heath family.

Bloom Season: June–August.

Habitat/Range: Wetlands and streamsides of the moist montane and subalpine forests.

Comments: The plant is called "trapper's tea" because the leaves were reportedly used as a beverage by early trappers and settlers. However, this practice could be dangerous. *Ledum* and several other genera in the heath family contain andromedotoxin, which causes slow pulse, low blood pressure, loss of coordination, convulsions, paralysis, and death. The Delaware Indians used the related eastern mountain laurel *(Kalmia latifolia)* in a potion for committing suicide.

Wood Nymph

WOOD NYMPH
Moneses uniflora (L.) A. Gray
(also *Pyrola uniflora* L.)
Heath Family (Ericaceae)

Description: This little forest herb displays a single white flower on the end of a stem that is less than 6" tall. The flower is about 2" across, open and nodding. Sepals are about ¼ the size of the petals and often bend back away from them. Oval, evergreen leaves about 1–2" long, toothed or wavy on the margin, are attached to the lower portion of the stem. About midway between the leaves and flower, 1 or 2 small bracts are often attached to the stem.

Bloom Season: June–July.

Habitat/Range: Damp forests, usually on rotting wood, from the valleys to the subalpine forests.

Comments: *Moneses* comes from the Greek *monos* (solitary), and *hesia* (delight), referring to the delightful solitary flower. In Greek mythology nymphs were nature goddesses, beautiful maidens living in rivers, mountains, and woods.

White Rhododendron

WHITE RHODODENDRON
Rhododendron albiflorum Hook.
Heath Family (Ericaceae)

Description: A few-flowered cluster of showy (up to 1" wide), broadly bell-shaped flowers circle the stem of this shrub a short distance below the terminal whorl of leaves. Although the petals are white (or buff), upon closer inspection red dots are seen on the surface of the upper 3 petal lobes, especially the uppermost one. The stigma is orange; the ovary is green and long-hairy. The 10 stamens are white, bearing dense hair on the lower half of the filaments. As much as 6½' tall, the woody stems support bright green, oval leaves that taper to both ends, especially the base. A rather copious (or sometimes thin) covering of coarse red hair covers the young leaves, twigs, and sepals.

Bloom Season: June–August.

Habitat/Range: Cool, damp woods, often growing in dense shrub communities under the canopy of subalpine forests.

Comments: White rhododendron is often mistaken for fool's huckleberry *(Menziesia ferruginea)*, with which it often occurs. However, fool's huckleberry has glandular, bluish green foliage and pink, urn-shaped flowers from the end of the branches. White rhododendron is considered a poisonous plant, and there are reports of livestock deaths resulting from animals grazing on its foliage. Some Northwest Indians are reported to have used the plant externally to treat swellings and internally for colds and as a stomach remedy.

Sheldon's Milkvetch

CREAM-FLOWERED PEAVINE

Lathyrus ochroleucus Hook.
Bean Family (Fabaceae)

Description: These are vines with well-developed, threadlike, branching tendrils from the end of the leaves, which support the plant in climbing. There are normally 6 egg-shaped leaflets per compound leaf, and a pair of large leaflike stipules where the leaf attaches to the stem. The white to pale yellow flowers are typical of the bean family, with banner, wings, and keel. Inside the petals the style is flattened and hairy on the inner surface (hand lens required). The ovary develops into pods about 2" long and ¼" wide at maturity.

Bloom Season: May–July.

Habitat/Range: Moist woods, in valleys and montane forests.

Comments: *Lathyrus* is the ancient Greek name for this plant. Other common names include "sweet pea" and "vetchling." These vines seem to prefer the rich soil where aspen and birch trees thrive.

SHELDON'S MILKVETCH

Astragalus sheldonii (Rydb.) Barneby
Bean Family (Fabaceae)

Description: The flowers of Sheldon's milkvetch are arranged in drooping or nodding racemes, while the pods stand erect on the stems. Black and/or white hairs are basally attached to the leaves and pods. The stems, up to 16" long, have several compound leaves, each about 6" long, with 13–41 small leaflets pinnately arranged in pairs on either side of the main leaf stalk. A raceme of 10–35 white (or cream-colored) pea-family flowers droop from the flower stalk. The sepals are tubular, with narrow teeth on the margin that are ⅓–⅘ the length of the tube. The pods are distinctly grooved and partially partitioned in cross section.

Bloom Season: April–June.

Habitat/Range: Dry slopes of the valleys and dry montane forests within the lower Snake, Salmon, and Clearwater drainages.

Comments: There are over 50 species of milkvetch in the Northern Rockies, several with white or cream-colored nodding flowers. Careful attention to detail is required to distinguish between them. Also compare with yellow sweetvetch *(Hedysarum sulphurescens)* and silky crazyweed *(Oxytropis sericea)*.

Cream-Flowered Peavine

SILKY LUPINE
Lupinus sericeus Pursh
Bean Family (Fabaceae)

Description: The flowers of silky lupine are usually blue, but sometimes yellow or white. The back surface of the banner petal is conspicuously hairy. The banner is broadly angled from the wings and keel, forming a wide V opening of about 60 degrees or more. Both surfaces of the leaves usually are densely silky-hairy; the leaflets are 1–3" long and less than ½" wide. The plants usually have solid stems, less than 32" tall.

Bloom Season: May–July.

Habitat/Range: Valleys, dry montane, and subalpine forest meadows.

Comments: *Sericeus* is from the Latin *sericum* (silk), referring to the silky hairs that cover the entire plant. Meriwether Lewis collected silky lupine near present-day Kamiah, Idaho, on June 5, 1806, while at Camp Chopunnish waiting for the snow to melt sufficiently to ascend Lolo Pass.

Silky Lupine

White Geranium

WHITE GERANIUM
Geranium richardsonii Fisch. & Trautv.
Geranium Family (Geraniaceae)

Description: The 5 white petals of this geranium have pink to purple veins and soft hair about half the length from the petal base. The flower stalks are covered with dense glandular hair, often with reddish tips. The leaves are deeply parted into 5–7 divisions that are coarsely toothed, with a distinctive geranium aroma.

Bloom Season: June–August.

Habitat/Range: Moist woods, in montane and subalpine forests.

Comments: *Geranium* is derived from the Greek *geranos* (crane). The style of geranium flowers expands into a long beak, like a crane's bill. *Richardsonii* is named in honor of Sir John Richardson (1787–1842), an English surgeon and naturalist. Richardson was the physician on three expeditions to the Arctic. Geraniums are medicinal herbs used to treat diarrhea, dysentery, ulcers, and hemorrhoids. They are also used to stop bleeding and reduce the inflammation of minor wounds.

Sticky Currant

STICKY CURRANT
Ribes viscosissimum Pursh
Currant Family (Grossulariaceae)

Description: This medium-sized shrub (to 6' tall) lacks the prickles of some gooseberries and currants. However, it is covered with glandular hairs that are sticky to the touch and give the plant its characteristic aroma. The flowers are greenish white to yellowish white and often tinged with pink. The flower tube is bell shaped and attached to the top of the ovary. The lobes of the sepals and petals (5 each) flare from the end of the "bell." The leaves are maplelike, with palmate veins (that radiate from the leaf base) and rounded lobes.

Bloom Season: May–August.

Habitat/Range: Damp woods and openings, especially after a fire, in montane and sub-alpine forests.

Comments: The first known botanical specimen was collected by Meriwether Lewis near Hungry Creek, Idaho. Lewis's label reads: "Fruit indifferent & gummy The hights of the Rocky mountain. Jun: 16th 1806." *Ribes* species are the alternate hosts for the blister rust disease that has been so devastating to western white pine, whitebark pine, and other 5-needled pines. The fungal disease was introduced to North America in 1921. Control once focused on removing the *Ribes* species from the immediate area of the pine stands to break the life cycle of the disease. With the failure of this control method, efforts have been redirected to locating and growing white pines that are genetically resistant to the disease.

Mockorange

MOCKORANGE
Philadelphus lewisii Pursh
Hydrangea Family (Hydrangeaceae)

Description: When in bloom, these flowers exude an arrestingly sweet orange-blossom aroma. Each flower has 4 petals, many stamens, and 4 styles. The fruit is a hard capsule that remains on the shrub through the winter. Mockorange is an erect shrub, up to 9' tall, stiff and densely branched. On older stems the reddish brown bark cracks open at a right angle to the stem and eventually falls away in small pieces, revealing the gray bark underneath. The leaves are in pairs, opposite each other on the stems.

Bloom Season: May–July.

Habitat/Range: Rocky hillsides, rock crevices, and stream banks, from valleys to the lower subalpine forests.

Comments: Mockorange is the state flower of Idaho, where it is often called "syringa." *Syringa* is also the botanical genus of ornamental lilacs, in the olive family. *Philadelphus* was derived from the Greek *philos* (love) and *adelphos* (brother). In 1814, Frederick Pursh named the plant *Philadelphus lewisii* in honor of Meriwether Lewis, from specimens that Lewis collected in 1806: one on May 6, along the Clearwater River in Idaho, and another on July 4, along the Blackfoot River in Montana.

Virgate Phacelia

VIRGATE PHACELIA
Phacelia heterophylla Pursh
Waterleaf Family (Hydrophyllaceae)

Description: These are tall, slender, herbaceous plants (1–4' tall), with either a single erect stem or a main stem having numerous short secondary branches. Bristly hairs cover the foliage and stems. The stem leaves are well developed; the larger ones have 1–4 lobes or leaflets at the base of the main leaf blade. Clusters of whitish flowers are arranged in scorpion-like coils, which unwind as blooming progresses. The stamens and stigma lobes protrude conspicuously from the much shorter flower petals.

Bloom Season: May–July.

Habitat/Range: Dry, open places in the valleys and montane forests.

Comments: *Heterophylla* is from the Greek *heteros* (different) and *phyllon* (leaf), referring to the varying types of leaves. "Virgate" means "shaped like a rod or wand," which describes these plants perfectly. A specimen of virgate phacelia was collected by Meriwether Lewis on June 9, 1806, the last day that the expedition was camped near present-day Kamiah, Idaho.

Geyer's Onion

GEYER'S ONION
Allium geyeri Wats.
Lily Family (Liliaceae)

Description: The flower cluster (umbel) of Geyer's onion is erect. The flowers are pink to white. The 6 stamens are hidden by the longer tepals (petals and petal-like sepals). The tips of the tepals are sharply pointed and erect. Sometimes many of the flowers in the floral cluster are replaced by small, stalkless bulbs clustered at the base. These bulbs are a means of asexual reproduction; they fall to the ground and sprout clones of the parent plant. Plants with bulbs in the flower cluster are in the variety *tenerum,* while those without are in the variety *geyeri.* The main stalk supporting the flower cluster is leafless and 4–20" tall. The 3 (or more) leaves rise from the base of the stalk. These leaves are concave to convex in cross section and solid.

Bloom Season: May–June.

Habitat/Range: Wet meadows and along streamsides in the montane and subalpine forests.

Comments: Geyer's onion was named in honor of Carl Andreas Geyer (1809–1853), a German botanist who collected plants in the Missouri River region and Oregon Territory. The flowers of Geyer's onion (and most others) begin blooming from the perimeter of the floral umbel and progress toward the center. Siberian chives *(A. schoenoprasum),* which often coexists with Geyer's onion, first blooms in the center and progresses outward to the perimeter of the floral arrangement.

Pointed Mariposa Lily

POINTED MARIPOSA LILY
Calochortus apiculatus Baker
Lily Family (Liliaceae)

Description: This breathtaking wildflower has three white petals (about 1" long) lined with soft, both white and yellowish hair on the petal surface and margin, especially below the middle. Just above the base of each petal is a small, round, dark spot; this marks a depressed nectar gland, fringed on the margin. There are 6 stamens having sharp-pointed anthers that are as long or longer than the filaments. The ovary is expanded on the sides into 3 wings and capped by a 3-lobed stigma. The fruit turns downward as the petals are shed. The stem is 4–12" tall; it bears 1–5 flowers, a single leaf (4–12" long) from the base, and a few (much smaller) leafy bracts farther up. The basal leaf is flat, tapering toward both ends, and seldom exceeds the stem in length.

Bloom Season: June–July.

Habitat/Range: Dry, rocky places in open woods of the valleys, montane, and lower subalpine forests within southwestern Alberta, southeastern British Columbia, northwestern Montana, northern Idaho, and northeastern Washington.

Comments: *Calochortus* is derived from the Greek *kalos* (beautiful) and *chortos* (grass). The bulbs do not transplant well and have not been successfully cultivated, despite many attempts by gardeners. They are best enjoyed in their wild native habitat. American Indians utilized the bulbs of various species of *Calochortus* for food and showed the starving Mormons in Utah how to dig them in 1848. Because of this, the Mormons consider the mariposa or "sego lily" to be a symbol of life and hope; it is the state flower of Utah.

Cat's Ear Mariposa Lily

CAT'S EAR MARIPOSA LILY
Calochortus elegans Pursh
Lily Family (Liliaceae)

Description: The cute little fuzzy petals of this wildflower do resemble the ears of kittens. White and/or purplish hair covers the surface of the 3 petals, and a fringe of hair lines the margin. There is a crescent purple blotch on the petals above (or below) the narrow, transverse gland. A similar purple blotch is also seen on the 3 sepals. The anthers are sharply pointed and longer than the filaments. As the flowers fall away, the winged ovary turns downward. The stems are 2–6" tall, much shorter than the single (4–8" long) flat, narrow basal leaf.

Bloom Season: May–June.

Habitat/Range: Dry, grassy slopes and open woods, from the valleys to the subalpine forests of northwestern Montana, north-central Idaho, and southeastern Washington (not known from Canada).

Comments: *Mariposa* is Spanish for butterfly. *Elegans* is a Latin word meaning "stylish," "graceful," or "pleasing to the eye." The botanist Frederick Pursh (1774–1820) named and described the new species from a specimen discovered by Meriwether Lewis in 1806 near present-day Kamiah, Idaho. Unable to place the plant in any known genus in the lily family, Pursh created and described the new genus *Calochortus* ("beautiful grass") to accommodate this discovery. The label on the specimen states: "A Small bulb of a pleasant flavour, eat by the natives. On the Kooskooske. May 17th 1806."

Queen's Cup Beadlily

QUEEN'S CUP BEADLILY
Clintonia uniflora (Schult.) Kunth
Lily Family (Liliaceae)

Description: A single white flower arising from between 2 (or 3) basal leaves is characteristic of queen's cup beadlily. Looking much alike, the 3 sepals and 3 petals are about ¾" long and twice the length of the filaments. A fine, woolly hair is present on the leaves, flower stalk, petals, and filaments. As the season progresses, the flower is replaced by a single, deep blue, beadlike berry. In flower, beadlily may be mistaken for the white phase of glacier lily *(Erythronium grandiflorum)*, except glacier lily is smooth (hairless), and its petals are bent backward toward the stem.

Bloom Season: June–July.

Habitat/Range: Shady woods of the moist montane and lower subalpine forests.

Comments: *Clintonia* was named in honor of DeWitt Clinton (1769–1828), a naturalist and governor of New York. Beadlily is so characteristic of the Northern Rockies that its range in effect distinguishes the Northern Rockies from the Central and Southern Rocky Mountains, where it is absent.

HOOKER'S FAIRYBELLS
Disporum hookeri (Torr.) Nichols.
Lily Family (Liliaceae)

Description: Two (or 3) creamy white, bell-shaped flowers hang down from the ends of the leafy branches of this lily. Each flower has 6 separate and similar tepals and 6 stamens. Hairs on the margin of the leaves point forward toward the leaf tip. The parallel leaf veins are conspicuous. The branching stems are brown and woody in appearance. The fruit is a round, bright red berry with only a few (4–6) seeds. The berry is often hairy, but not warty.

Bloom Season: May–July.

Habitat/Range: Montane and lower subalpine forests.

Comments: *Disporum* is derived from the Greek *di-* (double) and *spora* (seed), probably because of the two berries typical of the genus. Some American Indians considered the plant to be poisonous, while others used it to make a love potion. A kidney medicine was prepared from the berries by some Indian people.

Hooker's Fairybells

Wartberry Fairybells

WARTBERRY FAIRYBELLS
Disporum trachycarpum (Wats.) Benth. & Hook.
Lily Family (Liliaceae)

Description: These fairybell flowers hang down from the ends of the branches, often concealed under the broad leaves. There are usually 2 creamy white, bell-shaped flowers per branch, but sometimes 1 or 3. Each flower has 6 separate and similar tepals and 6 stamens. The leaves are egg shaped, abruptly pointed on the end, with a fringe of hair on the leaf margin that points outward. The berry is yellowish to orange-red, with numerous (6–12) seeds. The berry's surface has a warty or pebbly texture.

Bloom Season: May–July.

Habitat/Range: Montane and lower subalpine forests.

Comments: *Trachycarpum* is from Greek roots, meaning "rough fruit," describing the surface of the berries. These berries are edible; mild, tasting faintly like cantaloupe. An eye remedy was prepared from the seeds by the Blackfeet Indians for removing eye matter or treating snow blindness.

False Solomon's Seal

FALSE SOLOMON'S SEAL
Smilacina racemosa (L.) Desf.
Lily Family (Liliaceae)

Description: False Solomon's seal has erect, unbranched stems about 2' tall with numerous leaves that clasp the stem. The egg-shaped, mostly oblong leaves have an abruptly pointed tip. Numerous tiny flowers are arranged in a branching panicle that is upright on the end of the branches. Each flower has 6 creamy white floral tepals (petals and petal-like sepals) and 6 stamens that protrude beyond the tepals. The fruit is a red berry flecked with purple, becoming more uniformly red when fully ripe.

Bloom Season: April–July.

Habitat/Range: Moist woods and streams, from the valleys to the lower subalpine forests.

Comments: *Smilacina* means "a small Smilax," and refers to this plant's resemblance to plants in the genus *Smilax* (catbriers and greenbriers). *Racemosa* implies that the plant has a simple-branched raceme flower arrangement, but actually the flowers are arranged in a many-branched panicle. True "Solomon's seals" are plants in the genus *Polygonatum* (also in the lily family) and grow east of the Rocky Mountains. Because of their resemblance to *Polygonatum* species, the name "false Solomon's seal" was coined and applied to *Smilacina* species.

Wild Lily of the Valley

WILD LILY OF THE VALLEY
Smilacina stellata (L.) Desf.
Lily Family (Liliaceae)

Description: Wild lily of the valley has 5–10 small, creamy white flowers arranged in a simple raceme on the end of the stems. The stem "zigzags" noticeably. The numerous lance-shaped, stalkless leaves are often lined with fine hair on the lower side. The 3 sepals and 3 petals are similar in color and shape. Within the flower, the 6 stamens are distinctly shorter than the sepals and petals. The berries are greenish yellow, with 3 red stripes, aging to red or black.

Bloom Season: May–June.

Habitat/Range: Moist to rather dry habitats, from the valleys to the lower subalpine forests.

Comments: This common native wildflower was named for its resemblance to the introduced garden flower, lily of the valley *(Convallaria majalis),* which has bell-shaped and nodding flowers. These garden plants have dangerously poisonous compounds that are purgative and have a digitalis-like effect on the heart, disturbing the heartbeat. Our native wild lily of the valley has edible berries, but they are not very tasty, and eating too many will unleash their laxative properties. It is sometimes called "starry Solomon's seal."

Twisted Stalk

TWISTED STALK
Streptopus amplexifolius (L.) DC.
Lily Family (Liliaceae)

Description: The flowers of twisted stalk hide under the leaves, 1 flower per leaf. An unusual kink or twist in the flower stalk is the key distinguishing feature. The flowers have 6 white to greenish yellow floral tepals and 6 stamens. The fruit is a red (or yellow) berry with a smooth, tender skin. The stems are stout, erect, and branched, standing 1–3' tall. The leaves strongly clasp the stem.

Bloom Season: May–July.

Habitat/Range: Montane and subalpine streamsides.

Comments: *Streptopus* is from the Greek roots *streptos* (twisted) and *pous* (foot). *Amplexifolius* refers to the clasping leaves. The berries are edible. The green shoots may be eaten raw and are said to taste like cucumber. However, the young leaves could lead one to confuse this plant with false hellebore, a dangerously poisonous plant.

STICKY TOFIELDIA
Tofieldia glutinosa (Michx.) Pers.
Lily Family (Liliaceae)

Description: The leaves are long, narrow, 2-ranked, and folded to sheath the stem, like grasses. Above the leaves the stem is densely covered with short glandular hair. The plants are slender and 4–20" tall. At the top of the stem is a dense cluster of white to greenish flowers. The flowers are arranged in groups of 3 within the cluster. Each flower has 6 floral tepals (petals and petal-like sepals) and 6 stamens. The fruit is a 3-lobed capsule.

Bloom Season: June–August.

Habitat/Range: Wet meadows, streams, and ponds of subalpine forests.

Comments: *Tofieldia* was named in honor of the English botanist Thomas Tofield (1730–1779). *Glutinosa* means "sticky," referring to the glandular hairs on the stem that are sticky to the touch. Mosquitoes, common in the habitat of *Tofieldia,* are often trapped on the sticky stems, which are a natural flypaper.

Sticky Tofieldia

White Trillium

WHITE TRILLIUM
Trillium ovatum Pursh
Lily Family (Liliaceae)

Description: The 3 large, stalkless, broadly egg-shaped leaves of white trillium are very distinctive. They are arranged in a whorl (all 3 leaves are attached to the stem at a common point). A single flower normally blooms a few inches above the whorl of leaves. The flower has 3 green sepals, 3 white petals, 6 stamens, and 3 long stigma lobes. As the flower ages the petals turn from white to lavender and finally purple. Just as the snow is melting on the forest floor the blossoms of trillium emerge, often impatiently pushing through the last few inches of slush.

Bloom Season: March–June.

Habitat/Range: Boggy areas in montane and lower subalpine forests.

Comments: This genus was named *Trillium* for having all its parts in threes. *Ovatum* is for the ovate (egg-shaped) leaves of this species. It is also called "wake-robin," because trilliums and robins appear at about the same time in early spring. Another name is "birth-root," for its use by American Indian women to reduce uterine bleeding during childbirth. The Chippewa Indians also used trillium for rheumatism and cramps. Herbalists claim that species of *Trillium* are a tonic for the uterus and useful in reducing excessive blood flow during menses.

California False Hellebore

CALIFORNIA FALSE HELLEBORE
Veratrum californicum Durand
Lily Family (Liliaceae)

Description: California false hellebore is a 3–6' tall, herbaceous plant with white to greenish-tinged flowers. The flowers are arranged in a dense, upright panicle on the end of the main stem. Each small flower has 3 petal-like sepals, 3 petals, and 6 stamens. The distinctive leaves are pleated, with folds like a fan, and are quite large, with the largest leaves 12" long and 6" wide.

Bloom Season: June–August.

Habitat/Range: Wet meadows, swamps, and streamsides, from the montane to the sub-alpine forests.

Comments: *Veratrum* species are known to contain compounds with a variety of physiological effects. They are especially potent as a heart depressant, in lowering blood pressure, and inducing congenital malformation in the fetus. Pregnant ewes feeding on false hellebore often bear "monkey-face" lambs, a fatal deformity. Other compounds in the plant have been shown to have value as an insecticide. False hellebore is a dangerous, poisonous plant with potentially fatal results if ingested. Meriwether Lewis collected a leaf specimen of this plant on June 25, 1806, along Hungry Creek in Idaho, as the Lewis and Clark Expedition was on its return journey over the Lolo Trail.

BEARGRASS
Xerophyllum tenax (Pursh) Nutt.
Lily Family (Liliaceae)

Description: Beargrass consists of a dense clump of long, wiry, grasslike leaves and a dense cluster of small white flowers on a tall stalk. The leaves are evergreen, remaining on the plant for several years. Basal leaves are 1–2' or more in length. On the stem, the leaves get progressively shorter upward. Each flower has 6 narrow tepals and 6 stamens. The plants do not bloom every year, and the dead stalks often remain on them as a testament to the last flowering.

Bloom Season: May–August.

Habitat/Range: Well-drained areas of the montane and subalpine forests.

Comments: Xerophyllum is derived from Greek words meaning "dry leaf." A specimen was collected by Meriwether Lewis on June 15, 1806, east of Weippe Prairie, Idaho. Lewis mentioned the plant many times in his journals. He was especially impressed with the ability of the American Indians to weave watertight baskets and conical hats from the leaves of beargrass and cedar bark.

Beargrass

SHOWY DEATH CAMAS
Zigadenus elegans Pursh
Lily Family (Liliaceae)

Description: Death camas species have a distinctive gland near the base of the 6 floral tepals. Showy death camas has deeply lobed and heart-shaped glands. The petals are egg shaped, ¼" long or more. There are 3 distinct styles that persist as beaks on the dry capsule fruit. Arranged in a raceme, the flowers are greenish white. The leaves are long, narrow, and mostly basal.

Bloom Season: June–August.

Habitat/Range: Moist meadows and open woods, from the montane forests to the alpine.

Comments: *Elegans* means "elegant," "fancy," or "ornate." Showy death camas is a poisonous plant, responsible for the deaths of both livestock and humans. The bulbs may be mistaken for the edible meadow camas *(Camassia quamash)*. Although its leaves and bulbs are similar to death camas, meadow camas is distinguished by its blue flowers and unique capsule, which has but a single style that falls off as the capsule matures.

Showy Death Camas

Common Death Camas

COMMON DEATH CAMAS
Zigadenus venenosus Wats.
Lily Family (Liliaceae)

Description: With much smaller flowers than showy death camas, common death camas's petals are less than ⅛" long. A tiny, egg-shaped gland lies near the base of the 6 floral tepals (petals and petal-like sepals). The small, greenish white flowers are closely arranged in a many-flowered raceme. The ovary's 3 distinct styles become 3 beaks on the mature capsule. The leaves are grasslike, the longest at the base, with progressively smaller leaves upward on the stem. In cross section, the leaves are V-shaped.

Bloom Season: April–July

Habitat/Range: Dry meadows and openings, from the valleys to near timberline.

Comments: *Zigadenus* comes from the Greek *zugon* (yoke) and *aden* (gland), presumably because of the resemblance of the glands of some species to an oxen yoke. *Venenosus* is Latin for "very poisonous." Like showy death camas, human and livestock deaths have resulted from consumption of common death camas.

Spotted Coralroot

SPOTTED CORALROOT
Corallorhiza maculata Raf.
Orchid Family (Orchidaceae)

Description: Spotted coralroot has no green leaves. Clothed instead with membranous bracts that sheath the stems, the plants are reddish purple to brownish. A raceme of 10–30 dainty flowers adorns the top of the stem. The 3 sepals and 2 upper petals are reddish purple. The lip petal is white with dark red spots and 2 lateral lobes. Occasionally, one encounters an albino plant, which is pale yellow with white flowers that lack the purple spots.

Bloom Season: June–July.

Habitat/Range: Shady woods of the montane and lower subalpine forests.

Comments: Lacking chlorophyll, spotted coralroot does not produce food by photosynthesis, but rather through a complex relationship with soil fungi. By parasitizing fungi that take up residence in the spongy tissue of its rhizomes, the coralroot plant obtains its nutrients indirectly from rotting humus and tree roots. The fungus initially invades the coralroot seed coat, as it would any other piece of organic matter to be utilized as food. However, the plant embryo neutralizes the fungal attack and through a complex chemical exchange establishes a lifelong parasitic relationship with the fungus.

Mountain Lady's Slipper

MOUNTAIN LADY'S SLIPPER
Cypripedium montanum Dougl. ex Lindl.
Orchid Family (Orchidaceae)

Description: The flowers of mountain lady's slipper are almost identical to yellow lady's slipper *(C. calceolus)*, except for the color. The white lip petal is inflated and pouchlike, but without the flat platform in front of the pouch found on fairy slipper *(Calypso bulbosa)*. A few purple stripes often decorate the white lip, especially within the pouch. The sepals and lateral petals are 2½" long, brownish purple, twisted, and wavy. There is a large green leafy bract attached to the stem just below the flower. The leaves are about 2–6" long, about half as wide, and strongly parallel veined. The plants are up to 2' tall and typically have 2 flowers, although they may have 1 or 3.

Bloom Season: May–early July.

Habitat/Range: Dry to moist woods of the montane forests.

Comments: Meriwether Lewis mentioned this plant in his journal on June 30, 1806, as the expedition was descending Lolo Creek in present-day Montana. He wrote: "I also met with the plant in blume which is sometimes called the lady's slipper or mockerson flower. it is in shape and appearance like ours only that the corolla is white, marked with small veigns of pale red longitudinally on the inner side. after dinner we resumed our march."

Sparrow's Egg Lady's Slipper

SPARROW'S EGG
LADY'S SLIPPER
Cypripedium passerinum Richards.
Orchid Family (Orchidaceae)

Description: Although the lip petal is white like that of mountain lady's slipper, sparrow's egg lady's slipper is easily distinguished by its much shorter sepals and petals (½–¾" long). The lateral petals are white and the sepals are green. Reddish purple spots on the bottom of the lip petal look like the spots on a sparrow's egg. Long, silky, straight hairs cover the stem, which typically supports but a single flower. The plant is usually less than 14" tall.

Bloom Season: Late June–July

Habitat/Range: Boggy, mossy areas, often along streams in the lower subalpine forests. Rare in Montana, it is more common in the Canadian Rockies.

Comments: *Cypripedium* is from the Greek *kypris* (Venus) and *pes* (foot); the pouchlike lip is thus imagined to appear like the dainty foot or slipper of Venus, goddess of love and beauty. Found from the Bering Sea to Hudson Bay, this is one of the few orchids growing north of the Arctic Circle. It was first collected in 1820 by Dr. John Richardson, during a polar expedition.

Western Rattlesnake Plantain

WESTERN RATTLESNAKE PLANTAIN
Goodyera oblongifolia Raf.
Orchid Family (Orchidaceae)

Description: Look for the distinctive white midvein of the leaves (2–8" long) in a basal rosette lying snugly on the forest floor. Except for the white mottling of the veins, the leaves are dark green and leathery, lasting through the winter. The flowering stem is leafless and 8–16" tall. Many small, greenish white, hooded flowers are closely spaced on the stem, all tending to face in the same direction. Glandular hairs cover the stem and outer surface of the flower.

Bloom Season: July–August.

Habitat/Range: Dry to moist shady woods of the montane and subalpine forests.

Comments: *Goodyera* was named in honor of John Goodyer (1592–1664), an English botanist. *Oblongifolia* refers to the leaf shape. There is a history of herbal use of this plant for soothing inflammations and healing wounds. However, because of the relative rarity of these orchids, the more common true plantain (*Plantago* species) would be a better choice for these uses.

Northern Rattlesnake Plantain

NORTHERN RATTLESNAKE PLANTAIN
Goodyera repens (L.) R. Br.
Orchid Family (Orchidaceae)

Description: The small (1½" or less) leaves of northern rattlesnake plantain have distinctively white-mottled lateral veins, but without the white midvein of western rattlesnake plantain. A few, leaflike bracts are found on the flowering stem, which is otherwise leafless and less than 10" tall. A raceme of small, greenish white, hooded flowers are aligned, closely spaced, on one side of the stem. Glandular hairs cover the stem and outer surface of the flower.

Bloom Season: July–August.

Habitat/Range: Cool, mossy, and shaded woods of the subalpine forests. Rare in Montana and not known from Idaho, it is more common in the Canadian Rockies.

Comments: *Repens* is from the Latin word meaning "creeping," in reference to its spreading by horizontal underground stems. "Rattlesnake" probably refers to the resemblance of the leaves to snakeskin. Some true plantain species (*Plantago* species) have similar basal leaves and medicinal value; this explains why the same common name is used for these otherwise unrelated species.

White Bog Orchid

WHITE BOG ORCHID
Habenaria dilatata (Pursh) Hook.
(also *Platanthera dilatata* [Pursh] Lind.)
Orchid Family (Orchidaceae)

Description: White flowers, and the abruptly expanded base of the lip petal, help to distinguish this species from the similar northern green bog orchid and related species. There are several (more than 4) leaves on the stem, which get progressively smaller up the stem. The plants are slender and sometimes 3' tall or more. The lip petal has a spur that is about the same length as the lip, but it can vary from twice to half as long. The flowers have a pleasant and distinctive fragrance.

Bloom Season: June–August.

Habitat/Range: Bogs, wet meadows, and streams, from valleys to subalpine forests.

Comments: *Habenaria* is derived from the Latin *habena* (reins), referring to the reinlike appendages of the lip of some species. *Dilatata* (dilated) refers to the expanded base of the lip of white bog orchid.

SMALL ROUND-LEAVED ORCHIS
Orchis rotundifolia Banks ex Pursh
(also *Amerorchis rotundifolia* [Banks] Hul.)
Orchid Family (Orchidaceae)

Description: This plant has a single basal leaf that is oval or almost round. The leafless stem is usually about 6" tall. About 2–8 flowers are arranged in a loose raceme on the end of the stem. The petals and sepals range from white to pink. The lip has 3 prominent lobes and a slender spur and the lip is dotted or streaked with purple.

Bloom Season: June–July.

Habitat/Range: Limestone springs and wetlands of subalpine forests.

Comments: *Amerorchis* means "the orchis from America," and *rotundifolia* means "round-leaved." Montana is about the southern limit of the species. Plants in such peripheral populations often have greater genetic diversity than those in the main body of the population. This genetic diversity could be critical to the survival of the species as environmental changes occur, such as global warming.

Small Round-Leaved Orchis

Fringed Grass-of-Parnassus

FRINGED GRASS-OF-PARNASSUS
Parnassia fimbriata Koenig
Grass-of-Parnassus Family (Parnassiaceae)

Description: The peculiar flowers of fringed grass-of-Parnassus are garnished with a conspicuous tasseled border on the lower half of the 5 petals. Further embellishment is provided by staminodes (infertile stamens) opposite the petals, which look like strange little paws (use a 10x hand lens). The flowers also have 5 fertile, normal-looking stamens alternate with the petals. The 5 sepals (underneath the petals) have fine, irregular teeth toward the tip. The stems are 4–14" long and have a single small leaf on the upper half and a single flower on the end. The rest of the leaves are all basal and kidney shaped.

Bloom Season: June–October.

Habitat/Range: Wetlands of montane and subalpine forests to timberline.

Comments: *Parnassia* is named for Mount Parnassus in central Greece. Grass-of-Parnassus was first recorded from there by Dioscorides, a military physician for Nero, the emperor of Rome in the 1st century A.D. Dioscorides wrote *Materia Medica*, which was a description of about 600 species that he used for medicinal purposes—one of the earliest botanical works known. Some authors place this species in the saxifrage family (Saxifragaceae).

Hood's Phlox

HOOD'S PHLOX
Phlox hoodii Rich.
Phlox Family (Polemoniaceae)

Description: Forming compact, dense cushions or mats, Hood's phlox is seldom over 4" tall. Its very narrow leaves are less than ½" long, rigid, and sharply pointed. Loose, cobwebby hair is often found on the leaf margin, especially near the base. Solitary, stalkless flowers arise from the ends of the short stems. The 5 lobes of the petals are about the same length as the petal tube or slightly shorter. Flower color varies, changing from white to pink or bluish as the flowers age.

Bloom Season: April–June.

Habitat/Range: Dry, open, often rocky places, from the valleys to the dry montane forests.

Comments: Blackfeet Indians used Hood's phlox as a laxative and to relieve chest pains. A yellow dye was prepared from the plant.

HOODED LADIES' TRESSES
Spiranthes romanzoffiana Cham.
Orchid Family (Orchidaceae)

Description: As many as 60 densely spaced, white flowers coil around the end of the stem in 3 spiraling ranks. The stems are 4–24" tall. The sepals and upper petals jut forward, while the lip petal turns sharply downward. The lip petal is narrow at the base and wider at the apex, with fine teeth or tears on the margin.

Bloom Season: July–August.

Habitat/Range: Wetlands, from valleys to the subalpine forests.

Comments: *Spiranthes* comes from the Latin *spira* (coil) and Greek *anthos* (flower), which describes the coiled flower arrangement. "Ladies' tresses" refers to the resemblance of these flower coils to the braided hair of women. Named *romanzoffiana* in honor of Nicholas Romanzoff (1754–1826), a Russian minister of state. The species was discovered on the Aleutian island of Unalaska, while Alaska was still a Russian territory.

Hooded Ladies' Tresses

LONG-LEAVED PHLOX
Phlox longifolia Nutt.
Phlox Family (Polemoniaceae)

Description: Long leaves and loose, erect stems are characteristic of this species. The larger leaves are 1–3" long or more. The plants are usually 4" or more tall. The flowers have a well-developed slender flower stalk. The petals range from white to pink. The sepals have 5 prominent, slender teeth that lead to ribs on the sepal tube. Toward the base of the sepal tube there is a distinctive bulge between the ribs (use a hand lens). The long styles (several times as long as the stigmas) and unnotched petals distinguish long-leaved phlox plants from the similar showy phlox *(P. speciosa)*.

Bloom Season: April–July.

Habitat/Range: Dry, open, often rocky places, from valleys to the montane forests.

Comments: American Indians used long-leaved phlox for building the blood in anemic children and for treating eye problems, stomachache, diarrhea, and venereal disease.

Long-Leaved Phlox

Sulphur Buckwheat

SULPHUR BUCKWHEAT
Eriogonum umbellatum Torr.
Buckwheat Family (Polygonaceae)

Description: The basal leaves of sulphur buckwheat often form large, flat mats up to 2' wide. The leaves are green on the upper surface, grayish white beneath. The woolly flowering stems are 2–12" tall, with an umbel flower arrangement. The individual flowers are on long, slender flower stalks attached within a cuplike bract with 3–10 downturned lobes. The tepals are smooth on the back, creamy white, and often tinged with red or purple.

Bloom Season: June–August.

Habitat/Range: Dry open places, from mountain valleys to the alpine.

Comments: Cultivated buckwheat (*Fagopyrum* species) and cultivated rhubarb (*Rheum* species) are in the buckwheat family. The seeds of wild buckwheats (*Eriogonum* species) were also a food source for some Native Americans, but more often the plants were used for their medicinal value in treating wounds, stomach problems, and rheumatism.

Springbeauty

SPRINGBEAUTY
Claytonia lanceolata Pursh
Purslane Family (Portulacaceae)

Description: The flowers of springbeauty are normally white but may appear pink because of the reddish veins of the petals and the pink anthers. The tips of the petals are distinctly notched. There are only 2 green sepals, but there are 5 petals, 5 stamens, and 3 styles. The succulent leaves are lance shaped and opposite. The plants are usually less than 8" tall. The similar yellow springbeauty *(C. flava)* was once considered to be a variety of *C. lanceolata.* However, yellow springbeauty differs by having narrower leaves and petals that lack the notch and the pink veins. Note that the petals of yellow springbeauty may be yellow, but they are more often white.

Bloom Season: April–July.

Habitat/Range: Cool, moist soil of recent snowmelts, from the valleys to the alpine.

Comments: Springbeauty is in the same family as the bitterroot *(Lewisia rediviva),* and American Indians used both for food. All parts of the plant are edible, fresh or cooked. It is also a favorite food of pocket gophers and bears and it is rightfully left for them.

PYGMY BITTERROOT
Lewisia pygmaea (Gray) Robins.
Purslane Family (Portulacaceae)

Description: The small flowers of pygmy bitterroot vary in color from white to pink or purple. There are 2 small, opposite, leaflike bracts about midway up the flowering stem. Each stem has a single flower. The flowers have 2 oval sepals, with tiny teeth on the margin, and about 7 petals. The narrow leaves all originate from the plant base and are up to 6" long. The flowering stems are much shorter than the leaves.

Bloom Season: May–August.

Habitat/Range: Moist areas in the meadows of the subalpine forests and alpine tundra.

Comments: The German botanist Frederick Pursh (1774–1820) named the genus *Lewisia* in honor of Meriwether Lewis of the Lewis and Clark Expedition.

Pygmy Bitterroot

Broadleaved Miner's Lettuce

BROADLEAVED MINER'S LETTUCE
Montia cordifolia (Wats.) Pax. & Hoffm.
(also *Claytonia cordifolia* Wats.)
Purslane Family (Portulacaceae)

Description: A single, opposite pair of heart-shaped leaves is found about halfway up the stem of this plant, while the balance of the broad leaves arises from the plant base. The stems, 4–12" tall, support a raceme of 3–10 white flowers, without the bracts of related species. The flower includes 2 sepals, 5 petals, 5 stamens, and 3 stigmas. The fruit is a capsule, producing 3 shiny black seeds.

Bloom Season: May–September.

Habitat/Range: Wet soil along streams, from the valleys to the subalpine forests.

Comments: *Montia* is named for an Italian botanist, Giuseppe Monti (1682–1760). If miners made salad with the leaves of this plant, they likely learned it from the Indians, who ate the plants raw.

Sweet Rock Jasmine

SWEET ROCK JASMINE
Androsace chamaejasme Wulf.
(also *Androsace lehmanniana* Spreng.)
Primrose Family (Primulaceae)

Description: The mats of this striking, soft-hairy cushion plant are seldom even 4" tall. In dense basal rosettes, the leaves are lance shaped and about ⅜" long. A single, white-hairy stem (per leaf cluster) supports an umbel of 4–5 flowers. The petals are white, with a yellow to orange "eye," and have 5 flaring lobes fused into a tubular base. The aroma of the flowers sweetens the alpine air.

Bloom Season: May–July.

Habitat/Range: Rocky ledges, often on lime-stone bedrock and alpine fellfield, near the Continental Divide and its eastern slopes.

Comments: *Androsace* is from the Greek *androsakes,* thought to be a sea plant. *Chamae-jasme* is from the Greek *chamae* (dwarf; low on the ground) and *jasme* (jasmine). This plant is uncommon enough that it is always a treat to see (and smell) its lovely cushions in bloom.

PIPER'S ANEMONE
Anemone piperi Britt.
Buttercup Family (Ranunculaceae)

Description: A single, white, dainty flower adorns the end of the slender, erect stem of Piper's anemone. About 6–14" in total length, the stem supports a whorl of 3 leaves a few inches below the flower and a single leaf at the base of the stem. These leaves are all com-pound, with 3 toothed leaflets each. The flower consists of 5–7 white (petal-like) sepals, no true petals, and many stamens and pistils.

Bloom Season: Late April–early August.

Habitat/Range: Shady woods, in the moist montane and lower subalpine forests.

Comments: Named in honor of Charles Vancouver Piper (1867–1926) professor of botany and zoology at Washington State University. On June 15, 1806, Meriwether Lewis collected a specimen of this plant. That same day, the Lewis and Clark Expedition traveled from Weippe Prairie to a camp along Eldorado Creek, Idaho.

Piper's Anemone

Baneberry (flower)

(fruit)

BANEBERRY
Actaea rubra (Ait.) Willd.
Buttercup Family (Ranunculaceae)

Description: The clusters of shiny red or white berries of baneberry are more distinctive than the small white flowers. Both red- and white-berried forms of baneberry are the same species. The white berries are said to resemble "doll's eyes," and the plants that bear them are often referred to by that name. The "eye" is the dark, persistent stigma on the berry. When in bloom, 25 or more flowers are arranged in a large cluster at the end of the stem. A close look at a flower will show that there is only a single style, numerous stamens with long filaments, 5–10 cream-colored petals, and 3–5 whitish petal-like sepals. The leaves are large and compound, with 9 or more toothed leaflets, often in groups of 3.

Bloom Season: May–July.

Habitat/Range: Damp woods and streams, in the moist montane and subalpine forests.

Comments: *Actaea* is the Greek name for "elderberry," which has some superficial similarities in leaf and fruit to baneberry, but is not closely related. "Bane" means "poison" or "death"; this plant has poisonous berries that cause severe intestinal inflammation. There are reports of children who have died after eating the berries.

Marsh Marigold

MARSH MARIGOLD
Caltha leptosepala DC.
Buttercup Family (Ranunculaceae)

Description: The leaves of marsh marigold are simple, longer than broad, and shaped like an arrowhead with a rounded point. The margin of the leaf has blunt or rounded teeth, especially on the lower half. Most of the leaves are basal. Sometimes there is a single leaf near the base of the otherwise leafless stem. A single large flower is on the end of the stem. There are 5–12 petal-like sepals, no true petals, and many stamens. The sepals are white or yellowish and are tinged with blue on the back.

Bloom Season: Late May–August.

Habitat/Range: Wet meadows of the subalpine forests and alpine tundra.

Comments: Marsh marigold is most often confused with the closely related globeflower *(Trollius albiflorus);* the two often grow side by side. While the flowers are similar, the leaves of globeflower are deeply divided and sharply toothed. The leaves of some species of *Caltha* have been eaten in Europe and eastern North America, but only after boiling them in several changes of water to remove the bitter properties. Like many other plants in the buttercup family, marsh marigold has a poisonous, acrid juice capable of blistering the mucous membranes if eaten raw.

WHITE VIRGIN'S BOWER
Clematis ligusticifolia Nutt.
Buttercup Family (Ranunculaceae)

Description: These common woody vines often climb on shrubs for support. With stems up to 60' long, they sometimes cover their host completely. Compound leaves, with 5–7 leaflets each, are in opposite pairs on the stems. The small, creamy white flowers are unisexual; the male ones with many stamens but lacking pistils, while the female flowers have both pistils and sterile stamens. The dry fruit is hairy, with a long, plumelike style.

Bloom Season: June–July.

Habitat/Range: Creek bottoms of the valleys and dry montane forests.

Comments: *Clematis* was used by modern herbalists as a headache remedy, especially for migraines or cluster headaches. American Indians valued the herb for a variety of medicinal uses: a wash for skin eruptions, to treat sore throats and colds, and for aches and cramps.

White Virgin's Bower

Water Buttercup

WATER BUTTERCUP
Ranunculus aquatilis L.
Buttercup Family (Ranunculaceae)

Description: Water buttercup has dense clumps of threadlike leaves submerged in the water and white flowers floating on the surface. Some plants also have broader, 3-parted leaves floating on the surface. The threadlike leaves at times seem so dense as to almost clog the stream. Whether threadlike or not, the leaves have a distinct petiole (leaf stalk) and will collapse when removed from the water. The flowers have 5 sepals, 5–10 white petals, and 10–15 stamens and pistils.

Bloom Season: May–August.

Habitat/Range: Sluggish streams, ponds, and lakes.

Comments: Water buttercup is important cover for small fish and is a productive substrate for the aquatic invertebrates that fish eat.

False Bugbane

FALSE BUGBANE
Trautvetteria caroliniensis (Walt.) Vail
Buttercup Family (Ranunculaceae)

Description: Numerous, large, unique leaves distinguish false bugbane. The leaf stalks are up to 18" long and the leaf blades as much as 12" wide. These leaves are palmately lobed into 5–11 toothed segments. Most leaves are from the plant base, with only a few, smaller leaves on the flowering stem. Arranged in dense corymbs on the end of long (2–5' tall) stems, the flowers are small (⅜" long) and rather inconspicuous. Each flower has 3–5 greenish white sepals, no true petals, numerous white stamens, and green pistils. The filaments of the outer stamens are dilated and appear somewhat petal-like.

Bloom Season: May–August.

Habitat/Range: Streams and wet woodlands of the moist montane and lower subalpine forests. Found in Japan and scattered places in North America from Vancouver Island to the southern Appalachian Mountains.

Comments: *Trautvetteria* was named in honor of the Russian botanist Ernst Rudolph von Trautvetter (1809–1889). "Bugbane" suggests that it is poisonous to insects. A poultice of the pounded roots was prepared by the Bella Coola Indians to treat boils. The treatment was believed to be too strong to use on children.

Buckbrush Ceanothus

BUCKBRUSH CEANOTHUS
Ceanothus velutinus Dougl. ex Hook.
Buckthorn Family (Rhamnaceae)

Description: Buckbrush ceanothus is a medium-sized, evergreen shrub 2–6' tall, with shiny, dark green, aromatic leaves. The leaves have 3 prominent veins that radiate from the leaf base. A varnishlike sticky substance on the upper leaf surface gives it a shiny appearance and its strong, characteristic aroma. The lower leaf surface is dull gray. The leaves are arranged alternately on the rather stiff, woody stems. Flower parts are in groups of 5, except for the single pistil with a 3-lobed stigma. The fruit is a hard capsule that separates into 3 segments.

Bloom Season: June–August.

Habitat/Range: Well-drained slopes of the montane and subalpine forests, especially abundant after a forest fire.

Comments: "Red root" is the name often used for this plant by herbalists, who rely on the herb to improve lymphatic and capillary health and to treat inflammation of the throat, tonsils, and sinuses. American Indians used New Jersey tea *(C. americanus)* for stomach problems and snakebite.

Western Serviceberry

WESTERN SERVICEBERRY
Amelanchier alnifolia (Nutt.) Nutt. ex Roem.
Rose Family (Rosaceae)

Description: These can be stately shrubs up to 30' tall but are more often less than half that size. On drier sites or when trimmed by browsing animals, they may remain 3' tall or less. The stems are alternately branched. The larger stems have smooth gray bark, while the twigs of the current year are reddish brown. The base of the leaf is rounded, with a smooth margin. The upper half of the leaf margin is coarsely toothed. The young leaves have silky hair, at least on the lower surface. The flowers are arranged in 5–15 flower racemes on the ends of the twigs. The 5 white petals are rather long and showy, widest above the middle and tapering to a narrow base. The purple fruit looks like a blueberry but is technically more like an apple.

Bloom Season: May–July.

Habitat/Range: Streams and open slopes, from the valleys to the subalpine forests.

Comments: *Amelanchier* was adapted from the French name for a European species. *Alnifolia* means "leaves like an alder." Serviceberry (or "sarvisberry") is also called "saskatoon," "shadbush," or "juneberry." The berries were widely used by American Indians, who pounded them into large cakes, which were dried for storage, or mixed them with dried meat to make pemmican. Serviceberry is an important browse plant for deer and elk.

BLACK HAWTHORN
Crataegus douglasii Lindl.
Rose Family (Rosaceae)

Description: These tall (4–14') shrubs are beset with stout, straight or slightly curved thorns, about 1" long or less. The leaf blades are about 2" long, 1–2" wide, and toothed on the margin, often doubly toothed. The white flowers are arranged near the ends of the twigs and have 5 petals, many stamens, and 5 distinct styles. The fruit is the familiar black haw. A closely related species, Columbian hawthorn *(C. columbiana)* is distinguished by its much longer thorns (1½–3"), 3 styles, and red fruit.

Bloom Season: May–June.

Habitat/Range: Along streams in the valleys and montane forests.

Comments: *Douglasii* honors the Scottish botanist David Douglas (1798–1834), who collected hundreds of plants in the Northwest, especially along the Columbia River. Long used for food and medicine by American Indians, today hawthorn berries are valued by herbalists as a tonic for the heart and circulatory system, especially in treating high blood pressure.

Black Hawthorn

Woods Strawberry

WOODS STRAWBERRY
Fragaria vesca L.
Rose Family (Rosaceae)

Description: The 3-bladed leaves, creeping habit, and red fruit of strawberries are recognized by all, but few distinguish the subtle differences between the two common native species of the Rockies, woods strawberry and mountain strawberry. The surface of woods strawberry leaves is bright yellow-green, often bulged between the prominent veins. The tooth on the leaf tip is well developed, normally at least as long as the two adjoining teeth, or projecting beyond them. The main flower stalk and flower arrangement are often at least equal in length to the leaves, if not longer.

Bloom Season: April–June.

Habitat/Range: Moist open woods and meadows, from the valleys to the lower subalpine forests.

Comments: *Fragaria* is from *fraga,* the Latin name for strawberry. It is amazing how a single, tiny, wild woods strawberry packs more flavor than a flat of the fruit from the supermarket! The leaves, infused as a tea, are used by herbalists to treat diarrhea and other digestive system inflammations.

Mountain Strawberry

CREAMBUSH OCEANSPRAY
Holodiscus discolor (Pursh) Maxim.
Rose Family (Rosaceae)

Description: Looking like a spray of fine water particles from breaking waves, the numerous, tiny, cream-colored flowers are arranged in pyramid-shaped panicles, 4–7" long, on the ends of the branches. These are large, erect shrubs, 3–9' tall, with arching branches. The leaves are about 2–3" long, green on the upper surface, but paler on the lower surface, due to a dense mat of soft, woolly hair. The leaf margin is both shallowly lobed and finely toothed.

Bloom Season: June–August.

Habitat/Range: Rocky soil of the montane forests.

Comments: *Holodiscus* is from the Greek *holo-* (whole) and *diskos* (disk), which describes the entire (unlobed) disk, or swollen receptacle at the base of the flower. A specimen of this shrub was collected by Meriwether Lewis on May 29, 1806, near present-day Kamiah, Idaho. American Indians used the branches for arrow shafts, tipi pins, harpoon shafts, and drum hoops.

MOUNTAIN STRAWBERRY
Fragaria virginiana Duchn.
Rose Family (Rosaceae)

Description: Mountain strawberry leaves have a powdery coating on the surface, giving them a blue-green color. The leaves are compound, with 3 leaflets each and without the prominent vein of woods strawberry. The terminal tooth on the leaflets is normally much shorter than the two adjacent teeth, like a gun sight. The leaves generally extend beyond the main flower stalk and flower arrangement, often partially concealing the flowers and fruit. The plants reproduce vegetatively by creeping runners.

Bloom Season: May–August.

Habitat/Range: Open woods and meadows of the montane and subalpine forests.

Comments: The authority for this species is the French botanist, Antoine Nicholas Duchesne (1747–1827), the author of many works on useful plants, particularly strawberries. American Indians used the plant medicinally to treat diarrhea, liver and kidney problems, stomachache, and external sores.

Creambush Oceanspray

MALLOW NINEBARK
Physocarpus malvaceus (Greene) Kuntze
Rose Family (Rosaceae)

Description: Shredding bark that hangs in strips from the stems characterizes this medium-sized (2–6' tall) shrub. Its maplelike leaves have 3–5 lobes and a double-toothed margin. Star-shaped hairs densely cover the ovaries and the lower surface of the leaves. A cluster of white flowers is arranged on the ends of the stems. There are normally only 2 pistils, but occasionally 3, rarely more. The fruit is a dry follicle.

Bloom Season: May–June.

Habitat/Range: Dry to moist woods, from the valleys to the lower subalpine forests.

Comments: In northern Idaho, the closely related species Pacific ninebark *(P. capitatus)* is found in moist to wet woods. Pacific ninebark is taller (6–12' or more) and commonly has 3–5 pistils, without the star-shaped hairs on the ovary (or only sparsely hairy). Meriwether Lewis collected a specimen of Pacific ninebark along the Columbia River, while traveling through in 1805–1806.

Mallow Ninebark

Bitter Cherry

BITTER CHERRY
Prunus emarginata (Dougl.) Walp.
Rose Family (Rosaceae)

Description: The flowers (and fruit) of bitter cherry are arranged in few-flowered corymbs (5–8 flowers each) from axils near the ends of the leaf-bearing stems. Each flower has 5 sepals, 5 petals, about 20 stamens, and a single ovary. The single-seeded cherry fruit turns dark red to black as it ripens. The tips of the leaves are usually rounded, but if pointed, the point is not drawn out. These many-stemmed shrubs are 3–12' tall.

Bloom Season: April–June.

Habitat/Range: Streams and dry woodlands of the valleys and montane forests. Often abundant in brush fields after a forest fire.

Comments: Bitter cherry was widely used by American Indians for both food and medicine. The fruit was dried and stored for later use. Many ailments, from skin disorders to colds, were treated with the bark and roots. The fibers and bark were used for baskets, twine, fishing line, mats, and containers.

Chokecherry

CHOKECHERRY
Prunus virginiana L.
Rose Family (Rosaceae)

Description: The white flowers are arranged in long racemes of 15 or more at the ends of leafy twigs. Each flower has a superior ovary with a single style, 5 sepals, 5 petals, and about 25 stamens. The fruit is a round, dark purple to black cherry with a single round pit. The leaves are alternately arranged and are egg shaped to somewhat oval. They have a sharp tip and fine, forward-pointing teeth on the margin. The petiole (leaf stem) has a pair of dark, reddish glands just below the base of the leaf blade. The shrubs are alternately branched, up to 24' tall, and often form dense thickets. On dry sites or where heavily browsed, they are often much lower (2–6' tall).

Bloom Season: May–July.

Habitat/Range: Streams and dry slopes, from the valleys to the montane forests.

Comments: Plains Indians pounded the fruit into flat cakes and used the bark to treat diarrhea. Meriwether Lewis, whose mother was an herbalist, used the same treatment successfully on himself when he fell ill below the Great Falls of the Missouri on June 11, 1805. The fresh pits and leaves of chokecherry contain toxic compounds that release cyanide, causing poisoning and death if sufficient quantities are consumed.

RED RASPBERRY
Rubus idaeus L.
Rose Family (Rosaceae)

Description: Wild red raspberries are a welcome treat along the trails of the Northern Rockies. These spiny shrubs grow 3–6' tall. Their leaves are compound, with 3–5 leaflets and prominent veins. The white flowers have 5 sepals, 5 petals, and many stamens and soon develop into the familiar red aggregate fruit.

Bloom Season: May–July.

Habitat/Range: Common along streams and in rocky places, from the valleys to the alpine summits.

Comments: Red raspberry provided both food and medicine for American Indians. A tea brewed from the plant was administered to women to ease childbirth pain, speed recovery after childbirth, and slow menstrual bleeding. The tea was also used to treat many other conditions including boils, sores, bladder infections, liver problems, and diarrhea. Modern herbalists likewise value raspberry leaves and fruit for treating a wide range of conditions, from diarrhea to mouth ulcers.

Red Raspberry

THIMBLEBERRY
Rubus parviflorus Nutt.
Rose Family (Rosaceae)

Description: The large, maplelike leaves and red, thumb-sized fruit of this shrub are familiar along forest trails in the Northern Rocky Mountains. The shrubs are unarmed, without the thorns and prickles of the closely related red and blackcap raspberries (*Rubus* species). The older stems are 2–6' tall, with loose bark that peels off in long strips. The white flowers are 1–2" in diameter and are arranged in 3–7-flowered racemes. The fruit is an aggregate of fleshy, one-seeded segments that loosen and fall from the receptacle when ripe.

Bloom Season: June–August.

Habitat/Range: Streams and shady, moist woods of the montane and subalpine forests.

Comments: *Rubus* is the Latin name for "bramble" and is related to *ruber* (red). The fruits are juicy and delicious, if you can catch them before they fall to the forest floor or get too mushy. American Indians also ate the young shoots and brewed a tea from the leaves.

Thimbleberry

Cascade Mountain Ash

CASCADE MOUNTAIN ASH

Sorbus scopulina Greene
Rose Family (Rosaceae)

Description: The clusters of orange, berrylike fruits of this shrub are persistent from late summer through winter. Each fruit develops from an inferior ovary (with sepals, petals, and stamens attached to the top of the ovary) like an apple. With 70–200 white flowers arranged in flat-topped corymbs, the plants in flower are quite showy. This is a medium-tall shrub (3–12' tall) with compound leaves having 9–13 leaflets pinnately arranged in pairs on the leaf stalk. Teeth line the margin of the leaflets, and the tip tapers to a sharp point.

Bloom Season: May–early July.

Habitat/Range: Woods and brushy slopes of the montane and subalpine forests.

Comments: Sitka mountain ash *(S. sitchensis)* also occurs in the Northern Rockies. It is distinguished by having rounded-tipped leaflets that lack teeth on the basal ¼ (or more) of the margin. Mountain ash fruit was consumed by American Indians fresh, cooked, or dried. It was sometimes buried in the ground to keep fresh for winter use. As a medicine, mountain ash was used for treating rheumatism, stomach problems, bed-wetting, earache, and as a purgative. Wild-food enthusiasts today report mountain ash as bitter and mealy—for emergency use only.

White Spiraea

WHITE SPIRAEA
Spiraea betulifolia Pall.
Rose Family (Rosaceae)

Description: This low shrub (10–24" tall) spreads by underground runners, often forming a dense ground cover on the forest floor, alone or in combination with snowberry *(Symphoricarpos albus)* or other species. White spiraea is alternately branched, with egg-shaped leaves having sharp teeth on the margin. Small, dull white flowers appear in flat-topped corymbs on the ends of the stems. The fruit is a small, dry follicle.

Bloom Season: June–July.

Habitat/Range: Common in woods, from the valleys to the upper subalpine forests. Resprouts readily after a forest fire.

Comments: *Spiraea* is from the Greek *speira* (coil; rope; wreath), possibly for the use of the plants as garlands. *Betulifolia* means "leaves like a birch." Also called "meadowsweet," *Spiraea* species are medicinal plants used by herbalists in relieving pain, reducing inflammation and fever, and for treating heartburn, hyperacidity, and diarrhea. It was similarly used by American Indians for treating abdominal and menstrual pains. Babies were washed with an infusion of the bark to treat diarrhea and to make them stronger. The branches were used for drying and smoking fish laid in alternating layers over the fire.

Northern Bedstraw

NORTHERN BEDSTRAW
Galium boreale L.
Madder Family (Rubiaceae)

Description: Northern bedstraw has numerous erect, square stems, 4–32" tall. The leaves are whorled, with 4 narrow leaves that attach to the stem at the same level. Secondary branches often grow from the axils of the primary leaves, making the plant rather densely leaved. The numerous white flowers are arranged in panicles from the leaf axis of the upper leaves and ends of the branches. Each tiny flower consists of 4 petal lobes, 4 stamens, and 2 styles. The fruit is a dry, 2-parted pod.

Bloom Season: June–August.

Habitat/Range: Meadows and open woods, from valleys to subalpine forests.

Comments: *Galium* is from the Greek *gala* (milk); a species of *Galium* was used in Europe for curdling milk. *Boreale* refers to the northern (boreal) home range of the species. "Bedstraw" comes from the practice of using the dry foliage as a stuffing for mattresses and pillows.

BASTARD TOADFLAX
Comandra umbellata (L.) Nutt.
Sandalwood Family (Santalaceae)

Description: Bastard toadflax is a small herb 4–12" tall. The alternate leaves are thick and gray-green in color. The floral parts are attached to a greenish tube (hypanthium) from the top of the ovary. The flowers have 5 white to purple lobes that extend out from the top of the tube. Each floral lobe has a stamen at the base and a tuft of hairs behind each stamen. The fruit is blue to brown in color with a single seed.

Bloom Season: April–August.

Habitat/Range: Meadows of the valleys and dry montane forests.

Comments: *Comandra* comes from the Greek *kome* (hair) and *andros* (man), in reference to the tuft of hair behind the stamens. These plants are parasitic on a variety of associated plant species. They spread by underground stems and attach themselves to the roots of other plants. The fruits are reported to be edible, but they may accumulate selenium to toxic levels.

Bastard Toadflax

Mountain Boykinia

MOUNTAIN BOYKINIA
Boykinia major Gray
Saxifrage Family (Saxifragaceae)

Description: These are large, aromatic plants (1–3' tall) with broad leaves (up to 8" wide). The numerous kidney-shaped leaves have 3–7 deep lobes and are 2–3 times toothed on the margin. The upper leaves have large, leaflike stipules at the base of the leaf stalk. Numerous white flowers are arranged in cymelike panicles on slender, erect stems. Each flower consists of 5 sepals, 5 petals, 5 stamens, and 2 pistils attached to a flared, yellow, glandular, cuplike structure (hypanthium).

Bloom Season: June–September.

Habitat/Range: Streams and wet meadows of the moist montane and subalpine forests of northern Idaho and northwestern Montana.

Comments: *Boykinia* is named for Georgia naturalist Dr. Samuel Boykin (1786–1848). The distinctive aroma of mountain boykinia often fills the air along certain high mountain streams in the Northern Rockies. This aroma comes from glands on the plants and is especially strong if the plants are brushed or stepped on. The dried leaves of a species of *Boykinia* were worn in caps by some American Indians for its fragrance.

Round-Leaved Alumroot

ROUND-LEAVED ALUMROOT
Heuchera cylindrica Dougl.
Saxifrage Family (Saxifragaceae)

Description: The tall (6–32"), slender, and leafless stem of round-leaved alumroot is graced with panicled clusters of tiny, greenish yellow to cream-colored flowers. Glandular hairs line the sepals and upper stems, which thrust out of a dense tuft of basal leaves. These leaves are broadly oval to nearly kidney shaped, with both deep and shallow rounded teeth along the margin. The cylindrical flower consists of 5 sepals and 5 stamens attached to a glandular disk that lines the top of the partially inferior ovary. When present, the slender petals number fewer than 5 and are half (or less) the length of the sepals. More often they are entirely absent.

Bloom Season: April–August.

Habitat/Range: Crevices of rock cliffs, outcrops, and rocky slopes, from the valleys to timberline.

Comments: *Heuchera* was named in honor of Johann Heinrich von Heucher (1677–1747), a German botanist and physician. It is called "alumroot" because of its alumlike properties; it works as a styptic for stopping bleeding and closing wounds. The root contains a concentration of tannin, useful medicinally both internally and externally, where an astringent is beneficial. Alumroot has a long history of medicinal use by American Indians and folk medicine herbalists, who have used it for treating diarrhea, as a poultice for various sores, and for healing ulcers.

DOTTED SAXIFRAGE
Saxifraga bronchialis L.
Saxifrage Family (Saxifragaceae)

Description: The dense clusters of small, rigid, overlapping leaves of dotted saxifrage look like a moss growing in the cracks of boulders and in stony soil. The stems are less than 8" tall, with a few widely spaced, entire (unlobed) leaves. The dainty white petals have tiny dots that can be purple, red, or yellow. There are 5 petals, 10 stamens (somewhat shorter than the petals), and 2 styles.

Bloom Season: June–September.

Habitat/Range: Rock crevices or rockslides, from the valleys to the alpine summits.

Comments: *Saxifraga* is derived from the Latin *saxum* (rock) and *frango* (to break). The plants often grow in rock crevices where they appear to be splitting the rock apart. *Bronchialis* refers to the bronchial tubes of the lungs of animals, perhaps for the resemblance of the flower branching to the similar branching of the bronchial tubes.

Dotted Saxifrage

Brook Saxifrage

BROOK SAXIFRAGE
Saxifraga odontoloma Piper
(also *Saxifraga arguta* D. Don)
Saxifrage Family (Saxifragaceae)

Description: The peculiar basal leaves (mostly round in outline with very coarse teeth) and the habitat (cold, shady streams) are distinctive features of brook saxifrage. Each plant has a single, leafless stem, 8–24" tall, which supports more than 10 flowers in an open panicle arrangement. The small flowers consist of 5 green to purple sepals, 5 round, white petals, 10 stamens with expanded petal-like filaments, and a mostly superior ovary with 2 styles.

Bloom Season: May–September.

Habitat/Range: Stream banks, from montane forests to timberline.

Comments: The name *Saxifraga* (rock break) may have originated from the herbal use of the plants in Europe to treat urinary stones. *Odontoloma* comes from the Greek roots *odont-* (tooth), and *lomat* (fringe, border); these, plus *arguta* (sharp), probably all refer to the prominent teeth on the border of the leaves.

Coolwort Foamflower

COOLWORT FOAMFLOWER
Tiarella trifoliata L.
(also *Tiarella unifoliata* Hook.)
Saxifrage Family (Saxifragaceae)

Description: A low herb (less than 18" tall), coolwort foamflower is found in the shade on the forest floor. The basal leaves have 3 or 5 lobed blades less than 3" wide, and leaf stalks up to 4" long. The stem leaves are smaller and more deeply lobed. White flowers are arranged in open panicles well above the leaves. The 5 sepals are petal-like, while the 5 smaller, awl-shaped petals look similar to the filaments of the 10 stamens. Two hornlike extensions of the ovary (divided in the upper half) end in slender styles. The fruit is a capsule with a few shiny black seeds.

Bloom Season: June–August.

Habitat/Range: Damp woods and stream banks of the moist montane and subalpine forests.

Comments: *Tiarella* is named from the Greek *tiara,* an ancient Persian headdress with 2 outward curved horns that look like the fruit of this plant. Some American Indians of the Northwest chewed the leaves as a cough medicine. A species of foamflower *(T. cordifolia)* in eastern North America was more widely used by American Indians as medicine for a variety of ailments.

Edible Tobacco-Root

EDIBLE TOBACCO-ROOT
Valeriana edulis Nutt. ex T. & G.
Valerian Family (Valerianaceae)

Description: The thick taproot of edible tobacco-root easily distinguishes it from other *Valeriana* species in the Rocky Mountains, but please do not dig them up to find out. It is just as easy to identify this plant by looking at the abundant basal leaves. They are simple, widest well above the middle, and taper gradually from there to the narrow base. The opposite leaves on the stems are usually compound, each consisting of many narrow, pinnate segments. The cream-colored flowers are arranged in a panicle. The fruit is a round achene (like a sunflower seed) with plumes on the top for wind dispersal.

Bloom Season: June–August.

Habitat/Range: Moist meadows, from foothills to alpine summits.

Comments: *Valeriana* was possibly named for the Roman province of Valeria in southern Europe, now part of Hungary and Croatia. The Tobacco Root Range in Montana was named for this plant. The Blackfoot Indians called this plant "smell foot" and made a drink from it to treat stomach trouble. The plant was a major food source for other American Indians; they considered the root poisonous when raw, but they rendered it safe for eating by baking. It has a very strong and peculiar flavor that is an acquired taste, like Limburger cheese. Some liken the odor to that of dirty socks.

Parrot's Beak

PARROT'S BEAK
Pedicularis racemosa Dougl. ex Benth.
Figwort Family (Scrophulariaceae)

Description: Parrot's beak is named for the long, slender, downturned beak of the galea, or upper lip, of the petals. The lower lip of the petals consists of 2 large lateral lobes and a smaller central lobe. The calyx (sepal) tube has only 2 lobes. Parrot's beak has leafy stems less than 20" tall, bearing simple leaves with fine, sharp teeth on the margin. The several other species of *Pedicularis* in the Northern Rocky Mountains are distinguished by having compound leaves that are lobed or divided into many segments, and 5 calyx lobes.

Bloom Season: July–August.

Habitat/Range: Upper montane and subalpine forests.

Comments: There are two varieties of parrot's beak. The variety *alba,* with white flowers, is found east of the Cascade/Sierra crest, including the Northern Rocky Mountains. Plants with pink to purple flowers grow west of the summit of the Cascade Range and the Sierra Nevada.

WESTERN TOBACCO-ROOT
Valeriana occidentalis Heller
Valerian Family (Valerianaceae)

Description: These herbs are 12–32" tall with thin, fibrous roots. The basal leaves are spoon-like, with a long leaf stalk (up to 8" long) and an oval terminal segment (up to 4" by 2"), sometimes with 2–3 pairs of much smaller lateral segments. The leaves on the stem have shorter leaf stalks and several segments. The bright white (or pinkish) flowers are very small (⅛" long). Other similar species of tobacco-root in the Northern Rockies have either larger flowers (⅛–¾" long) or shorter stems.

Bloom Season: April–July.

Habitat/Range: Moist meadows and woods, from the montane forests to timberline.

Comments: The name *Valeriana* may come from the Latin *valere* (to be strong), in reference to the strong odor and medicinal value of these plants. The related *V. officinalis* has long been used by herbalists as a sedative for relaxing and soothing the nerves and reducing tension and anxiety.

Western Tobacco-Root

LAMB'S LETTUCE
Valerianella locusta (L.) Betcke
Valerian Family (Valerianaceae)

Description: A small, annual weed, 4–16" tall, with opposite leaves having short, fine hairs along the leaf margin. The stems curiously branch by repeated divisions into two, with a pair of leaves at the junction of each branching. At the ends of the branches are dense clusters of small, white flowers. The floral petals are tubular, slightly swollen or spurred on the back, and with 5 lobes. There are 3 stamens and a 3-lobed stigma.

Bloom Season: April–July.

Habitat/Range: Introduced from Europe; found here in moist meadows and disturbed places in the valleys and montane forests.

Comments: *Valerianella* means "small *Valeriana*." These little introduced annuals are often mistaken for our native annual species of *Plectritis*, which is distinguished by having a simple stem (or with axillary branches) and a 2-lobed stigma (rarely 3).

Lamb's Lettuce

Canada Violet

CANADA VIOLET
Viola canadensis L.
Violet Family (Violaceae)

Description: Rather large as violets go, Canada violet has erect stems 4–16" tall and large, heart-shaped leaves with fine teeth and a fringe of hair on the margin. The leaf stalks of the basal leaves are up to 12" long. The flowers are mostly white but are marked with a purplish tinge on the outer surface and purple lines on the inner surface of the lower 3 petals. The flowers often turn lavender as they age.

Bloom Season: May–July.

Habitat/Range: Damp woods in rich, loamy soil of the moist montane and subalpine forests.

Comments: Like other violet species, Canada violet is known for its edible and medicinal properties (see *V. orbiculata* and *V. glabella*). However, collecting wildflowers for this purpose must be done with special care to avoid damage to the plants and their native habitat.

GREEN AND BROWN FLOWERS

Western Goldthread

*Pale green to deep green and yellowish green
flowers are included in this section, as are
brown or purplish brown flowers. You may
want to check the white and yellow sections for
very pale green or pale yellowish green flowers
if you cannot find what you are looking for here.
Some purplish brown flowers may appear in the
blue and purple section.*

Mountain Maple

MOUNTAIN MAPLE
Acer glabrum Torr.
Maple Family (Aceraceae)

Description: This familiar, 8–30'-tall shrub has graceful, widely spreading branches and bright fall foliage. Appearing in early spring, the inconspicuous and short-lived flowers are yellowish green. Each tiny flower is about ⅜" wide and typically has 5 slender sepals, 5 petals, and 8–10 stamens. The pair of broadly winged fruits, joined at the point of attachment, is known as a samara. The opposite leaves are 3-lobed, typical of maples, with an unequally and sharply toothed margin. Shrubs with leaves having 3 separate leaflets are occasionally seen. The young twigs are smooth and cherry red, turning gray as they age. The buds are valvelike, with 2 bud scales.

Bloom Season: April–June.

Habitat/Range: Moist slopes and along draws and streams, from montane to subalpine forests. It is tolerant of shade, often growing under the canopy of conifer trees.

Comments: *Acer* is the Latin name for maple. *Glabrum* means "smooth; without hair." Mountain maple was employed by American Indians for a variety of uses, including medicine, cordage, cradle frames, snowshoes, tepee pegs, bows, fish traps, and drum hoops.

Western Sweet Cecily

WESTERN SWEET CECILY
Osmorhiza occidentalis (Nutt.) Torr.
Parsley Family (Apiaceae)

Description: The pleasant aroma of this plant, reminiscent of anise or licorice, is often noticed when the foliage is bruised. This medium-to-large herb (1–4' tall) has compound leaves with numerous broad, toothed leaflets. The tiny, yellow or greenish flowers are arranged in compound umbels on the ends of leafy stems. The fruit is smooth, long (½–¾") and very narrow and linear (having sides parallel).

Bloom Season: April–July.

Habitat/Range: Moist, rich soils in both montane and subalpine forests.

Comments: *Osmorhiza* comes from the Greek *osme* (odor) and *rhiza* (root), aptly named for its strongly odorous root. The Blackfeet name for the plant translates to "smell mouth." American Indians valued the herb for treating toothache, stomachache, eye troubles, skin rashes, and lice. Sweet cecily tea is a useful tonic for the digestive system and soothing for sore throats. Hikers often nibble the fruits along the trail, but one must be careful not to mistake it for the poisonous water hemlock *(Cicuta maculata)*.

Wild Sarsaparilla

WILD SARSAPARILLA
Aralia nudicaulis L.
Ginseng Family (Araliaceae)

Description: The unusual compound leaves of wild sarsaparilla are 12–20" long, arising singly from an underground stem. Each leaf includes a long, bare stalk with 3 branches that terminate in 3–5 leaflets each. The leaflets are 2–5" long, with sharp teeth on the margin, and have an abruptly pointed tip. Inconspicuous flowers arise on short stems from near ground level, well below the spreading leaflets. The tiny flowers are greenish and arranged in 3 globe-shaped umbels. A dark purple berry develops from each ovary.

Bloom Season: May–June.

Habitat/Range: Damp woods of the moist montane forests.

Comments: First collected for botanical science in Quebec, the genus name *Aralia* was derived from the French-Canadian *aralie*. Wild sarsaparilla was widely used by American Indians for a variety of medicinal applications both internally and externally. It was applied to skin disorders and wounds to draw out infection, and it was made into a tea for treating kidney problems, stomach pain, colds, coughs, and internal bleeding.

Devil's Club (flower)

(fruit)

DEVIL'S CLUB
Oplopanax horridum (J. Smith) Miq.
Ginseng Family (Araliaceae)

Description: Devil's club gets its unsavory reputation from its stout, club-shaped woody stems (3–9' tall), plagued with stiff, sharp spines up to ¾" long. The huge leaves, often over 12" broad, are beautifully deceptive; they bear similar sharp spines on their veins and leaf stalks. The leaves are shaped like those of maple trees, palmately 3–9 lobed, with sharp teeth on the margin. Small, globe-shaped umbels of greenish white flowers are arranged along a central flower stalk up to 10" long. The fruit is a cluster of bright, shiny red berries.

Bloom Season: May–July.

Habitat/Range: Streams and seeps of the moist montane forests, often in association with old-growth western red cedar and western hemlock.

Comments: The scientific name *Oplopanax* is derived from the Greek *hoplon* (tool; weapon); *horridum* needs no explanation. American Indians and modern herbalists alike value devil's club for its medicinal properties. It is an expectorant, useful for coughs, colds, and bronchitis. It has also been used to treat arthritis, diabetes, cataracts, pain, indigestion, and other complaints.

Prairie Sagewort

PRAIRIE SAGEWORT
Artemisia ludoviciana Nutt.
Aster Family (Asteraceae)

Description: This aromatic herb is often mistaken for silver sagebrush *(Artemisia cana)*, which is easily distinguished by its 2–4'-tall, woody stems. In contrast, prairie sagewort is an herbaceous plant, 1–3' tall, that dies back to the ground each winter, growing again from perennial roots and underground stems the following spring. Prairie sagewort has silvery leaves covered with dense woolly hair, at least when young, but often becoming less so with age. Leaf shape is also highly variable; some plants have leaves entire and lance shaped, and others have leaves deeply divided into many narrow lobes. Numerous small flower heads, having only disk flowers, are in a panicle-like arrangement on the ends of the stems.

Bloom Season: June–October.

Habitat/Range: Dry, open places in the valleys and dry montane forests.

Comments: *Artemisia* was named in honor of a noted botanist of 400 B.C, Artemisia, queen of ancient Caria (now within Turkey). Queen Artemisia was in turn likely named in honor of the Greek goddess Artemis. In Greek mythology Artemis was the goddess of the moon, wild animals, and hunting. The Blackfeet Indians called this plant by a name that is said to be translated as "man sage." It was widely used by many Plains Indian tribes as a sacred cleansing herb in smudging, in the sweat lodge, and during the sun dance and many other ceremonies.

Sitka Alder

SITKA ALDER
Alnus viridis (Vill.) DC.
Birch Family (Betulaceae)

Description: Sitka alder is a medium-tall shrub (6–30' high) having egg-shaped leaves with a pointed tip and a double sawtoothed margin. The buds are stalkless, with 4–6 overlapping bud scales and a sharply pointed tip. Unisexual male and female flowers are borne in separate flower arrangements, but on the same plant. The yellow male flowers hang downward in long, spiraling clusters, or catkins. The green female flowers are borne upright in stout, egg-shaped, woody catkins that look like miniature pinecones. These "cones" remain intact on the shrub through the winter.

Bloom Season: May–July.

Habitat/Range: Streamsides and wooded slopes, from the moist montane forests upward to timberline. It often forms dense glades on steep, cool mountain slopes, especially in avalanche chutes.

Comments: Alder bark is loaded with tannin, a chemical compound valuable for tanning hides. A reddish brown to orange dye is also obtained from the bark. Some American Indians used it to dye moccasins, feathers, and even their hair. An astringent, medicinal tea was made from the bark. Herbalists consider this tea useful internally for improving digestion and externally for poison ivy rash and insect bites. Medical research has isolated compounds from one species of alder that shows promise in cancer chemotherapy.

Western Coneflower

WESTERN CONEFLOWER
Rudbeckia occidentalis Nutt.
Aster Family (Asteraceae)

Description: Black, cone-shaped flower heads easily distinguish this species. At maturity these flower heads are 2" or more long, with narrow, tapering bracts that sweep downward away from the head. Tiny yellow disk flowers briefly decorate the black disk, but there are no showy ray flowers. The leaves are normally simple and broadly egg shaped, tapering to a sharp point. These are tall (2–6'), herbaceous perennials.

Bloom Season: June–August.

Habitat/Range: Moist places in montane and subalpine forests.

Comments: *Rudbeckia* species have been used in folk medicine to stimulate urination and ease menstruation. Poisoning of livestock has also been reported for the plants. However, livestock tend to avoid them, resulting in local increases of this plant in areas that are heavily grazed.

CHAMISSO'S COTTON SEDGE
Eriophorum chamissonis C. A. Mey
Sedge Family (Cyperaceae)

Description: A flower of the Chamisso's cotton sedge has many flexible floral bristles about ¾" long. Looking like a ball of cotton on the end of a stick, many of these flowers are arranged in a single dense, cottony tuft (spikelet) on the end of a tall (12–28" long) slender stem. The color of the "cotton" ranges from off-white to tan or pale reddish brown. The plants spread by underground runners, forming dense colonies.

Bloom Season: June–July.

Habitat/Range: Cold wetlands, often at the margin of ponds, of the moist montane and subalpine forests.

Comments: *Eriophorum* is from the Greek *eiron* (wool) and *phoros* (bearing), referring to the appearance of the flowers. While Chamisso's cotton sedge is not uncommon where its wetland habitat is found, it is sometimes associated with green-keeled cotton sedge *(E. viridicarinatum)* and other rare species.

Chamisso's Cotton Sedge

GREEN-FLOWERED WINTERGREEN

Pyrola chlorantha Sw.
Heath Family (Ericaceae)

Description: This is a 4–8"-tall herbaceous plant. The flower petals are pale green. The style is curved downward, sticking out beyond the petals on the lower part of the flower. Arranged in a raceme, the flowers are few (2–8), sparsely spaced, and distributed on all sides of the flowering stalk. The leaves are pale green on the upper surface and darker underneath. The usual shape of the leaves is round, but they are sometimes broadly egg shaped.

Bloom Season: June–August.

Habitat/Range: Shady woods of montane and subalpine forests.

Comments: *Pyrola is* Latin for "little pear," because of the pear-shaped leaves of some species. *Chlorantha* is a Greek word meaning "green-flowered." Species of *Pyrola* were used by American Indians externally to treat wounds, and internally for coughs, constipation, stomach problems, and to aid in childbirth.

Green-Flowered Wintergreen

ONE-SIDED WINTERGREEN

Pyrola secunda L.
(also *Orthilia secunda* [L.] House)
Heath Family (Ericaceae)

Description: This is a small (2–6" tall) plant of the forest floor. The flowers lie on one side of the arching flowering stalk, arranged in a raceme of 6–20 flowers. The flower petals are pale yellowish green to white. The style is straight, sticking out beyond the petals, with a flat, 5-lobed stigma. The margin of the leaves is finely toothed. Leaf shape varies from egg shaped and rounded at the base to rather round overall.

Bloom Season: June–August.

Habitat/Range: Montane and subalpine forests, often in deep shade.

Comments: *Orthilia* is from the Greek *orthos* (straight), in reference to the straight style. *Secunda* is derived from the Latin *secundus,* meaning "next" or "following," referring to the flowers, which follow one another on the same side of the stem. Wintergreens are medicinal herbs used as a diuretic to treat kidney weakness and chronic kidney infections.

One-Sided Wintergreen

Green Gentian

GREEN GENTIAN
Frasera speciosa Dougl.
(also *Swertia radiata* [Kell.] Kuntze)
Gentian Family (Gentianaceae)

Description: Green gentian was once thought to be a biennial, completing its life cycle in two years. However, botanical research has shown that the vegetative phase actually lasts 20–60 years or more. In the vegetative phase, the plant grows as a circle of large, radiating basal leaves at ground level. Each smooth leaf is 10–20" long and up to 6" wide. The relative age of the plants can be estimated by comparing the number of leaves per plant: the more leaves, the older the plant. When sufficient food reserves are stored, and the year is right, the plant expends all of its energy in flowering. The climactic flowering stalk is up to 6' tall. Whorls of 3–5 leaves are arranged on this stem in tiers, which get progressively smaller up the stem. The numerous flowers arise at the junctions of these leaves with the stem. Each flower is wheel shaped, with "spokes" consisting of 4 sepals, 4 petals, and 4 stamens surrounding a prominent, superior ovary. The petals are pale green, flecked with purple, and decorated at the base with a corona of fringe and a pair of hair-lined pits. Once reproduction is complete, the plant dies, leaving a straw-colored skeleton monument.

Bloom Season: June–August.

Habitat/Range: Grasslands and meadows, from the valleys to the alpine summits.

Comments: As a medicinal plant, green gentian is used as a bitter herb to stimulate the digestive system. However, since this plant only flowers once in its long life, collecting it before flowering effectively removes it from the population gene pool. And remember, it may be older than you.

SEASIDE ARROWGRASS
Triglochin maritimum L.
Arrowgrass Family (Juncaginaceae)

Description: The narrow leaves of this plant are grasslike, they are thicker and more fleshy than grasses. It has 6 greenish yellow floral parts and 6 stamens. Arrowgrass flowers are densely crowded in a long, cylindrical arrangement. The flowering stem is 1–3' tall, leafless, and twice the length of the basal leaves. As the fruit dries, it splits open into 6 segments that fall away, revealing a round, central axis.

Bloom Season: May–August.

Habitat/Range: Wet meadows, from the valleys to the subalpine forests.

Comments: *Triglochin* is named from the Greek *treis* (three) and *glochin* (point), because of the 3 points on the fruit of some arrowgrass species. Seaside arrowgrass is poisonous to livestock, causing death from cyanide poisoning. American Indians are said to have parched the seeds and eaten them, but do not try this at home.

Seaside Arrowgrass

Copper Bells

COPPER BELLS
Stenanthium occidentale Gray
Lily Family (Liliaceae)

Description: Copper bells are bulb-bearing lilies with primarily basal leaves and a single stem 4–16" tall. The bell-shaped flowers hang downward from the main stem on flower stalks ½–1" long in a raceme or panicle flower arrangement. The unusual greenish yellow to purplish green flowers resemble tarnished copper. Each flower has 3 petal-like sepals plus 3 petals (that is, 6 tepals), 6 stamens, and 3 styles. Upon maturity the ovary develops into a dry capsule with 3 slender beaks.

Bloom Season: June–August.

Habitat/Range: Wet, rocky places and meadows, from subalpine forests to the alpine.

Comments: *Stenanthium* comes from the Greek *stemos* (narrow) and *anthos* (flower), words that describe the narrow flower segments.

Green False Hellebore

GREEN FALSE HELLEBORE
Veratrum viride Ait.
Lily Family (Liliaceae)

Description: Green false hellebore is a 3–6'-tall, herbaceous plant with yellow-green to deep green flowers. The flowers are arranged in open panicles with several branches on the end of the main stem. The lower flower branches droop downward, as if they are wilting. Each small flower has 3 petal-like sepals, 3 petals, and 6 stamens. The distinctive leaves are pleated with fanlike folds and are quite large, with the largest leaves 12" long and 6" wide.

Bloom Season: June–September.

Habitat/Range: Swamps, streamsides, and seepage slopes, from the montane to the subalpine forests.

Comments: *Veratrum* is said to be derived from *vere* (true) and *ater* (black), because of the black rhizomes of some species. The Blackfeet and other Indian tribes were known to dig these rhizomes as a medicinal herb called "makes-you-sneeze-root." The shavings from the dry root were sniffed up the nose to relieve nasal congestion. Other American Indians used the plant as a permanent contraceptive and to treat snakebites. In Western medicine these practices seem very hazardous, considering the high toxicity of these plants. False hellebore is a dangerous, poisonous plant with potentially fatal results if ingested.

EARLY CORALROOT
Corallorhiza trifida Chatel
Orchid Family (Orchidaceae)

Description: This small (2–10" tall) orchid is leafless, but it has 2 or 3 tubular bracts that sheath the stem. The stems and bracts are yellowish green. The plant bears 3–15 flowers. These short-lived flowers have a white lip, sometimes with a few purple spots. The sepals and petals range from yellow to green and thrust forward past the lip.

Bloom Season: June–early August.

Habitat/Range: Montane and subalpine forest floors rich with organic matter.

Comments: Coralroots derive nutrients and energy by parasitizing fungi, that in turn parasitize trees and digest wood. The recycled wood is thus put to good use supporting these lovely plants. Early coralroot also has some chlorophyll in all of its plant parts, enabling it to capture the sun's energy through photosynthesis and supplement that derived from the fungi.

Early Coralroot

Northern Green Bog Orchid

NORTHERN GREEN BOG ORCHID
Habenaria hyperborea (L.) R. Br.
(also *Platanthera hyperborea* [L.] Lind.)
Orchid Family (Orchidaceae)

Description: Northern green bog orchid has numerous green flowers crowded in a dense, spikelike raceme in which the flowers overlap. The flowers have a long-tapering, entire (without teeth), strap-shaped lip petal. At the base of the lip petal is a tubular, cylindrical spur, about the same length as the lip petal. Numerous lance-shaped leaves overlap on the lower half of the 8–40"-tall stem.

Bloom Season: June–August.

Habitat/Range: Stream banks, bogs, and seepy slopes of the moist montane and subalpine forests.

Comments: In the Rockies, northern green bog orchid is most often mistaken for the frog orchis *(H. viridis)* and slender bog orchid *(H. saccata)*, which have pouchlike spurs. Frog orchis is further distinguished by the 3 teeth on the end of its lip petal.

Small Northern Bog Orchid

SMALL NORTHERN BOG ORCHID

Habenaria obtusata (Banks ex Pursh) Rich.
(also *Platanthera obtusata* [Banks ex Pursh] Lind.)
Orchid Family (Orchidaceae)

Description: The solitary leaf and small, greenish white flowers of this bog orchid make it easy to distinguish from others in the Rocky Mountains. The single leaf is oblong, blunt on the end, and gradually tapers toward the sheathing base. The stem is about 3–12" tall and bears 3–15 widely spaced flowers. The flowers have a long-tapering, strap-shaped lip petal, slightly upturned at the tip. The spur is also long-tapering and about as long as the blade of the lip petal.

Bloom Season: June–July.

Habitat/Range: Stream banks, bogs, and seepy slopes of the moist montane and subalpine forests.

Comments: *Platanthera* comes from the Greek *platys* (wide) and *anthera* (anther) and refers to the unusually wide anthers in these plants. Bog orchids are included in the genus *Habenaria* or *Platanthera*, depending on the floral manual consulted. Small northern bog orchid is pollinated by mosquitoes, which are abundant in the plant's habitat.

Large Round-Leaved Rein Orchid

LARGE ROUND-LEAVED REIN ORCHID
Habenaria orbiculata (Pursh) Torr.
(also *Platanthera orbiculata* [Pursh] Lind.)
Orchid Family (Orchidaceae)

Description: A pair of large (about 4" by 3"), nearly round leaves, flat on the ground, quickly distinguishes large round-leaved rein orchid. The leafless stem is 8–24" tall and graced with 5–25 greenish white, distinctly orchid flowers. Strap-shaped and long tapering, the lip petal has a long, curved spur from its base. The spur is much longer than the lip petal and is distinctly greenish at the tip, fading to a paler and translucent shade toward the base.

Bloom Season: June–August.

Habitat/Range: Mossy woods of the moist montane and subalpine forests, from Van-couver Island east across the Northern Rockies and boreal Canada to Nova Scotia and south down the Appalachian Mountains to Georgia.

Comments: Three moth species have been identified as pollinators for large round-leaved rein orchid, including two small gray moths and the larger, night-flying hawk moth. This species was first described to botanical science by Frederick Pursh (1774–1820), who described it in 1814 in his *Flora Americae Septentrionalis* as growing in shady beech woods on the mountains of Pennsylvania and Virginia, where it was known as "heal-all." Today this species is much too rare to consider using medicinally.

Northwest Twayblade

NORTHWEST TWAYBLADE
Listera caurina Piper
Orchid Family (Orchidaceae)

Description: Northwest twayblade has a pair of opposite leaves above the middle of the stem and a raceme of 5–25 tiny green flowers. The entire plant grows up to 14" tall. The leaves are dark bluish green and as large as 2" long and 1" wide. The flower includes a lip petal that is broadest on the end and gradually tapering to the base. Two darker green stripes on the lip petal terminate near the base, where there are two dark, shiny bulges that look like two black, beady eyes. Two tiny, hornlike projections arise from the base of these "eyes." The other sepals and petals are swept back away from the lip petal, like ears. The flower is reminiscent of a strange, short-horned, green cow that must belong to some forest leprechaun.

Bloom Season: June–August.

Habitat/Range: Mossy woods of the moist montane and subalpine forests.

Comments: *Listera* was named in honor of an English physician, Martin Lister (1638–1711). *Caurina* is from the Latin *caurinus* (of the northwest wind). Orchids are highly evolved plants that have developed specialized and complex reproductive systems. Twayblades have an unusual mechanism for ensuring cross-pollination. A trail of nectar on the lip attracts small insects and leads them to the base of the column where the stigma and anthers reside. Movement of the insect there triggers the plant to forcefully eject a droplet of liquid glue onto the insect, and some pollen becomes firmly fixed to the droplet. Fright-ened by this action, the insect flies away to another flower, where the pollen is then deposited on the stigma at the base of the column.

HEART-LEAVED TWAYBLADE
Listera cordata (L.) R. Br.
Orchid Family (Orchidaceae)

Description: The lip petal of heart-leaved twayblade is distinctly forked into 2 pointed lobes, about halfway from the base, where there are 2 tiny prongs. A raceme of 5–15 tiny green flowers is arranged near the tip of the stem. The entire plant grows up to 10" tall, with a pair of opposite leaves about midway on the stem. The leaves are usually less than 1½" long, heart shaped or triangular, with a short bristle on the tip.

Bloom Season: June–August.

Habitat/Range: Damp, mossy woods of the moist montane and subalpine forests. The most widely distributed *Listera* species, ranging around the boreal region of the earth in the northern hemisphere.

Comments: Heart-leaved twayblade was first collected in North America in the Rocky Mountains near Spanish Basin, Montana, in 1895.

Heart-Leaved Twayblade

COMMON PLANTAIN
Plantago major L.
Plantain Family (Plantaginaceae)

Description: This is a perennial plant with large basal leaves (about 5" long and 3" wide). The plants are sometimes called "ribgrass" because of the prominent, parallel veins of the leaf. The leafless stem is about 6" tall, with a dense, narrow, cylindrical flower arrangement on the end. The numerous flowers are tiny and unnoticeable without a hand lens. The petals are thin, dry, and turn downward on the end. The 4 stamens extend well beyond the petals.

Bloom Season: May–August.

Habitat/Range: Introduced; in disturbed places, from the valleys to the montane forests.

Comments: American Indians used plantain externally to treat wounds and infections and to draw out thorns or splinters. It was also taken internally for colds and various stomach complaints. A commonly used bulk laxative is made from the seed of *P. psyllium*. Herbalists have long relied on common plantain leaves for soothing inflamed mucous membranes, from sore throats to hemorrhoids.

Common Plantain

Mountain Sorrel

MOUNTAIN SORREL
Oxyria digyna (L.) Hill
Buckwheat Family (Polygonaceae)

Description: The abundant kidney-shaped basal leaves of this plant are distinctive. A leafy sheath (stipule) encloses the stem at the attachment of the leaf petiole. The stems are 4–16" tall, crowded with numerous flowers and fruit. The flowers are green, tinged with red, and consist of 4 floral (tepal) segments (2 narrow, 2 broad), 6 stamens, and an ovary with a curious, fringed stigma. The floral segments are tiny when in bloom, but they expand as the fertilized ovary rapidly grows into a flattened and winged fruit about ¼" long.

Bloom Season: July–August.

Habitat/Range: Rock crevices on subalpine and alpine ridges.

Comments: *Oxyria* comes from the Greek *oxys*, meaning "sharp." The juice of mountain sorrel is sharply acidic, like lemon juice. The foliage is edible, and a taste of the leaves is a refreshing treat. However, the oxalic acid, which is responsible for the sharp taste, is known to change to a precipitate of calcium oxalate in the bloodstream, where it tends to impede kidney function.

Western Goldthread

WESTERN GOLDTHREAD
Coptis occidentalis (Nutt.) T. & G.
Buttercup Family (Ranunculaceae)

Description: The shiny, evergreen leaves of western goldthread often form a deep green ground cover on the forest floor. The leaves are compound, having 3 leaflets; each with 3 primary lobes and a sharply toothed margin. The short-lived and inconspicuous flowers also occur in threes, in an open arrangement on the end of a stalk about 4–8" tall, or about the same height as the leaves. Each flower consists of 5–7 narrow, lancelike sepals and an equal number of petals. There is a small nectar gland near the base of each petal.

Bloom Season: May–August.

Habitat/Range: Cool, moist woods of the montane and lower subalpine forests.

Comments: *Coptis* was derived from the Greek *kopto* (cut), in reference to the cuts on the leaflets that form the lobes. "Goldthread" refers to the bright yellow inner bark of the roots, valued as an herbal medicine for treating mouth ulcers, healing cold sores, and improving digestion. A related species, three-leaved goldthread *(C. trifolia)* is distinguished by having 3 leaflets that are not again appreciably lobed, much broader sepals, and hollow petals with a nectar gland on the tip. That species is found in the Northern Rockies of British Columbia and Alberta.

Cascara Buckthorn

CASCARA BUCKTHORN
Rhamnus purshiana DC.
(also *Frangula purshiana* [DC.] J.G. Cooper)

Buckthorn Family (Rhamnaceae)

Description: A rather large shrub or small tree (up to 33' tall), cascara buckthorn has inconspicuous greenish flowers that develop into purplish black berries as they mature. The flowers are arranged in clusters of 8–50 from the axils of the leaves. Each flower consists of a cuplike enlargement of the base of the sepals (hypanthium), with 5 pointed sepal lobes. The tiny petals are alternate with the sepals, appearing just inside the notch between sepals. The flowers may be unisexual or bisexual; some having only stamens or pistil, and some having both. The alderlike leaves have more than 8 prominent lateral veins per leaf half. The curious buds are naked, lacking any bud scales.

Bloom Season: April–June.

Habitat/Range: Streamsides and mixed woods of the valleys and moist montane forests.

Comments: The bark of cascara buckthorn and other *Rhamnus* species has a long history of herbal use as a laxative. American Indians also prepared a poultice from it and applied it to wounds. The name *purshiana* is in honor of the early botanist Frederick Pursh (1774–1820), who first described cascara buckthorn for botanical science in *Flora Americae Septentrionalis* (1814). In this book Pursh states: "Berries purple, very highly esteemed by the Indians of that country." He is thus describing the specimen collected on May 29, 1806, by Meriwether Lewis along the Clearwater River.

Sweet-Scented Bedstraw

SWEET-SCENTED BEDSTRAW
Galium triflorum Michx.
Madder Family (Rubiaceae)

Description: A low, trailing perennial herb of the forest floor, sweet-scented bedstraw's leaves occur in whorls of 6, which radiate from a common point on the stems. Each narrow leaf is less than 2" long, tipped with a sharp, needlelike point. A sweet aroma, like vanilla or sweetgrass, is emitted from the leaves. The tiny, greenish white flowers are in groups of 3 and originate in the leaf axils, with 4 petals per flower.

Bloom Season: June–August.

Habitat/Range: Streamsides and damp, often dense woods of the valleys, moist montane, and subalpine forests.

Comments: *Galium* is from the Greek *gala* (milk); a European species was used for curdling milk. It was named "bedstraw" for the practice of using the plant as a stuffing for pillows and mattresses. Sweet-scented bedstraw is most likely to be mistaken for cleavers *(G. aparine)*, which has 3–5 flowers from the axil of the 6 or 8 whorled leaves. Both species have stiff, hooked hairs on the stem angles and on the margin and lower midrib of the leaves. However, those of cleavers are much more prominent. Cleavers is further distinguished by being an introduced, weedy annual plant often growing in more open disturbed habitats. Cleavers is a medicinal herb, long used by herbalists to tone the lymph system and treat inflammations of the urinary tract.

Tweedy's Willow

TWEEDY'S WILLOW
Salix tweedyi (Bebb) Ball
Willow Family (Salicaceae)

Description: Almost everyone recognizes willows as a group and knows the "pussy willow" flower clusters (catkins) that they bear. Distinguishing individual species of willow requires careful attention to detail (and a hand lens). Willow flowers are tiny and unisexual, with male and female flowers on separate plants. An individual flower consists simply of 2 stamens (male) or a pistil (female). Attached to the base of each flower is a scalelike bract, often covered with hair. Tweedy's willow has scales that are distinctly black and covered with dense, long hair. The pistil of its female flower is smooth (hairless) and has an unusually long style (up to ⅛" or more). The catkins are attached directly to the twigs, often from the end of the previous year's twig growth. The leaves are broad, equally dark green on both surfaces, and thinly clad with long hairs. This is a tall shrub, up to 9' or more, with hairy and unusually stout twigs. The "pussy willow" catkins often appear before the leaves, or just as they are breaking bud.

Bloom Season: June–early July.

Habitat/Range: Stream banks, lakeshores, and wet meadows in high subalpine forests.

Comments: *Salix* is said to be derived from the Celtic *sal* (near) and *lis* (water), because it is frequently found near water. Tweedy's willow is named in honor of Frank Tweedy (1854–1937), who collected the type specimen at the head of Big Goose Creek in the Bighorn Mountains of Wyoming in 1896.

Rock Willow

ROCK WILLOW
Salix vestita Pursh
Willow Family (Salicaceae)

Description: Rock willow has strongly veined, leathery leaves that are dark green, smooth and "shiny" on the upper surface, and covered with white silky hair on the lower surface. Tiny glands are scattered on the leaf margin, which is slightly rolled toward the underside of the leaf. Leaves are egg shaped, more or less rounded on the tip. The flower-bearing catkins often extend from the tip of the twigs. Bracts of the unisexual flowers are brown, with long, silky, straight hair.

Bloom Season: July–September.

Habitat/Range: Upper subalpine forests and alpine.

Comments: Willows have a long history of medicinal use from the time of the Greek physician Dioscordes in the 1st century A.D., if not earlier. American Indians also used willow to relieve pain and other complaints. The bark contains salicin, which changes to salicylic acid when ingested. Salicylic acid is effective in treating skin diseases and in bringing relief for headaches, neuralgia, and arthritis. In 1899, the Bayer Company synthesized aspirin in the laboratory as a substitute for salicylic acid, with the side effect of stomach irritation much reduced.

Bog Saxifrage

COMMON CATTAIL
Typha latifolia L.
Cattail Family (Typhaceae)

Description: The long, flat, straplike leaves and the cylindrical, dense flower masses of cattails are familiar to all. Cattails, also know as "flags," have unisexual flowers. The top ⅓–½ of the "cattail" consists of pollen-bearing male flowers. The bottom portion consists of the tightly packed pistillate flowers, which are green when young but turn dark brown as the plant matures. In the common cattail the male and female segments are normally right next to one another, with no space in between.

Bloom Season: June–August.

Habitat/Range: Streams and lakes, from the valleys to the montane forests.

Comments: Every part of the cattail plant was important to the American Indians. The pollen, the young flower spikes, and the long rhizomes were eaten. The leaves were woven into mats. On November 21, 1805, near the mouth of the Columbia River, William Clark recorded in his journals: "we also purchased hats made of Grass &c. of those Indians, Some very handsom mats made of flags."

BOG SAXIFRAGE
Saxifraga oregana Howell
Saxifrage Family (Saxifragaceae)

Description: Bog saxifrage is 1–2' tall, with 2–7"-long leaves that originate from the base. The leaves are usually widest above the middle and taper gradually to the base. The stems are leafless, often purple, and covered with fine, gland-tipped hairs. About 100 flowers are arranged in small clusters on the stems. Each tiny flower has 5 sepals, up to 5 petals, 10 stamens, and a pistil parted into 2 segments above the middle. The petals are greenish white when present but are usually absent.

Bloom Season: May–August.

Habitat/Range: Wet meadows or along streams of the subalpine forests and alpine tundra.

Comments: The name *Saxifraga* comes from the Latin *saxum* (rock) and *frango* (to break). According to the doctrine of signatures, a physical character of a plant indicated which illness it could heal. Early herbalists believed that the granular bulblets found in certain species of saxifrage indicated that it would dissolve urinary stones.

Common Cattail

Nettle

NETTLE
Urtica dioica L.
Nettle Family (Urticaceae)

Description: Unfortunately, this plant is more often identified accidentally by touch (ouch!) than by sight! The leaves and stems are covered with stinging hairs that contain histamine-like substances causing acute allergic dermatitis. The plants often grow to 3' or more tall. They have opposite, toothed leaves and inconspicuous, green, unisexual flowers from the leaf axils.

Bloom Season: June–September.

Habitat/Range: Streams and seepy slopes, from valleys to the subalpine forests.

Comments: *Urtica* comes from Latin *urere* (to burn), which describes the sensation on the skin when the plant is touched. Surpris-ingly, the plant is considered an important edible and medicinal plant, rendered harmless by cooking. Nettle greens are rich in minerals, vitamins, and protein. Modern herbalists value the plant for its astringent and diuretic properties, especially for treating internal bleeding or water retention.

Lodgepole Pine Dwarf Mistletoe

LODGEPOLE PINE DWARF MISTLETOE

Arceuthobium americanum Nutt.
Mistletoe Family (Viscaceae)

Description: It takes a keen observer to notice these small parasitic shrubs growing out of the branches of lodgepole pine trees. The delicate, branching stems are seldom over 2" long, or about the length of the needles of the pine tree. There are no broad leaves as there are on Christmas mistletoe, only pairs of opposite scales, joined at the base. The unisexual flowers are equally obscure, consisting of 2–4 greenish tepals and either anthers or pistils. The male (staminate) flower, has a single anther attached directly to the inner surface of each tepal. The tepals of the female (pistillate) flower are attached to the ovary. The ovary requires a full year to progress from flowering to mature fruit.

Bloom Season: April–July.

Habitat/Range: This species of dwarf mistletoe is parasitic on lodgepole pine *(Pinus contorta)* but has also been reported on whitebark pine *(P. albicaulis)*. There are 2 other dwarf mistletoe species, which are parasitic on several other coniferous trees in the Northern Rockies.

Comments: As the ovary of dwarf mistletoe matures, pressure builds up in the tissues until it explodes, forcefully ejecting the seed across distances of 30' or more. The seed has a sticky coating, which adheres to the bark of a host conifer, where it will germinate and penetrate the bark. Here the dwarf mistletoe plant establishes its parasitic relationship, with its "root system" in the inner bark, drawing nutrients from the tissues of the host tree. The response of the host tree is to form swellings on the infected stems and abnormal, dense masses of stems called witches'-brooms.

GLOSSARY

Achene. A small, dry, one-seeded fruit that does not split open upon maturity.

Alternate. Placed singly along a stem or axis, one after another, usually each successive item on a different side from the previous; often used in reference to the arrangement of leaves on a stem.

Angular. Having angles or sharp corners; generally used in reference to stems, in contrast to round stems.

Annual. A plant completing its life cycle, from seed germination to production of new seeds, within a year and then dying.

Anther. The portion of the stamen that bears the pollen.

Awn. A slender, stiff bristle or fiber attached at its base to another part, such as a leaf tip.

Axil. The upper angle formed between the main stem and any organ that arises from it, like a leaf.

Axillary. Situated in the axil.

Banner. The upper petal of a typical flower of the bean family (Fabaceae). Another name for standard.

Basal. At the base or bottom of; generally used in reference to leaves.

Biennial. A plant that completes its life cycle in two years; normally not producing flowers during the first year.

Bog. Wet, spongy ground, often dominated by sphagnum mosses.

Boreal. Northern.

Bract. A reduced or modified leaf, often associated with flowers.

Bractlet. A small bract.

Bristle. A stiff hair, usually erect or curving away from its attachment point.

Bulb. An underground plant part derived from a short, usually rounded shoot that is covered with scales or leaves.

Calyx. The outer set of flower parts, composed of the sepals, which may be separate or joined together; usually green.

Capsule. A dry fruit that releases seeds through splits or holes.

Catkin. A spikelike flower arrangement in which the flowers are unisexual and often hang downward.

Circumboreal. Found around the world at high latitudes or elevations.

Circumpolar. Found around the world in alpine or polar regions.

Clasping. Surrounding or partially wrapping around a stem or branch.

Cluster. Any grouping or close arrangement of individual flowers that is not dense and continuous.

Compound leaf. A leaf that is divided into 2 to many leaflets, each of which may look like a complete leaf but which lacks buds. Compound leaves may have leaflets arranged along an axis like the pinnae of a feather or radiating from a common point like the fingers on a hand.

Corm. An enlarged base or stem resembling a bulb.

Corolla. The set of flower parts interior to the sepals composed of the petals, which may be free or united; often brightly colored.

Corymb. A broad, flat-topped flower arrangement in which the outer flowers open first.

Cyme. A broad, flat-topped flower arrangement in which the inner, central flowers open first.

Dioecious. Having unisexual flowers, with male and female flowers borne on separate plants.

Disk flower. Any of the small, tubular flowers in the central portion of the flower head of many plants in the aster family (Asteraceae).

Disturbed. Referring to habitats that have been impacted by actions or processes associated with European settlement such as ditching, grading, or long intervals of high-intensity grazing.

Draw. A small, elongate depression with gentle side slopes in an upland landscape resembling a miniature valley or ravine.

Ecosystem. A complex interacting system of organisms and their environment.

Entire. A leaf edge that is smooth, without teeth or notches.

Erect. Upright, standing vertically or directly perpendicular from a surface.

Escape. A plant that has been cultivated in an area and spread from there into the wild.

Family. A group of plants having biologically similar features such as flower anatomy, fruit type, etc.

Fellfield. An area within the alpine zone made up primarily of broken rock, possibly interspersed with accumulations of soils and plant life.

Fen. A specialized wetland permanently supplied with mineralized groundwater.

Filament. The part of the stamen that supports the anther; also can refer to any similar threadlike structure.

Flower head. As used in this guide, a dense and continuous group of flowers without obvious branches or space between them; used especially in reference to the aster family (Asteraceae).

Follicle. A dry fruit that splits open along one suture at maturity.

Forb. A nonwoody, herbaceous plant.

Generic name. A name applied to a group of closely related species, for example, the generic name *Viola*, is applied to all the violet species.

Gland. A bump, projection, or round protuberance, usually colored differently than the object on which it occurs, and often sticky or producing sticky or oily secretions.

Herbaceous. Having a fleshy stem; not woody.

Hood. A curving or folded, petal-like structure interior to the petals and exterior to the stamens in certain flowers, including milkweeds. Since most milkweeds have petals that are bent backward, the hoods are typically the most prominent feature of the flowers.

Hooded. Arching over and partially concealing or shielding.

Horn. A small, round, or flattened projection from the hood of a milkweed flower.

Host. As used here, a plant from which a parasitic plant derives nourishment.

Hypanthium. An enlargement of the floral receptacle, bearing on its rim the sepals, petals, and stamens.

Incomplete flower. A flower lacking sepals, petals, stamens, pistils, or one or more other parts.

Inferior ovary. An ovary with the sepals, petals, and stamens attached on the top.

Inflorescence. The way the flowers are arranged on an individual plant.

Infusion. A tealike beverage made by steeping plant parts (usually leaves) in hot water.

Irregular flower. A flower that is not radially symmetrical, with petals that differ in shape and size.

Keel. A sharp, lengthwise fold or ridge, referring particularly to the two fused petals forming the lower lip in a typical flower of the bean family (Fabaceae).

Krummholz. The horizontal, wind-deformed tree growth found at timberline; the German word for "crooked wood."

Leaflet. A distinct, leaflike segment of a compound leaf.

Lobe. A segment of an incompletely divided plant part, typically rounded; often used in reference to leaves.

Margin. The edge of a leaf or petal.

Mat. Densely interwoven or tangled, low plant growth.

Mesic. Referring to a habitat that is well drained but generally moist throughout most of the growing season.

Monoecious. Having unisexual flowers, with separate male and female flowers on the same plant.

Opposite. Paired directly across from one another along a stem or axis.

Ovary. The portion of the flower where the seeds develop, usually a swollen area below the style (if present) and stigma.

Ovate. Egg shaped.

Ovule. The organ that becomes the seed after fertilization.

Palmate. Spreading like the fingers of a hand; usually used in reference to leaf shape.

Panicle. A flower arrangement with a central axis with branches that are again branched before bearing a flower.

Pappus. Thistledown; the scalelike or fine bristlelike sepals of flowers in the aster family (Asteraceae).

Parallel. Side by side, approximately the same distance apart, for the entire length; often used in reference to veins or to the edges of a leaf.

Perennial. A plant that normally lives for three or more years.

Petal. A component part of the corolla, the inner floral envelope, often the most brightly colored and visible part of the flower.

Petiole. The stem of a leaf.

Pinnate. Having leaflets, lobes, or other divisions along each side of a leaf stalk, resembling a feather.

Pistil. The seed-producing, or female, unit of a flower, consisting of the ovary, style (if present), and stigma; a flower may have one to several separate pistils.

Pod. A dry fruit that splits open along the edges.

Pollen. The tiny, often powdery, male reproductive microspores formed in the stamens and necessary for sexual reproduction in flowering plants.

Prickle. A small, sharp, spinelike outgrowth from the outer surface.

Raceme. A flower arrangement with a central axis along which simple pedicels of equal length bear flowers.

Ray. The radiating branches of an umbel.

Ray flower. A flower in the aster family (Asteraceae) having a single, strap-shaped corolla resembling one flower petal; ray flowers may surround the disk flowers in a flower head, or, in some species, such as dandelions, the flower heads may be composed entirely of ray flowers.

Regular flower. A radially symmetrical flower whose petals are all alike.

Resinous. Containing or covered with sticky to semisolid, clearish sap or gum.

Rhizome. An underground stem that produces roots and shoots at the nodes.

Rosette. A dense cluster of basal leaves from a common underground part, often in a flattened, circular arrangement.

Runner. A long, trailing stem.

Sap. The juice within a plant.

Sedge. Any of the many members of the sedge family (Cyperaceae); many of these grasslike plants grow in wetlands.

Sepal. A component part of the calyx, the outer floral envelope; typically green but sometimes enlarged and brightly colored.

Serrate. Possessing sharp, forward-pointing teeth.

Shrub. A multistemmed, woody plant.

Simple leaf. A leaf that has a single leaflike blade, although this may be lobed or divided.

Specific name. The second portion of a scientific name, identifying a particular species; for instance, in Colorado columbine *(Aquilegia coerula),* the specific name is *coerula.* Also called the specific epithet.

Spike. An elongate, unbranched cluster of stalkless or nearly stalkless flowers.

Spine. A thin, stiff, sharp-pointed projection.

Spreading. Extending outward from; at right angles to; widely radiating.

Spur. A hollow, tubular projection from the base of a petal or sepal; often producing nectar.

Stalk. As used here, the stem supporting the leaf, flower, or flower cluster.

Stalkless. Lacking a stalk. A stalkless leaf is attached directly to the stem at the leaf base.

Stamen. The male unit of a flower, which produces the pollen; typically consisting of a long filament with a pollen-producing tip (the anther).

Standard. The upper petal of a typical flower of the bean family (Fabaceae). Another name for banner.

Steppe. An arid land with drought-tolerant vegetation.

Sterile. In flowers, referring to an inability to produce seeds; in habitats, referring to poor nutrient and mineral availability in the soil.

Stigma. The portion of the pistil receptive to pollination; usually at the top of the style, and often appearing fuzzy or sticky.

Stipule. A bract or leafy structure occurring in pairs at the base of a leaf stalk.

Style. The portion of the pistil between the ovary and the stigma; typically a slender stalk.

Subspecies. A group of plants within a species that has consistent, repeating, genetic, and structural distinctions.

Succulent. Thickened and fleshy or juicy.

Superior ovary. An ovary that is above the sepals, petals, and stamens, which are attached at its base.

Swale. A depression or shallow hollow in the land, typically moist.

Taproot. A stout, main root extending downward.

Tendril. A slender, coiled, or twisted filament with which climbing plants attach to their support.

Tepals. Petals and sepals that cannot be distinguished from each other.

Ternate. Arranged in threes, as the leaflets of a compound leaf.

Timberline. The zone of limit of tree growth on the landscape, where the forest and alpine zone (or prairie) meet.

Toothed. Bearing teeth or sharply angled projections along the edge.

Trifoliate. Having three leaves.

Tuber. A thick, creeping underground stem; sometimes also used for a thickened portion of a root.

Tubercle. A small, rounded projection, as on a cactus or on a plant root.

Tubular. Narrow, cylindrical, and tubelike.

Umbel. A flower arrangement in which the flower stalks (pedicels) have a common point of attachment, like an umbrella.

Variety. A group of plants within a species that has a distinct range, habitat, or structure.

Vein. A small tube that carries water, minerals, and nutrients.

Whorl. Three or more parts attached at the same point along a stem or axis and often surrounding the stem.

Wing. One of two side petals flanking the keel in a typical flower of the bean family (Fabaceae).

Winged. Having thin bands of leaflike tissue attached edgewise along the length.

Woody. Firm-stemmed or branched.

NATIVE PLANT DIRECTORY

To find out more about wildflowers and other plants native to the Northern Rockies, you may wish to contact the native plant societies and natural heritage data centers listed below. The state and provincial native plant societies are diverse groups of amateur and professional plant enthusiasts organized to share information about the study and conservation of plants native to their states. The natural heritage data centers maintain comprehensive databases that list the rare, threatened, and endangered plants, animals, and ecosystems within their states and provinces.

NATIVE PLANT SOCIETIES

Alberta
Alberta Native Plant Council
Box 52099, Garneau Postal Outlet
Edmonton, AB T6G 2T5
www.anpc.ab.ca/

British Columbia
Native Plant Society of British Columbia
2012 William Street
Vancouver, BC V5L 2X6

Idaho
Idaho Native Plant Society
P.O. Box 9451
Boise, ID 83707-3451

Montana
Montana Native Plant Society
P.O. Box 8783
Missoula, MT 59807-8783

Washington
Washington Native Plant Society
P.O. Box 28690
Seattle, WA 98118
www.wnps.org

NATURAL HERITAGE DATA CENTERS

Alberta
Alberta Natural Heritage Information Centre
Alberta Environment
2nd Floor, Oxbridge Place
9820 - 106th Street
Edmonton, AB T5K 2J6
780-427-5209
www.gov.ab.ca/env/parks/anhic/anhic.html/

British Columbia
British Columbia Conservation Data Centre
Ministry of Environment, Lands and Parks
P.O. Box 9344, Station Provincial
Government
Victoria, BC V8W 9M1
250-356-0928
www.elp.gov.bc.ca/rib/wis/cdc/

Idaho
Idaho Conservation Data Center
Idaho Department of Fish and Game
600 South Walnut/P.O. Box 25
Boise, ID 83707-0025
208-334-3402
www2.state.id.us/fishgame/cdchome.htm

Montana
Montana Natural Heritage Program
State Library Building
1515 East Sixth Avenue
Helena, MT 59620
406-444-3009
www.nris.state.mt.us/mtnhp/

Washington
Washington Natural Heritage Program
Department of Natural Resources
P.O. Box 47016
Olympia, WA 98504-7016
360-902-1340
www.wa.gov/dnr/htdocs/fr/nhp/

SELECTED REFERENCES

Arno, Stephen F. 1979. *Forest Regions of Montana.* USDA Forest Service Intermountain Forest and Range Experiment Station, Research Paper INT-218.

Bailey, Robert G. 1995. *Description of the Ecoregions of the United States.* 2d ed. USDA Forest Service Misc. Pub. no. 1391. Washington, D.C.

Cooper, Stephen V., Kenneth E. Neiman, Robert Steele, and David W. Roberts. 1987. *Forest Habitat Types of Northern Idaho: A Second Approximation.* USDA Forest Service Intermountain Research Station, General Technical Report INT-236.

Daubenmire, R., and Jean B. Daubenmire. 1968. *Forest Vegetation of Eastern Washington and Northern Idaho.* Washington Agricultural Experiment Station, Washington State University.

Davis, Ray J. 1952. *Flora of Idaho.* Dubuque, Iowa: Wm. C. Brown.

Dorn, Robert D. 1984. *Vascular Plants of Montana.* Cheyenne, Wyo.: Mountain West Publishing.

Dowden, Anne Ophelia. 1978. *State Flowers.* New York: Crowell.

Featherly, H. I. 1965. *Taxonomic Terminology of the Higher Plants.* New York: Hafner Publishing.

Furman, T. E., and J. M. Trappe. 1971. "Phylogeny and Ecology of Mycotropic Achlorophyllous Angiosperms." *Quarterly Review of Biology* 46:219–25.

Garman, E. H. 1973. *The Trees and Shrubs of British Columbia.* Handbook no. 31. Victoria: British Columbia Provincial Museum.

Harrington, H. D. 1967. *Edible Native Plants of the Rocky Mountains.* Albuquerque: University of New Mexico Press.

Hart, Jeff. 1976. *Montana: Native Plants and Early Peoples.* Helena: Montana Historical Society.

Hitchcock, C. Leo, and Arthur Cronquist. 1973. *Flora of the Pacific Northwest.* Seattle: University of Washington Press.

Hitchcock, C. Leo, Arthur Cronquist, Marion Ownbey, and J. W. Thompson. 1955–1969. *Vascular Plants of the Pacific Northwest.* 5 vols. Seattle: University of Washington Press.

Hoffmann, David. 1983. *The Holistic Herbal.* The Park, Forres, Scotland: Findhorn Press.

Hopkins, A. D. *Periodical events and natural law as guides to agricultural research and practice.* U.S.D.A. Monthly Rev., Supp. No. 9, 1918.

Inouye, D. W., and O. R. Taylor Jr. 1980. "Variation in Generation Time in *Frasera speciosa* (Gentianaceae), a Long-lived Perennial Monocarp." Oecologia 47:171–74.

Johnston, Alex. 1987. *Plants and the Blackfoot.* Lethbridge, Alta.: Lethbridge Historical Society.

Kingsbury, John M. 1964. *Poisonous Plants of the United States and Canada.* Englewood Cliffs, N.J.: Prentice-Hall.

Kuijt, Job. 1982. *A Flora of Waterton Lakes National Park.* Edmonton: University of Alberta Press.

Lackschewitz, Klaus. 1986. *Plants of West-Central Montana—Identification and Ecology: Annotated Checklist.* USDA Forest Service Intermountain Research Station, General Technical Report INT-217.

Layser, Earle F. 1980. *Flora of Pend Oreille County, Washington.* Pullman: Washington State University Cooperative Extension.

Lesica, Peter. 1985. *Checklist of the Vascular Plants of Glacier National Park, Montana, U.S.A.* Montana Academy of Sciences Supplement to the Proceedings, vol. 44, Monograph no. 4.

Lewis, Walter H., and Memory P. F. Elvin-Lewis. 1977. *Medical Botany: Plants Affecting Man's Health.* New York: John Wiley and Sons.

Mantas, Maria. 1999. *Vascular Plant Checklist for the Flathead National Forest.* USDA Forest Service, Flathead National Forest.

Moerman, Daniel E. 1998. *Native American Ethnobotany.* Portland: Timber Press.

Moore, Michael. 1993. *Medicinal Plants of the Pacific West.* Santa Fe: Red Crane Books.

Morin, Nancy R., ed. 1993–1997. *Flora of North America.* Vols. 1–3. Oxford: Oxford University Press.

Moss, E. H. 1959. *Flora of Alberta.* Toronto: University of Toronto Press.

Ody, Penelope. 1993. *The Complete Medicinal Herbal.* London: Dorling Kindersley.

Parish, Roberta, Ray Coupé, and Dennis Lloyd, eds. 1996. *Plants of Southern Interior British Columbia.* Vancouver: Lone Pine Publishing.

Patterson, Patricia A., Kenneth E. Neiman, and Jonalea R. Tonn. 1985. *Field Guide to Forest Plants of Northern Idaho.* USDA Forest Service Intermountain Research Station, General Technical Report INT-180.

Pfister, Robert D., Bernard L. Kovalchik, Stephen F. Arno, and Richard C. Presby. *Forest Habitat Types of Montana.* USDA Forest Service Intermountain Forest and Range Experiment Station, General Technical Report INT-34. Ogden, Utah.

Reese, Rick. 1981. *Montana Mountain Ranges.* Helena: Montana Magazine.

Strickler, Dee, Zoe Strickler, and Anne Morley. 1997. *Northwest Penstemons: Eighty Species of Penstemon Native to the Pacific Northwest.* Columbia Falls, Mont.: Flower Press.

Szczawinski, Adam F. 1962. *The Heather Family of British Columbia.* Handbook no. 19. Victoria: British Columbia Provincial Museum.

Williams, Kim. 1984. *Eating Wild Plants.* Missoula, Mont.: Mountain Press.

Wuerthner, George. 1986. *Idaho Mountain Ranges.* Helena, Mont.: American Geographic Publishing.

INDEX

ABOUT THE AUTHOR

Wayne Phillips, formerly a Forest Service ecologist, range manager, and forester, is now devoting his time to teaching and writing about the flora of the Rocky Mountains and Great Plains. He has taught botany and wildflower classes at the Yellowstone Institute in Yellowstone National Park since 1982. His teaching experience also includes botany classes as a faculty affiliate at the University of Montana, Montana State University–Northern, and the University of Great Falls. He is currently the president of the Montana Native Plant Society.

Wayne's hobbies include ethnobotany, herbalism, wildflower photography, canoeing, and mountaineering. His ongoing botanical studies include collecting and photographing all of the plant species that were collected and described by Meriwether Lewis in 1804 to 1806. He is contributing this collection to the Lewis and Clark Expedition Interpretive Center in Great Falls, Montana. Wayne is also the author of *Central Rocky Mountain Wildflowers* (Falcon Publishing, 1999).

FALCON GUIDES ® Leading the way™

FalconGuides® are available for where-to-go hiking, mountain biking, rock climbing, walking, scenic driving, fishing, rockhounding, paddling, birding, wildlife viewing, and camping. We also have FalconGuides on essential outdoor skills and subjects and field identification. The following titles are currently available, but this list grows every year. For a free catalog with a complete list of titles, call FALCON toll-free at 1-800-582-2665.

BIRDING GUIDES
Birding Georgia
Birding Illinois
Birding Minnesota
Birding Montana
Birding Northern California
Birding Texas
Birding Utah

PADDLING GUIDES
Paddling Minnesota
Paddling Montana
Paddling Okefenokee
Paddling Oregon
Paddling Yellowstone & Grand
  Teton National Parks

WALKING
Walking Colorado Springs
Walking Denver
Walking Portland
Walking Seattle
Walking St. Louis
Walking San Francisco
Walking Virginia Beach

CAMPING GUIDES
Camping Arizona
Camping California's
  National Forests
Camping Colorado
Camping Oregon
Camping Southern California
Camping Washington
Recreation Guide to Washington
  National Forests

FIELD GUIDES
Bitterroot: Montana State Flower
Canyon Country Wildflowers
Central Rocky Mountain
  Wildflowers
Chihuahuan Desert Wildflowers
Great Lakes Berry Book
New England Berry Book
Ozark Wildflowers
Pacific Northwest Berry Book
Plants of Arizona
Rare Plants of Colorado
Rocky Mountain Berry Book
Scats & Tracks of the Pacific
  Coast States
Scats & Tracks of the Rocky Mtns.
Sierra Nevada Wildflowers
Southern Rocky Mountain
  Wildflowers
Tallgrass Prairie Wildflowers
Western Trees

ROCKHOUNDING GUIDES
Rockhounding Arizona
Rockhounding California
Rockhounding Colorado
Rockhounding Montana
Rockhounding Nevada
Rockhounding New Mexico
Rockhounding Texas
Rockhounding Utah
Rockhounding Wyoming

HOW-TO GUIDES
Avalanche Aware
Backpacking Tips
Bear Aware
Desert Hiking Tips
Hiking with Dogs
Hiking with Kids
Mountain Lion Alert
Reading Weather
Route Finding
Using GPS
Wild Country Companion
Wilderness First Aid
Wilderness Survival

MORE GUIDEBOOKS
Backcountry Horseman's
  Guide to Washington
Family Fun in Montana
Family Fun in Yellowstone
Exploring Canyonlands & Arches
  National Parks
Exploring Hawaii's Parklands
Exploring Mount Helena
Exploring Southern California
  Beaches
Hiking Hot Springs of the Pacific
  Northwest
Touring Arizona Hot Springs
Touring California & Nevada
  Hot Springs
Touring Colorado Hot Springs
Touring Montana and Wyoming
  Hot Springs
Trail Riding Western Montana
Wilderness Directory
Wild Montana
Wild Utah
Wild Virginia

■ *To order any of these books, check with your local bookseller*
*or call FALCON ® at **1-800-582-2665**.*
Visit us on the world wide web at:
www.Falcon.com

FALCON®

FALCONGUIDES ® Leading the Way™

---

www.Falcon.com

Since 1979, Falcon® has brought you the best in outdoor recreational guidebooks. Now you can access that same reliable and accurate information online.

❏ Browse our online catalog for the latest Falcon releases on hiking, climbing, biking, scenic driving, and wildlife viewing as well as our Insiders' travel and relocation guides. Our online catalog is updated weekly.

❏ A Tip of the Week from one of our guidebooks or how-to guides. Each Monday we post a new tip that covers anything from how to cross a rushing stream to reading contour lines on a topo map.

❏ A chance to Meet our Staff with photos and short biographies of Falcon staff.

❏ Outdoor forums where you can exchange ideas and tips with other outdoor enthusiasts.

❏ Also Falcon screensavers and panoramic photos of spectacular destinations.

And much more!

Plan your next outdoor adventure at our web site. Point your browser to www.Falcon.com and get FalconGuided!

FALCON®

FALCON GUIDES ® Leading the Way™

FALCON GUIDES ® are available for where-to-go hiking, mountain biking, rock climbing, walking, scenic driving, fishing, rockhounding, paddling, birding, wildlife viewing, and camping. We also have FalconGuides® on essential outdoor skills and subjects and field identification. The following titles are currently available, but this list grows every year. For a free catalog with a complete list of titles, call FALCON® toll-free at 1-800-582-2665.

SCENIC DRIVING GUIDES

Scenic Driving Alaska and the Yukon
Scenic Driving Arizona
Scenic Driving the Beartooth Highway
Scenic Driving California
Scenic Driving Colorado
Scenic Driving Florida
Scenic Driving Georgia
Scenic Driving Hawaii
Scenic Driving Idaho
Scenic Driving Indiana
Scenic Driving Kentucky
Scenic Driving Michigan
Scenic Driving Minnesota
Scenic Driving Montana
Scenic Driving New England
Scenic Driving New Mexico
Scenic Driving North Carolina
Scenic Driving Oregon
Scenic Driving the Ozarks
Scenic Driving Pennsylvania
Scenic Driving Texas
Scenic Driving Utah
Scenic Driving Virginia
Scenic Driving Washington
Scenic Driving Wisconsin
Scenic Driving Wyoming
Scenic Driving Yellowstone and
    the Grand Teton National Parks
Scenic Byways East & South
Scenic Byways Far West
Scenic Byways Rocky Mountains
Back Country Byways

HISTORIC TRAIL GUIDES

Traveling California's Gold Rush Country
Traveling the Lewis & Clark Trail
Traveling the Oregon Trail
Traveler's Guide to the Pony Express Trail

WILDLIFE VIEWING GUIDES

Alaska Wildlife Viewing Guide
Arizona Wildlife Viewing Guide
California Wildlife Viewing Guide
Colorado Wildlife Viewing Guide
Florida Wildlife Viewing Guide
Indiana Wildlife Vewing Guide
Iowa Wildlife Viewing Guide
Kentucky Wildlife Viewing Guide
Massachusetts Wildlife Viewing Guide
Montana Wildlife Viewing Guide
Nebraska Wildlife Viewing Guide
Nevada Wildlife Viewing Guide
New Hampshire Wildlife Viewing Guide
New Jersey Wildlife Viewing Guide
New Mexico Wildlife Viewing Guide
New York Wildlife Viewing Guide
North Carolina Wildlife Viewing Guide
North Dakota Wildlife Viewing Guide
Ohio Wildlife Viewing Guide
Oregon Wildlife Viewing Guide
Puerto Rico & the Virgin Islands
    Wildlife Viewing Guide
Tennessee Wildlife Viewing Guide
Texas Wildlife Viewing Guide
Utah Wildlife Viewing Guide
Vermont Wildlife Viewing Guide
Virginia Wildlife Viewing Guide
Washington Wildlife Viewing Guide
West Virginia Wildlife Viewing Guide
Wisconsin Wildlife Viewing Guide

■ *To order any of these books, check with your local bookseller
or call FALCON ® at **1-800-582-2665**.
Visit us on the world wide web at:*
www.falcon.com

FALCON®

FALCONGUIDES ®Leading the Way™

HIKING GUIDES

FALCON®